Preface

The aims of this book

Various writers have attributed computer systems failures to two complementary causes.

- A lack of knowledge of business needs and operations on the part of technically biassed computer systems analysts and designers.

- A lack of technical confidence on the part of general and departmental managers which makes them reluctant to intervene in computer system design decisions.

This book is aimed at students who will become the next generation of managers and developers, and is intended to address the deficiences identified above.

For the business student it provides an Information Systems perspective to facilitate their future role in system development. This perspective is centred around *information*, rather than *technology*, so that a business orientation is retained.

For the computing student it gives an insight into the business framework that ultimately justifies most technical activity.

It is essentially a business orientated computing text. In comparison with any perceived competitors it probably;

- dwells less on hardware technologies, hardware descriptions and the detail of file organisation;

- places more emphasis on software packages, microcomputers and issues of audit, privacy and security.

Furthermore, an attempt has been made to build each chapter around a 'framework'. Too many texts fail to convey successfully the evaluative nature of Information Systems development, leaving many students with the impression that it is a rather flat, mechanistic and largely uninteresting descriptive subject. Nothing could be further from the truth! Hence, the provision of frameworks of understanding in preference to exhaustive descriptions of technologies, methods and applications. It is more important to realise what needs to be achieved than to grasp all the intricacies of trying to achieve it.

Thus, in summary, this book is primarily aimed at giving business students an introduction to Information Systems development and computing students a business framework into which they can place their technical skills. It is suitable for both undergraduates and students studying for a Higher National Diploma (or Certificate). However, material from the text has also been used successfully to:

- provide MSc. computing students with a basic appreciation of business activities;

- provide course material for professional qualifications, supplementing the rather dour 'cook-book' approach of many correspondence courses.

Book Layout

The book is presented in six parts. Each part is reasonably independent of each other and so this permits variations in teaching or studying order. Furthermore, whole parts may be omitted if they are inappropriate for a particular course or circumstance. The aim is to present business computing from six different perspectives. A teaching scheme for using this book is available to bona fide lecturers from the publishers, Edward Arnold.

About the Author

Steve Skidmore developed information systems in both public and private sectors before joining Leicester Polytechnic where he is currently a Principal Lecturer in Systems Analysis. He is also a Senior Partner in the Assist Partnership, the Bedford based systems and training company, where he has specific responsibility for systems development and training. He is also a regular lecturer for the Association of Certified Accountants.

Steve Skidmore

Business Computing

Steve Skidmore

Principal Lecturer in Systems Analysis
Leicester Polytechnic

Edward Arnold

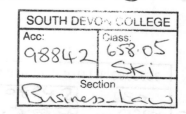

© Steve Skidmore 1987

First published in Great Britain 1987 by
Edward Arnold (Publishers) Ltd, 41 Bedford Square, London WC1B 3DQ

Edward Arnold (Australia) Pty Ltd, 80 Waverley Road, Caulfield East,
Victoria 3145, Australia

Edward Arnold, 3 East Read Street, Baltimore, Maryland 21202, U.S.A.

British Library Cataloguing in Publication Data

Skidmore, Steve
Business computing.
1. Business——Data processing
I. Title
658′.05   HF5548.2

ISBN 0 7131 3633 2

Text set in 10/11pt Times Roman, Linotron 202,
by TecSet Ltd, Wallington, Surrey.
Printed and bound in Great Britain
by J. W. Arrowsmith, Bristol

Acknowledgements

Many people have directly and indirectly contributed to the material included in this book. Where I have adopted a particular model or framework I hope that I have sufficiently acknowledged this in both the detail of the text and in the appropriate Further reading. In addition, there are four people who I would wish to single out for particular acknowledgement.

David Benyon. Many of the ideas of Part 2 were developed jointly with David before he left Leicester to join the staff of the Open University. It is difficult to know where many of the original ideas came from, although I am conscious of particular 'borrowings' — such as the model of physical resources.

Frank Land. I was a part-time student of Frank's at the LSE in the late seventies. Much of his teaching again permeates parts of Part 2, particularly the sections on input and output, where the guidelines are the ones that he presented.

The chapter on project management (Chapter 14) is based upon a correspondance course written for NALGO. The author wishes to acknowledge their agreement for this material to be reproduced in this book. The section on dataflow diagrams is expanded upon in an article in the Certified Accountants Newsletter, October 1986: *A Tutorial in Data Flow Diagrams*.

Martin Abram and Mike Crawford of the Assist Partnership who have consistently given me the opportunity to practice what I preach and then the time to write about it.

Thanks are also due to David Wolf, Martyn Wroe, Peter Messer and Vikki Galloway for commenting on parts of the text. However, all mistakes and idiosyncracies are mine!

Steve Skidmore

Trademarks

CP/M is a trademark of Digital Research
dBase III is a trademark of Ashton-Tate
Delta is a trademark of COMPSOFT
Framework is a trademark of Ashton-Tate
Hornet is a trademark of Claremont Controls
Lotus 1-2-3 is a trademark of the Lotus Development Corporation
MS-DOS is a trademark of MicroSoft
Multiplan is a trademark of MICROPRO
Open Access is a trademark of S.D.I. (Computers Systems Ltd.)
Symphony is a trademark of the Lotus Development Corporation
Supercalc IV is a trademark of Computer Associates
Superproject is a trademark of Computer Associates
UNIX is a trademark of AT & T Bell Laboratories

Contents

Part 1
Computer Fundamentals

This part examines the technical computer resource available to the builder of business information systems. It is difficult to achieve balance in such a subject and to steer an informative and relevant course through the barrage of technical detail that could be included. Similarly, at the other extreme, it is necessary to avoid a superficial approach which defines rather than explains. The end result is, of course, a compromise between highlighting certain issues and only referencing others.

The first chapter begins by examining this technical dilemma in a little more detail and attempts to justify the emphasis of the book on business rather than technological aspects of information systems. A number of elementary concepts are introduced, including the binary notation — fundamental to all digital processing — before the structure of a computer is considered in more detail. The three parts of the central processing unit are all described and their interactions and limitations identified. This leads naturally to an examination of secondary storage devices, with a brief historical review included to give perspective.

Chapter 2 introduces three aspects of software — programming, operating systems and files. Four generations of programming languages are identified and some of their principal features contrasted. The *activity* of programming is then considered in some depth to give the reader an insight into this very fundamental building block of business computing. This is followed by a review of the tasks of the operating system and observations are made about their evolution and the fundamental design issues that confront them. Finally, files and data bases are introduced, concentrating on organisation and access method. This is a subject that will be examined again in Part 3 when the design of file content is considered.

Two technical areas not included in this introductory part are communications and office automation. The omission of both of these deserves a brief discussion.

There are obvious benefits to be gained from linking machines, terminals, microcomputers, etc. and clear costs and problems associated with doing just that. Data communication is concerned with the technical, operational and economic feasibility of providing and implementing those links. It is a task that will be complicated by geographical distance, machine incompatibility, security constraints and software difficulties. On reflection, I felt it was a subject best referenced rather than simplistically explained. This was due to the difficulty of writing anything concise that was neither too technical (so that the average reader would not understand it) nor too simple (so that no useful information was actually imparted). The decision to leave this out of the text was made easier by one of the reference books also being a key source for office automation (Hirschheim — see Further reading).

I see office automation as an *application* rather than a *technology*. Many of the analysis and design issues considered in subsequent parts are applicable to implementing office systems. Unfortunately, this has not always been recognised by office automation implementors themselves and this has undoubtedly contributed to the failure of some projects. Hirschheim's book examines office automation in commendable depth and should be essential reading for business students and businessmen alike.

Further reading

Data communications

Cole, Robert, *Computer Communications*, Macmillan (1981)
Doll, Dixon, *Data Communications*, Wiley (1978)
Tannenbaum, A, *Computer Networks*, Prentice-Hall (1981)

Office automation

Hirschheim, R, Office Automation — Concepts, Technology and Issues, Addison-Wesley (1985)

1
Elements of hardware

1.1 Introduction

This book deliberately concentrates on the *business* aspect of *business computing*, not the technology that supports it. There are four main reasons for this.

- Business objectives are considered to be more important than technical ones and that, ultimately, most failures in computer systems are not due to technical reasons but to misunderstanding the systems that the technology was supposed to support.

- Technology changes rapidly. Most texts can only hope to be 'up-to-date' for a year or so. In contrast, the business systems that underlie most organisations are relatively stable. An understanding of the principles of business computing should hold the reader in good stead as the technology changes.

- There is a danger of a business student or practitioner becoming too fascinated with the technology at the cost of understanding its operational implications. Grindley and Humble (see Further reading) once stated that

  '. . . it is no more necessary for the average manager to understand the theory and technical detail of the computer than it is for him to understand the theory of electrical generation before he switches on a light. A sensible grasp of the essential features is all that is required.'

- There are already a considerable number of bulky textbooks on the technical aspects of computing. A few have been selected for the further reading at the end of this chapter. A particularly helpful (and cheap) text is Day and Alcock's fine little book *Ilustrating Computers (Without Much Jargon)*.

The study of computing is also made more confusing by the different levels at which the computer and its application may be studied. This is illustrated in Bell and Newell's hierarchy of systems (Fig 1.1). This multi-level study of a phenomenon is not unique to computing. As Sloan (see Further reading) has pointed out, the same is true of the study of human activity. This may also be examined at various levels — 'the anatomical, the neurological, the biochemical, the psychological, the social and the anthropological to name just a few'. Usually each level interacts but is unlikely that many people may be found who understand all levels with equal comprehensiveness and insight. The same holds true for computer systems. An expert in hardware may not be competent at implementing an actual business system, whilst a senior business analyst may be unable to take the top off the machine and insert a memory expansion board. This multi-level nature of computing must be recognised and acknowledge. It is unfortunate that many people 'in computing' ignore this multi-level hierarchy and hang grimly on to their selected level claiming loudly that this alone is 'real computing'. Such people are largely counter-productive and do the profession a disservice.

IMPLICATION   The effect of computer systems on employment levels and structure. Privacy and Data Protection. Fraud.
BUSINESS SYSTEMS   Examining how computer systems may be effectively harnessed by organisations. Problems of establishing project priority and of ensuring smooth implementation.
COMPUTER SYSTEMS   Effectively organising hardware and software resources to fulfill the information needs of the organisation. Detailed analysis and design of systems.
PROGRAMMING   The skills of providing the software required by the computer system. Unique to digital devices with central processors that interpret or compile a programming language.
LOGIC LEVEL   Unique to digital technology. Concerned with the principles of truth tables, Boolean algebra, flipflops and gates.
CIRCUIT LEVELS   The physical realisation of the logical level. Resistors, capacitors, inductors, voltage and current sources.

Fig. 1.1   A computer system hierarchy

I have adopted this hierarchy from Sloan (see Further reading). This textbook is primarily concerned with levels 1, 2 and 3 of the hierarchy.

1.2   Some elementary concepts

1.2.1   Hardware and software
There is a distinction (although it is slightly blurred at times) between the **hardware** and **software** of a computer system. The term hardware refers to the *physical units* — the various electrical and electromagnetic devices described later in this chapter, while software is used to describe the *programs and protocols* that make the hardware work. Certain aspects of software are covered in Chapter 2.

The difference between hardware and software may be illustrated by using a road transport example. The physical aspects of the transport system (hardware) include cars, buses, roads and traffic lights. The software encompasses drivers, routes, traffic light sequences (and their meaning) and the highway code. A bus and a road are aspects of hardware but the feat of transporting the bus from point A to point B, picking up and discharging passengers as required, cannot be achieved without recourse to software. The same is true of the computer. Plugging in and switching on a computer will not perform the payroll calculations; it will just give a little noise and a little light. Only when the computer is given the instructions necessary to perform such operations will processing be possible.

1.2.2   Digital and analogue
Computers use electrical voltages to represent values and they can do this in two distinct ways. In **analogue** computers the value stored is represented by a certain voltage level — for example the value 10 may be associated with a voltage level of 5 volts, the value 9 by $4\frac{1}{2}$ volts, 8 by 4 volts etc. Thus different numbers are represented by physical differences in the voltage level. In **digital** computers numbers are stored by a combination of a series of electrical voltages. Each number, letter, symbol etc. is represented by a unique code built up from a number of **binary digits**. All digital computers use the binary principle and so it is worth examining the binary notation in a little more detail.

Most readers will probably be familiar with the decimal number system using a base of 10. In this system each number is worth ten times the number on its immediate right. For example:

```
1              0              3
1 × 100        0 × 10         3 × 1
hundreds       tens           ones
        × 10           × 10
```

However, the decimal notation is not the only number method and the binary system based on similar principles, has a base of 2. Thus:

```
1          0          1          0
1 × 8      0 × 4      1 × 2      0 × 1
eights     fours      twos       ones
8   +      0   +      2   +      0          = 10
```

and so the value of the first eight places is

	128	64	32	16	8	4	2	1
binary number	1	0	1	0	0	0	0	1

i.e. $128 \times 1 + 32 \times 1 + 1 \times 1$
$= 128 + 32 + 1 = 161$

The binary format may look bulky but, from a computer's point of view, it is an attractive way of holding data.

It means that only two states have to be represented — zero and one. For example the value of 9, represented in an analogue computer by $4\frac{1}{2}$ volts, can be stored in a digital computer by a combination of four devices each representing a **binary digit** (or **bit**).

Binary 9 (1001)   1   0   0   1

a device a device a device a device
repr 1   repr 0   repr 0   repr 1

Given that only ones and zeros have to be represented, only two voltages are necessary — say $+3\frac{1}{2}$ volts to represent a one and +0.2 volts for a zero. This means that changes in the current of, for example $\frac{1}{2}$ volt, do not distort the data stored in the computer. If such a fluctuation occurred in the analogue computer then the value for 9 ($4\frac{1}{2}$ volts) would either become 5 volts (10) or 4 volts (8) and so the data would have been corrupted in some way. Analogue computers demand expensive hardware to ensure the high degree of accuracy required for reliable computation. In contrast digital computers may tolerate quite sizeable changes in current and still preserve the accuracy of the data. Indeed, in practice, the ones and zeros may be represented by band widths rather than exact voltages; 2.2 volts to +5 volts equalling a one and 0 to 1.2 volts a zero. As a result of this the vast majority of commercial computers are based on digital principles with analogue computers confined to scientific and specialised industrial applications.

Binary notation is also attractive because of the relative simplicity of binary arithmetic. All addition is covered by four rules.

$$0 + 0 = 0$$
$$0 + 1 = 1$$
$$1 + 0 = 1$$
$$1 + 1 = 1 \text{ carry } 1$$

and multiplication may be carried out (as in the decimal system) by repeated addition. The binary notation can also be extended to letters and symbols, so that certain combinations of zeros and ones may denote the letter A, a semi colon ;, or a dollar sign $. An arrangement of eight bits permits 2^8 (= 256) combinations of zero and one and this is sufficient to represent all numbers, special characters and upper and lower case letters. In practice a ninth bit is added known as a **parity bit**. This is an additional bit designed to permit a certain degree of internal checking. For example, a computer may utilise an even parity checking system and check each combination of bits to see if there is an even number of ones. If an odd number results then an error message would be recorded. The parity bit has no arithmetic or logical significance; it is only designed to check correct internal transfer of data. In fact, the most common code for representing data is the ASCII standard (American Standard Code for Information Interchange) which actually uses only seven bits providing 2^7 (128) different characters. The eighth bit may be used for extra graphical characters, alternate character sets or, indeed, for parity checking.

An additional attraction of using the binary notation is that it is possible to harness the mathematics of Boolean algebra (or logic) devised by an Englishman, George Boole, a century before computers. The algebra is concerned only with logical operations and so the physical representation of the digits is irrelevant. This provided an important, consistent, theoretical underpinning for digital computation. The existence of this logical basis has left designers free to concentrate on improving the methods of representing these logical ones and zeros. In essence computers are boxes full of two state devices, all of which are in a state representing a one or in a different state denoting a logical zero. For example, an electrical switch being ON may represent one and OFF is zero. These electronic switches are customarily termed **flip-flops**. The logical output of an operation — say adding two binary numbers — is determined by the rules of **Boolean logic** and is performed by **logic gates.** These gates are arrangements of switches designed to carry out a certain operation. Although they are conceptually simple their combination in a computer may lead to complicated circuit patterns. The design of such circuits will determine the speed and functions of the different devices. Some will be used in computers, others in washing machines!

Furthermore, the large number of flip-flops required in a computer will not only impose logical problems, but also physical difficulties of bulk and cost. The task of reducing size and price, as well as improving speed, function and reliability has been pursued through four **generations** of computer. These can briefly be summarised as:

- First generation. Valve technology producing slow, cumbersome machines, with restricted functions and low reliability.

- Second generation. Transistors used rather than valves. Machines became cheaper, faster and more reliable.

- Third generation. Integrated circuits. Computers enter mass production.

- Fourth generation. Very large scale integration. Large, complicated circuits etched onto wafers of silicon producing very cheap, reliable and powerful functions.

The result of this progress through the generations is that hardware costs are fast becoming a negligible part of business system development. Some machines are now being purchased as a disposable product. When they fail, they are replaced — not repaired.

1.3 Elements of hardware

In its simplest form the computer performs a number of processes on input data to produce the required output, e.g. adding 2 and 5 to make 7

input	processor	output
2, 5	+	= 7

Mechanisms of input and output will be discussed in Part 3. This section concentrates on the processing part of the computer system — the central processing unit (CPU). It has three main sections.

1.3.1 The control unit
The control unit is, if anything deserves the term, the 'brain' of the machine. It coordinates and controls the activities of the rest of the computer system using appropriate circuits. For example, in the task of adding 2 and 5 it is the control unit that determines the operation that has to be performed (i.e. addition) and the location of the data (the two and the five) that are required for this particular task. The control unit also determines where the data is to be stored when the result has been computed. However, the control unit does not perform the actual arithmetic operation. This task is sub-contracted to the arithmetic and logic unit.

1.3.2 Arithmetic and logic Unit (ALU)
This section of the CPU has special circuits designed to undertake the common arithmetic operations (addition, division etc.) and also to perform certain logical functions such as comparison (is $X > Y$?). The arithmetic unit uses areas of temporary storage to aid it in its arithmetic (just like we would use a notepad) called **registers** — usually constructed from high speed flip-flops. Once the arithmetic and logic unit has completed its task the control unit again takes over to determine where the result should be placed in the primary store.

1.3.3 Primary store
This section (also called **main memory**) is where the data (2 and 5) and the instructions about what to do with it are stored. It can be conceived as a large collection of pigeon holes with a piece or pieces of data in each hole.

It is worth emphasising that the required data is found by the address associated with it and not by its content. Thus the control unit tells the arithmetic and logic unit to use the data stored in memory cells address 'A' and address 'B'. It does not tell it about the values of the data. Entering data into the memory is termed **writing** and extracting data is **reading**. This is performed by external devices using a **read/write** head — a term that will be introduced in Section 1.4. The time taken to complete a memory access, either reading or writing, is termed the memory **cycle time**. The amount of memory is usually described in terms of **bytes**.

A byte is the term attached to eight bit patterns, usually with an additional parity bit. The name was originally introduced to distinguish the eight bit representation from the old six bit character. In this text the terms byte and character are used interchangeably (usually character is preferred) to represent 'a piece of data' e.g. a two, an A, an exclamation mark. The storage capacities of both memory and secondary storage (see Section 4.4) are usually described in bytes. These figures are conventionally given in terms of thousands (kilobytes) or millions (megabytes) because of the large numbers involved.

The **wordlength** is also important in understanding the configuration of the computer. The *size* of the memory is usually given in bytes but it is likely that the memory is actually organised in words, and it is the wordlength that gives the normal size of each pigeon hole available for data storage. The wordlength is usually given in bits and common wordlength examples are 32 bits, 16 bits and eight bits. In general it will be some multiple of character length, for example a 32 bit **word** may be built up from four eight bit characters (bytes). The general trend is for machines to migrate to larger wordlengths. For example, the eight bit generation of microcomputers (e.g. Superbrains, Apple IIs, PETs) has now been largely superceded by its 16 bit successors (IBM PC, Olivetti M–24, Compaq etc.).

The main memory area may also be commonly referred to as the **random access memory (RAM)**. It is termed random because it takes the same time to access data irrespective of which memory cell it is residing in. Thus the access time is **independent** of the position of the data and, as we shall see later, this is not necessarily true for other types of storage. The main memory may also have a section of **read only memory (ROM)**. This may be envisaged as random access memory which can be read from — but not written onto. The ROM may be used to store instructions which are required frequently or for instructions which the computer user has no need or right to alter. On microcomputers it is common to have part of the operating system (see Chapter 2) in ROM so that the machine is almost ready to use when it is switched on. Similarly, larger machines may store special purpose programs and function tables, such as logarithms, in ROM so that they are easily available. The RAM is often constructed from **volatile** semi-conductors so that when the power is switched off all the contents of the RAM are lost. In contrast a ROM has fixed data patterns established at manufacture which remain if there is any loss of power.

Despite the importance of the CPU its outward appearance is usually unspectacular. In most data processing departments the most striking physical units are the secondary storage devices (described in the Section 1.4) and the input and output hardware examined in Part 3. The most important part — the CPU remains relatively anonymous.

1.3.4   Further hardware considerations

Thus data and instructions are stored in the memory section of the CPU. This may be accessed very quickly and the position of the data within this store does not affect its retrieval time. Access time to data stored in this primary memory is measured in nanoseconds (typically 100–400 ns) where a nanosecond is a thousandth of a millionth of a second. To put this speed in perspective Fuori (see Further reading) stated that a nanosecond is to a second what a second is to 30 years.

However, it is not possible for an organisation to store all its data in the primary memory. There are three contributory reasons for this.

- It is likely to be uneconomic. RAM is the most expensive storage method per byte of data so when data or instructions are not being used there is economic sense in storing it in a cheaper way.

- If the RAM is volatile then the machine has to be left switched on all the time otherwise the data will be lost.

- Finally, it is unlikely that there will be sufficient room in the RAM to store all the organisation's data. For example, consider the storing of name, address and occupation.

Stephen Richard Skidmore
17 Bell Lane
Market Harborough
Leicestershire
Lecturer in Systems Analysis

will require approximately 100 bytes.

Thus a machine with 512 000 bytes primary storage could only store approximately 5120 of these records even if all the store was dedicated to this purpose. So, organisations storing, say, personnel records for 30 000 staff, stock control records for 200 000 items etc. will not be able to store all this data within the primary store. As a result it is necessary to transfer the data from primary to **secondary storage devices** and to hold in the primary store only the data and instructions which are currently being used. A number of secondary storage devices exist but in all instances the data must be transferred back into the primary store before any processing can take place. In general, secondary storage media is everything that primary storage is not. It is non-volatile, cheap and large. The price paid for these advantages is the speed of access to the data, a factor which is considered in more detail in the brief descriptions given in Section 1.4.

1.4   Secondary storage

1.4.1   A brief historical perspective
There is little practical justification for including an exhaustive description of punched card and paper tape technology. These methods have long been superceded as a method of secondary storage although they may still remain in use for certain input and output tasks. However, they do represent a useful *perspective* and *contrast* to the magnetic technologies, particularly in their storage capacity, and so a brief review has been included for that reason.

Both methods represent a character as a combination of punched holes with different combinations of holes representing different characters. The hole patterns are detected by a reader which transfers the data to the CPU. Punched cards are expensive and bulky and the speed of data transfer into the CPU, via the card reader, is relatively slow. Paper tape is also slow but is a cheaper medium to use and it still enjoys a certain popularity as a method of controlling automatic machinery. Paper tape is typically 1 inch wide with data represented by punched hole patterns, similar in principle to the punched card.

Punched cards and paper tape both use physical hole/no hole as the method of representing the binary digits 0 and 1. Thus if a hole is detected this may be interpreted as a logical 1 and vice versa. This physical representation places constraints on the storage density; paper tape, for example, typically permits only 10 characters to the inch. Thus a standard 1000 foot tape will store about 120 000 characters of data. If this storage capacity is to be improved then a technology is required that is not constrained by the physical limits of the hole/no hole method.

1.4.2   Magnetic media
The efficient alternative to this physical representation of binary digits is the principle of recording data as magnetic patterns. This method builds up a pattern of local magnetised areas on magnetic material with each of these patterns representing a unique character. Thus each character is represented by a combination of magnetic spots rather than by physical holes. There are a number of possible coding mechan-

isms of which the 'return to zero' method is an example. In this method a positive pulse represents 1 and a brief negative pulse 0 with the current returning to zero (hence its name) in between pulses. Thus the bit pattern is represented by positive and negative pulses. This is the basis of a whole range of 'magnetic' storage devices.

Magnetic tape

Magnetic tape is available in three forms, each with close equivalents in the home audio market — reels, cassettes and cartridges. The tape reel is typically $\frac{1}{2}$ inch wide and in a spool 2400 feet long. Each character is represented by a magnetic bit pattern across the tape (analogous to the paper tape principle) with the number of characters stored per inch varying from 800 to 6250. This clearly represents an enormous improvement on the densities offered by paper tape. For example, a 2400 foot tape holding data at 1600 characters per inch gives approximately 46 megabytes of data storage.

Data stored on the tape is entered into the CPU by first locating the correct tape and loading it onto a tape **drive**. This loading is accomplished by threading the tape through rollers, over a read/write head and onto a take up reel, similar indeed to the audio equivalent. The drive may then be started and once the tape has achieved a constant speed data may be transferred via the read head into the CPU. The inertia involved in mechanically stopping and starting the tape effectively prevents the transfer of single characters. As a result 'blocks' of characters are transferred at a time with each block separated by blank segments of tape known as inter block gaps. Clearly we would wish to store related data in each of these blocks as this is data we are likely to use together (see Part 3 for more on this). The rate at which data is transferred into the CPU is determined by the number of characters stored per inch and the speed of the tape across the read/write head. However, although quite high transfer speeds can be achieved, these do not generally represent a significant part of the time taken to transfer a piece of data stored on a tape into primary storage and hence available for processing. Time taken to identify, locate and load the correct tape and to find the relevant block in that tape is likely to be relatively time-consuming. Indeed this type of 'linear' storage (appropriate also to punched cards and paper tape) is representative of **serial access devices** where unwanted data has to be physically passed over before the relevant block can be retrieved. Hence the speed of access to data held on such devices varies considerably with the position of the data on the media.

Thus access to a piece of data is relatively slow — usually in terms of minutes — and this compares unfavourably with the access times of the RAM. However, magnetic tape is a cheap, reliable way of storing data, characteristics shared by **cassettes** and **cartridges**. Both these methods employ similar principles of storage to the magnetic tape. Cassettes are widely used with small home computers giving cheap storage at the cost of slow transfer speeds. Cartridges are more expensive but their higher capacity ensures that their cost per bit stored is lower.

Magnetic disk

Magnetic disk (disc) storage uses magnetic patterns organised in concentric circles. The term '**tracks**' used to describe these bands again suggests audio equivalents. Usually both surfaces of the disk are used to record data.

Fixed disks are permanently linked to the CPU and so may not be loaded or unloaded — unlike the tape which may be removed from its tape drive. Disks may be organised as one large disk or a stack of disks — known as **diskpacks**. These latter devices are particularly popular in an 'exchangeable' form which permits the diskpack to be loaded or unloaded from the drive in a similar way to the tape.

In a diskpack each disk surface has its own read/write head. These heads move together and so the most efficient way of storing data is in a cylinder form as this minimises the amount of head movement. Access time to a particular piece of data will be made up of the following.

- A head movement time as the head moves to the appropriate track. The time taken to get to that track depends the last track accessed, but it is likely to be in terms of nanoseconds.

- A rotational delay. Once the correct track is located the head has to wait until the relevant data arrives. At most this is just under one revolution of the disk and this is again measured in nanoseconds.

- Data transfer rate. The time taken to read data into the CPU. This will again be relatively quick.

Thus the average access time is likely to be in terms of hundredths of a second, giving much faster access than the serial access devices outlined in Section 1.3. This is primarily due to the fact that the device can go (more or less) directly to the data that is required and so large quantities of unwanted data does not have to pass the read/write head. Devices which have this circular storage method are called **direct access devices** (**DADs**) and much development work has gone into the design of these devices aimed at producing faster access times and increased storage capacity. This has included the development of 'flying heads' or 'head off' designs where the head does not come into physical contact with the disk but 'flies' just above the surface so reducing disk wear. Storage capacity of disks and diskpacks varies, but capacities of 20–500 megabytes are typical.

Other variations on the disk principle

Floppy disks or **diskettes** are used mainly in microcomputer systems. These are plastic disks coated with ferrite enclosed within a plastic envelope. The envelope is loaded into a diskette drive and the diskette rotates inside the envelope. Data is again stored in tracks with capacities of around 1 million bytes for 8 inch diskettes and 350 000 bytes for $5\frac{1}{4}$ inch diskettes. In floppy disk systems there is physical contact between the head and the surface of the diskette so creating some problems of wear.

Winchester disks introduced by IBM in 1973 represent an increasingly popular storage device for minicomputer systems. Conceptually similar to a fixed diskpack the winchester disk incorporates several differences in design which have contributed to lower prices. $5\frac{1}{4}$ inch, 8 inch and 14 inch disks are available with storage capacity varying typically from 5 million to 400 million bytes of data.

Other secondary storage devices

A number of other devices have been developed over the years designed to store data at low cost with relatively slow access times (e.g. mass storage systems, data cells and magnetic cards). However, it is the disk and tape technologies which dominate the secondary storage market place. These two methods offer reasonably complementary facilities, the disks providing fast access at a higher unit cost — suitable for data that has to be located quickly, while the tapes are slower and cheaper, ideal for data that has to be retrieved infrequently.

Thus a number of secondary storage devices exist with varying characteristics, costs and access times. However, access to a particular piece of data not only depends on the device but on how the data has been organised. This will briefly be examined when file design is encountered in Part 3.

1.5   Summary

Digital computers use the principles of binary notation and Boolean algebra to establish and organise hundreds of two state devices wired together in complex circuits and packaged in an innocuous box. This CPU has three main sections — storage, arithmetic and logic unit, and the control unit. The primary storage in the CPU is limited and so a number of secondary storage devices have been developed providing different facilities at differing costs. In all instances data in secondary storage has to be transferred into primary storage before any processing can be undertaken. This transmission of data is achieved by using data lines and channels of varying sophistication.

A general schematic view of the computer is given in Fig. 1.2.

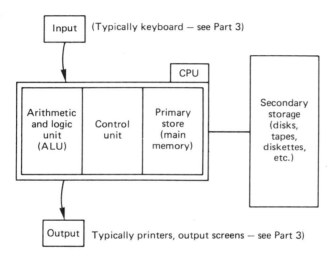

Fig. 1.2   Simple schematic view of a computer

Further reading

Alcock D and Day C, *Illustrating Computers (without much jargon)*, Pan (1982)

A very useful 'hand-written' text with plenty of diagrams and images. Greatly recommended for all those wishing to know more about hardware.

Fuori W M, Introduction to the Computer, Prentice-Hall (1983)

Sheldon N A, *Fundamentals of Computing*, Hutchinson (1984)

A well written book that presents the material in short accessible chapters. Fairly detailed coverage of the logical basis of computing and its physical realisation.

Sloan M, *Computer Hardware and Organisation*, Science Research Associates (1976)

A detailed, comprehensive but very readable book. The Bell and Newell hierarchy is introduced in this text. Reference — Bell C G and Newell A, *Computer Structures*, McGraw-Hill (1971)

2
Elements of software

It is software that turns the computer into a useful business tool and hence issues about software functions, selection and testing occupy significant later sections of this book (see Part 4 in particular). This chapter is used to introduce three important software areas which are developed, to varying extents, in the following chapters — programming, operating systems and files. Appropriate further reading is again suggested at the end of the chapter.

2.1   Programming

Programming languages have, like hardware, passed through four generations of development. However, unlike hardware, the 'first generation' is still in legitimate everyday use and hence the four periods tend to co-exist rather than completely to supercede each other.

2.1.1   Machine code
Chapter 1 discussed how the digital computer uses the binary principle in its storage and manipulation of data. It is important to recognise that this is the computer's only direct level of understanding and so if it is necessary to address the machine directly a binary based **machine code** will be required. An example of instructions at this level is given below (from Coats — see Further reading).

```
241 00 111 010        op code
242 00 000 000                      address 1
243 00 000 001                      address 2
244 01 000 111        op code
245 00 111 010        op code
246 00 000 001                      address 1
247 00 000 001                      address 2
248 10 000 000        op code
249 00 110 010        op code
250 00 000 010                      address 1
251 00 000 001                      address 2
```

This uses the bit patterns introduced in Chapter 1. Machine code programs are difficult and tedious to write and correct with their size and inaccessibility giving many opportunities for error. However, they do permit very close control of the hardware operations and give a precise insight into what is actually happening when a computer executes an operation.

2.1.2   Assembler language
An assembler language uses simple English statements (such as ADD) together with appropriate symbols to represent variables in the program. These names and symbols are much easier to remember and use than their machine code equivalents. The

example given below performs exactly the same operation as the machine code program given above. It is important to note that each assembler language instruction has a direct equivalent in machine code, although this may not be evident from the example. This is because the assembler level instructions do not have to specify **addresses** where data has to be placed and retrieved from. This task is undertaken by a piece of software called an **assembler** that translates the instructions into the machine code that can be understood by the computer. If an assembler is not present then the computer cannot execute the assembler language instructions.

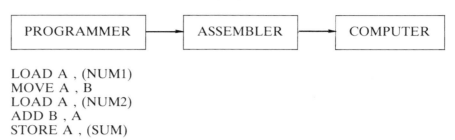

```
LOAD A , (NUM1)
MOVE A , B
LOAD A , (NUM2)
ADD B , A
STORE A , (SUM)
```

Assembler language programming is attractive because it retains the efficiency of the machine level, but it does so with more economy and a more readable notation. You should now be able to guess what that machine program was doing!

2.1.3   High level languages
The task performed by the programs given in the preceding two sections is executed by the high level language BASIC in one line.

```
LET SUM=NUM1+NUM2
```

High level languages permit powerful arguments to be expressed in brief statements. They require a **compiler** to translate the code of the language into the instructions understandable by the machine.

It is important to be clear on this point. A computer does not directly understand statements in a language such as BASIC. These BASIC statements must pass through a compiler and so an appropriate BASIC compiler has to be purchased and resident in the machine.

A compiler translates the program instructions of the high level language (the source code) into machine code. If one of the source code instructions is incorrect then it has to be modified and the whole program passed through the compiler once more to give a new machine code version. This recompilation of programs may be very time consuming and so some languages are interpreted. An **interpreter** is a piece of software that permits the source code to be understood and executed by the CPU. It translates and executes instructions one at a time and permits editing of those instructions without resorting to the overhead of recompilation. However, the result of this facility is that interpreted programs are much slower than their compiled equivalents. A useful assessment of the scope and relative merits of compilers and interpreters is given in Coats (see Further reading).

Most computer programming is performed using the variety of high level languages available on the market. Commercial programming is still dominated by COBOL, scientific programming by FORTRAN and ALGOL. Other common languages include BASIC, Pascal, APL, PL/1, Logo and C. Smaller markets exist for programming languages aimed at specific applications, e.g. SNOBOL for string handling. A useful distinction can be drawn between **procedural** languages which require statements about *how* a certain problem must be undertaken and **non-procedural** languages which state *what* the problem is. Traditional high level programming languages such as COBOL and FORTRAN are procedural while newer fourth generation languages are largely non-procedural. It is difficult to give an adequate definition of a fourth generation language, and Lobell's survey of the field (see Further reading) ranged from simple program generators to complete application development tools. Examples of fourth generation products are given later in the book, (Part 3).

2.2   Programming as a craft

The variety of programming languages, together with the competing claims of their advocates, tends to divert attention away from the actual craft of *writing* programs. In fact it is perhaps easier to view the programming task as three inter-related activities.

- Problem definition. Getting to understand the problem itself. A requirement to write a 'pay calculation' routine will need detailed research and analysis before it can be completed successfully. All the elements of a pay calculation will have to be understood — basic hours, pay rates, overtime, tax tables etc. and their relationships understood. For example, is national insurance calculated from gross or net pay? To gain this understanding the programmer will be aided by an appropriate model.

- Problem description. Modelling the problem definition. Flowcharts, decision tables and Structured English are typical examples of such techniques. In constructing these models the programmer will use program structures that are supported by most programming languages.

- Problem coding. Implementing the problem definition. This is the actual task of program coding. The programmer will write the programming code that will perform the operations defined in the problem description. This will employ the syntax of an appropriate programming language.

It is important to stress that this three-fold division will seldom be clearcut. For example, the understanding of the problem may proceed into testing and implementation before it is discovered that certain information has been omitted. It is also likely that the techniques used to describe the problem will vary with the stage of program development, the urgency of the task and the preference of the programmer. The model may vary from a scribbled diagram to a fully documented flowchart.

However, if it is unwise to constrain the method of expression, experience suggests that the structure of that expression can and should be limited in some way. This is because the logic and flow of programs quickly becomes very difficult to follow and poor program construction can lead to programs that are very hard to correct and change. This is brought forcibly home when you are asked by a 'friend' to 'look at my program' because it has 'a bug in it somewhere'!

Structured programming is an attempt to reduce the control problems of programming by suggesting a restricted set of control structures. It claims that any program can be written using three types of statement, **sequence, selection** and **repetition** together with the facility to switch control to other programs. It is useful to examine these in greater detail because it will help you gain an understanding of the structures of programs. dBASE III is used to illustrate the program structures. This has the advantage of being relatively easy to understand and also shows the use of such structures in a non-procedural programming language.

2.2.1   Structured programming — Control structures

Sequence
A number of statements that are executed in the order that they are written.

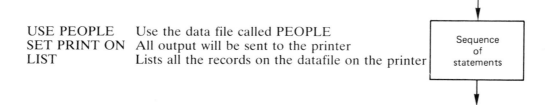

USE PEOPLE   Use the data file called PEOPLE
SET PRINT ON   All output will be sent to the printer
LIST   Lists all the records on the datafile on the printer

Selection
All selections are based on the existence of a condition. When a program meets a condition it tests it against the value that it currently holds. The result determines the subsequent path of the program. Selection permits three types of branching.

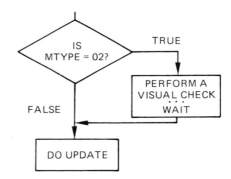

• Single branch

    IF MTYPE=02
    @ 12, 12 SAY "Perform a visual check"
    WAIT
    END IF
    DO UPDATE

In this example the condition check is contained in the IF line. If the category entered is 02 then the data entry operator is requested to perform a visual check on the data before proceeding. This is because 02 entries are rare and so the program must check that it is not a mistake before proceeding to the command DO UPDATE.

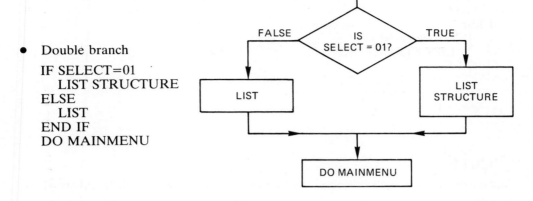

- Double branch

IF SELECT=01
    LIST STRUCTURE
ELSE
    LIST
END IF
DO MAINMENU

In this example two routes are provided, one through SELECT=01 (the structure of the file is listed) and the other through any other value of SELECT (the contents of the file are listed).

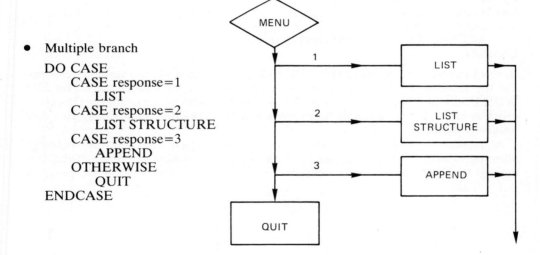

- Multiple branch

DO CASE
    CASE response=1
        LIST
    CASE response=2
        LIST STRUCTURE
    CASE response=3
        APPEND
    OTHERWISE
        QUIT
ENDCASE

This control is useful in establishing 'menus' where the user is requested to input a certain value corresponding to the option required. The use of the CASE structure in the example could be replaced by a number of IF statements, the result would be the same.

```
IF response=01
   LIST
ELSE
   IF response=02
      LIST STRUCTURE
   ELSE
      IF response=03
         APPEND
      ELSE
         QUIT
      END IF
   END IF
END IF
```

This illustrates how the same result can be obtained by using two different selection structures.

Repetition
This permits the repeated execution of a number of statements until a condition is met.

```
STORE 'Y' TO response
DO WHILE response='Y'
      DO ADDREC
      ACCEPT 'Enter Y to add another record'
ENDDO
```

In this example the command DO ADDREC is repeated while the variable response has the value of Y. If it has any other value then the commands between the DO WHILE and the ENDDO are not executed. The two forms of the conditional loop are given in Fig. 2.1. One example loops *while* a certain condition is satisfied, the other *until* it is satisfied.

A number of other loop structures are permitted (see Coats Further reading) allowing variations which need not concern us here. A particularly common requirement is the incremented index whereby a certain value is increased in the program

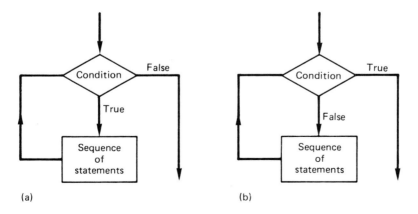

(a)   (b)

Fig. 2.1 Two forms of conditional loop (a) Loop *while* condition is satisfied (b) Loop *until* condition is satisfied.

until a condition becomes true and the loop is terminated. Fig. 2.2 shows the flowchart for such a structure together with the dBASE code for a simple example.

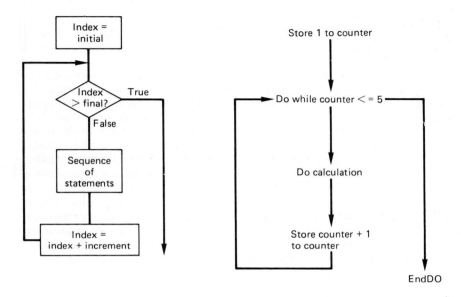

Fig. 2.2 Loop statement using a simple increment

2.2.2 Observations

These structures form the basis of the programming craft. Once these have been mastered it is a case of using the correct programming commands to map the structure into a coded program. The success of this is determined by the programmer's knowledge of the syntax of the programming language being used. However, it must be recalled that most programming languages have a fairly limited vocabulary (much less than a foreign language) and their similarities tend to be more striking than their differences. Most difficulties in programming are due to poor problem definition and expression and not to a lack of knowledge of the programming commands. Thus if you can learn to program well in one particular language it should be relatively easy to transfer that skill to another language because two parts of the task remain the same (problem definition and expression); only the syntax changes.

2.3 Operating systems

The operating system may be viewed as the lowest layer of software on the computer, acting as a cushion between the raw hardware and other software such as compilers and application packages. In general the operating system tries to achieve two major objectives.

- To provide a friendly and useful interface between the computer user and the hardware components.

  This takes the form of relieving the computer user of much of the detail of computer operation. For example, an operating system will organise the storage of a file on a disk, record its presence on a directory and store details about where it can be found so that the file may be reliably retrieved when it is required. The operating system will also provide error messages to inform the user of errors he/she has made (putting in a disk the wrong way round, requesting a file which does not exist) and suggest possible remedial actions.

- To manage the computer's resources efficiently so that fast devices such as processors are not slowed down by slow devices such as printers and human beings sitting at terminals!

  This is critical in multi-user systems where the processor cannot be dedicated to one task. In such an environment the operating system has to ensure that the processor is used as much as possible and is not left idle waiting for further input. In effect the operating system 'swaps' jobs in and out of the processor so that while one task is waiting for further input the CPU can be processing one of the other tasks. It should be evident that this complicates the work of the operating system. For example, it has to record exactly where a task has been interrupted so that it may be resumed correctly when the CPU is free. This function of processor management is further complicated by the fact that demand for processor time is almost certain to exceed availability. Thus processor time has to be allocated to programs in accordance with some **scheduling policy**. Such policies vary from one operating system to another. However, a common method used on multi-user systems is that of **time slicing** where each program is accorded a slice of processor time and if the program is not completed in that time it returns to a queue of programs awaiting execution.

2.3.1   Other operating system tasks

Memory management
The processor can only work on data and programs resident in the primary store. Thus if a number of programs are to be run simultaneously then they must all be loaded into RAM. This effectively means that the number of programs that can be run at the same time is limited by the amount of primary store available. It also means that much of this storage is wasted as only a small part of each program is actually active at any one point in time. To counteract this most operating systems have memory management facilities which allocate primary store to those programs or part of programs that need it most whilst everything else is written out to disk. This leads to continual swapping between memory and disk and appears to give the user much more memory than is actually available.

Input and output control
An example of this is provided by the **spooling** facility. When a user wishes to print a file the request is spooled — added to a queue of files waiting to be printed. Each file is printed in turn and the user can continue with other tasks and is not held up waiting for the completion of printing. If a spooling facility is not available then processor time is wasted as it waits for pages of output to be printed before it can begin its next operation. Users of single user micros with certain operating systems will be all too aware of the frustration caused by the absence of a spooling utility.

Accounting information
An operating system will record how long it spends on a task so that the use of the processor can be charged out to the relevant department. It will also record information about file accesses, such as source, time and date of last update, time and date of file creation etc. This information will be particularly useful in detecting fraud (see Part 6).

Housekeeping commands
The operating system will have a number of commands that permit the deletion and renaming of files, the display of the amount of disk space available, the transfer of files, etc.

2.3.2 Observations
Manufacturers of mainframe computers have tended to develop their own proprietary operating systems designed around the characteristics of their hardware. Typical examples are the OS/VM series from IBM and the GEORGE series from ICL. In contrast the microcomputer, and to some extent the minicomputer, industry has used a limited number of common operating systems. Indeed the microcomputer market place has been dominated by CP/M and MS-DOS (PC-DOS), and firms that have tried to introduce their own hardware dependent operating system have generally been unsuccessful. The large number of application packages now available for these two operating systems has further encouraged standardisation.

Microcomputers are usually single user machines where the processor is dedicated to the tasks required by that user. This means that no multi-programming or memory management facility is required and their only major disadvantage, in terms of resource management, comes if the processor is tied up by extensive printing requirements. This can be overcome by spooling or by making the operating system **multi-tasking**. This permits the user to undertake a number of tasks simultaneously so that he/she is not confined within one software area. These **concurrent** operating systems are still restricted to one user but that user may undertake a number of simultaneous tasks.

The multi-tasking facility must be distinguished from **multi-user** systems where more than one terminal is attached to the computer. Many microcomputers are now being made multi-user, using an operating system derived from a single user system (e.g. MP/M — the multi-user relation of CP/M), or from systems that have been used successfully in the minicomputer market such as UNIX. In making this leap from single to multiple users the operating systems begin to encounter some of the processor and memory management problems that have always faced mainframe operating systems. Further complications are caused by the need to ensure an adequate response time for users at every terminal together with minimising the size of the operating system itself so that it does not take up a disproportionate amount of memory and disk space. The difficulty of achieving an adequate compromise between the conflicting requirements of an operating system ensures the continued debate of the relative merits of different systems!

2.4   Files and data bases

Chapter 1 included a brief review of the secondary storage devices used to hold the data required by an organisation. This section examines how this data may be arranged and accessed and considers the basic building block of data storage, the **file**.

The concept of a file may be illustrated by a simple example. Consider the data shown in the table below.

ISBN	Book Title	Author
0–471–90645	Data, Delta and You	Abram & Skidmore
0–7131–3472	Software Engineering	Coats
0–07–070132	Database Design	Wiederhold

This table holds certain items of data — ISBN, Book Title and Author together with specific instances of that data — Data, Delta and You, Coats etc. The columns represent data **fields**, the rows data **records** and all the records in the table constitute an embolden file.

A field of particular significance is the **key field**. This is the field whose value can be used to uniquely identify a record. In the example given above the key field is likely to be ISBN because the other fields are unlikely to produce unique retrievals as the file becomes longer.

A file is subject to addition (adding a new record), deletion, editing (changing a field) and retrieval (who wrote Software Engineering?). The nature and frequency of these operations will affect how the file is both organised and accessed.

Serial files

A file is in serial order if records are stored one after another on the storage medium with no regard to order or storage location. Any ordering of the data is purely a result of the input operation — for example putting invoices in date order before entering them — and is not associated with the file itself. This method of organisation is usually adopted where it is necessary to capture a number of transactions which can then be subsequently sorted into some order. Thus serial files are often **temporary** files used to store **transactions** as they occur.

Sequential files

A sequential file stores all the records in ascending or descending order of some numerical or alphabetical key field. One of the major merits of sequential organisation is the efficiency with which transactions stored in the sequence of some key field may be used to update the permanent records of a **master file** also held in that sequence. This is a common data processing requirement so it will be considered in a little more detail. A master file of accounts is held in ascending order of the key field Account Number.

Master file

Accout Number	Account Name	Balance
001	Shortland Holdings	$2345.00
002	Marker Computing	$3210.00
003	Cruise Engineering	$4560.00
004	Wakeland Security	$2310.00
005	Abram Computers	$4567.00
006	Attila Videos	$6785.00
007	Quoin Computing	$2000.00

Orders placed during the day

Serial transaction file

008	Cottage Bakery	$1000.00
004	Wakeland Security	$2769.00
006	Attila Videos	$3000.00

These orders are then SORTed into account order.

Sequential transaction file

004	Wakeland Security	$2769.00
006	Attila Videos	$3000.00
008	Cottage Bakery	$1000.00

This sequential transaction file can then be run against the master file. The simplified logic is as follows.

Read the first record in the transaction file.

004	Wakeland Security	$2769.00

Locate the record with the same key in the master file.

004	Wakeland Security	$2310.00

Because 004 is the first located record on a sequential file it may be assumed that no transactions have occurred on the first three records. Therefore these may be written out onto a new master file unchanged.

001	Shortland Holdings	$2345.00
002	Marker Computing	$3210.00
003	Cruise Engineering	$4560.00

The record 004 is now updated and written to the new master file.

004	Wakeland Security	$5079.00

This process is now repeated. The next transaction is read, all preceding records are written to the master file, and the altered account is updated before being added to the new master file. The result is the following updated master file.

Master file

001	Shortland Holdings	$2345.00
002	Marker Computing	$3210.00
003	Cruise Engineering	$4560.00
004	Wakeland Security	$5079.00
005	Abram Computers	$4567.00
006	Attila Videos	$9785.00
007	Quoin Computing	$2000.00
008	Cottage Bakery	$1000.00

Random files

In a random file the records are not stored in key field order but in an order dictated by the result of applying a mathematical transformation to the key. This is to permit **direct access** to a requested record so that irrelevant records do not have to be read and rejected. Random files are common in systems which demand fast response times.

In some instances it may be possible to use the key field numbers to locate directly the position of the record. However, this may require the imposition of a key field which has no relevance at all to the operational system and so it is common to derive positions by the application of the mathematical transformation mentioned above. A simple example is given below:

Key field
   Account number

109866	10	Take the last two digits	74
	98		
	66		
	174		
234542	23	Take the last two digits	10
	45		
	42		
	110		

Thus the record for account number 109866 is stored at address 74 and 234542 at 10. This is an example of one of the so-called **hash functions** that can be applied to the key field to derive the storage position. The basic requirement of such a function is to reduce both storage waste (i.e. addresses that cannot be derived by the function) and clashes (two account numbers requiring the same storage address).

Indexed files

So far two distinct ways of accessing records have been introduced. The first required the reading of consecutive records until the required record was found (serial and sequential files) and the second concerned direct access to a record based upon a procedure applied to the key field (random files). A third possibility uses the concept of an **index**.

A file index contains only the key values of the records together with a pointer to where the rest of that record may be found. Thus the key field of a record is first located in the small index file which then retrieves the rest of the record directly by accessing the address given in the index file. In small files it may be possible to index all records but as the file gets larger the storage overhead of the index becomes more significant. In such circumstances it is common to establish an index for a **group** of records where the index refers to a range of records. The address of this group is accessed and consecutive records searched until the requested record is located. The use of ranges in the index demands that the file is organised **sequentially**, i.e. that the records are in ascending or descending order of the values of the key field. Such **indexed sequential** files are popular because the use of the index permits fairly fast access to a record without creating too much of an index overhead or wasting the storage space associated with the direct access of random files.

Thus both the **order** and **access** method of the file is of interest to us. An indexed sequential file whose records are in sequential order may be accessed sequentially or directly via an index. The **medium** of file storage will also be important. Serial access devices, such as magnetic tapes, do not support direct access to records and serial and sequential files are dominant. Direct access devices such as disks are suited to the direct access possible in random and indexed sequential files. In the end it comes down to the *type of processing* and *speed of record retrieval* required by the system. Processing a large amount of ordered data with little need to access specified records lends itself to sequential file organisation, perhaps using one of the cheaper storage media such as magnetic tape. In contrast systems which have unpredictable retrieval

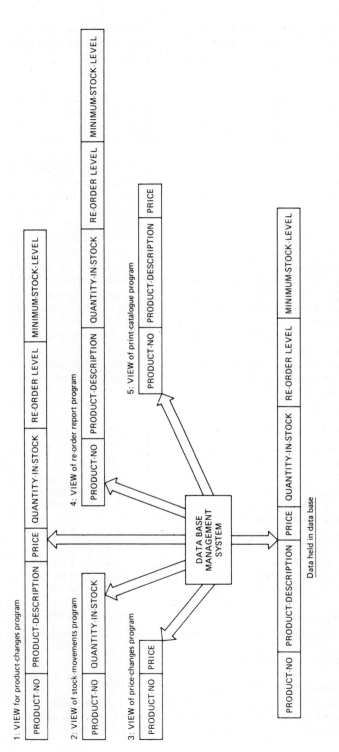

Fig. 2.3 Local views of data held in a data base (Adopted from D R Howe, *Data Analysis for Date Base Design*, Edward Arnold)

requirements that have to be quickly performed demand fast access methods, perhaps using random files, and fast storage media. Some aspects of these issues are explored again in Part 3 when the design of files is examined in a little more detail.

2.4.2   Data bases

Data base management systems (DBMS) free the programmer from the tasks of data organisation and location. The data base can be conceived as a common pool of data which is both organised and accessed by the DBMS. Individual users have specific *views* of the data base which reflect their needs and requirements. Such a view is likely to exclude large sections of the data base and indeed users may be unaware that they are actually using a selected sub-set of the organisation's data resources. The DBMS has to arrange physical storage, access requests, security, as well as data amendment, deletion and addition. It attempts to produce a data resource independent of individual application requirements. An example of this is given in Fig. 2.3 (adopted from Howe — see Further reading). Data base literature distinguishes between the external view of the DBMS — what the data base appears to look like for each application — and the internal organisation — how the stored data is actually implemented. The latter aspect will include elements of the file arrangements and access methods already considered. The actual organisation and architecture of the DBMS will vary from vendor to vendor. Some claimed 'data bases' are actually conventional file systems while more sophisticated products achieve a great deal of independence between the external and internal arrrangements. In general, DBMSs have forced organisations to re-assess their data needs and to control the data resource in a much more disciplined fashion. The task of co-ordinating and undertaking these activities has often been given to a **data administrator**. The data base is a shared organisation resource; therefore it is essential to have a person, or group of persons, responsible for co-ordinating its design, implementation and maintenance.

Further reading

Coats R B, *Software Engineering for Small Computers*, Edward Arnold (1982)

Sub-titled '*A Programmer's Companion*'; Coats has produced a book for those who have learnt the basic principles of programming but who 'now want to learn how to produce reliable, robust and well structured programs'. A valuable insight into competent programming and largely language independent so that it is of interest to the more casual reader.

Howe D, *Data Analysis for Data Base Design*, Edward Arnold (1983)

Howe's book is discussed again in the Further reading recommended for Chapter 5. However, for the reader who is interested in seeing examples of a DBMS in action in detail Part 4 of the book — Implementation — is particularly useful.

Lobell R F, *Application Program Developers — A State of the the Art Survey*, NCC (1981)

Discusses the problems of defining what is meant by a Fourth Generation Language (called Application Program Developers by Lobell) and then surveys the field. Not a book for the casual reader to purchase but well worth requesting from a local library.

Martin J, Fourth Generation Languages, Two Volumes, Prentice-Hall (1986)

Those interested in future developments should dip into this book. Far too expensive to buy for the casual reader but very comprehensive and enjoyable reading. Martin attempts to define what is required in a Fourth Generation Language and then looks at some of those on offer.

Part 2
Systems Analysis

This Part examines how candidate systems for computerisation may be identified and analysed. Chapter 3 looks at the identification and selection of projects and introduces simple concepts of technical, operational and economic feasibility. This stems from a discussion of how competing claims for resources may be placed in order of priority, so that key systems receive immediate attention.

Once an appropriate project has been selected, detailed analysis may begin. This is the subject of Chapter 4. It is split into three basic parts.

- Fact finding techniques. How to find facts about the system.

- Organising collected facts. The role of documentation, marshalling facts into defined standards.

- What facts should be recorded. What facts are being collected and documented. These are organised into five main areas:

  physical resources
  document flow
  processes and procedures
  personnel and jobs
  data.

A representative model is introduced to illustrate each of these areas of interest.

At the end of Chapter 4 the person undertaking the analysis, (henceforth called the analyst, designer or developer), should have a good understanding of the current operational system, of requirements not met by that system, and of the *logical system* that must underlie any subsequent design. Furthermore, the very act of appraisal may have discovered fundamental problems and suggested significant improvements. Analysis provides a baseline for future planning and development. Someone once said (I seem to recall that it was attributed to Walt Whitman) that 'a problem understood was half-solved'. This homily is particularly applicable to computer systems development.

3
Preliminary analysis

3.1 Introduction

This chapter looks at early stages of computerisation examining some of the issues that will be encountered at the start of a project.

3.2 Problem identification and selection

Every organisation faces two fundamental problems when it considers the role of computers.

- It has to identify opportunities for computerisation.
- It needs to give these opportunities appropriate priority.

It is important not to jump to conclusions when establishing areas of the enterprise that might benefit from computerisation. For example, payroll is a common and relatively simple application, but there is no reason why this should *necessarily* be computerised in every organisation. The fact that something *can* be computerised does not mean that it *should* be. Computer systems that aid the organisation's aims and prosperity should receive priority. A simple, slightly fictionalised, example illustrates this.

LDF Engineering was a small engineering firm based in the Midlands. It appointed a keen and aggressive accountant who set about the task of acquiring the firm's first computer to support his planned computerisation of the accounting ledgers and payroll. The hardware and software selection was performed meticulously and an appropriate system was purchased and installed. Just over one year later the firm went into voluntary liquidation. At the post mortem it was felt that over-stocking of certain product lines and poor production planning and control had been major contributors to the company's decline. Yet these are applications suited to computerisation! In retrospect, the firm appeared to have successfully computerised the *wrong* system. If better stock and production controls had been applied through using a computer system they may have resulted in something that the accounts application could not offer — the organisation's survival.

Unfortunately, the selection of relevant applications is much easier with the benefit of hindsight. However, it is a problem that cannot be passed over and so it is necessary to examine ways of analysing an organisation's activity that may lead to a better chance of identifying the most appropriate computer applications.

Two different illustrative approaches to this problem are considered. The 'Soft Systems' approach which explores the problem area, and the Grindley and Humble Effective Computer method based around MBO or Management by Objectives.

3.2.1 Soft systems methodology
Some of the most interesting work in systems understanding is being carried out by Peter Checkland (see Further reading) and his colleagues at the Department of

Systems, University of Lancaster. Their research and practice is primarily concerned with tackling the ill structured problems of the real world and suggesting solutions that may, or may not, include computers. Their 'Soft Systems Methodology' attempts to solve the fuzzy and complicated problems of organisations where there often appears to be insurmountable problems in *defining* the problem, let alone solving it.

Although Checkland's work has gained academic favour, it has often been too complex for students and too abstract for the practising systems analyst. Wood-Harper et al (see Further reading) have incorporated the Checkland model into their Information System Design approach called Multiview and in doing so they have also made it more accessible to the lay reader. They have also extended the idea of the **rich picture**, a model which is worth considering in more detail, because it provides a diagrammatical way of exploring complexity.

At the beginning of a systems project the people involved are likely to have only a fuzzy idea of what they want to achieve. Even if the proposed objectives can be sorted out, they still need to be formulated in such a way that they can be explained to analysts and potential suppliers. A useful technique for modelling the overall system under consideration is the rich picture. It attempts to show what the organisation is *about*.

The picture is constructed by first putting the system area under consideration into a large bubble in the centre of the page. Other symbols are sketched in to represent people, activities and physical objects of interest and importance to that system. Arrowed lines show relationships, crossed swords indicate conflict and 'think' bubbles may be used to show the main worries of the participants. The relative importance of people and things may be reflected in the size of the symbols.

Rich pictures should be largely self-explanatory as they are designed to aid communication as well as helping the analyst visualise the problem setting. It is a method of pictorially representing three important considerations in information systems design.

- Elements of structure in the problem area. This might include departmental boundaries, physical or geographical layout and product types and activities.

- Elements of process. What takes place in the system.

- Elements of relationships. The relationship between structure and process is the climate of the problem area. This will include conflicts, worries and mismatches between new processes and old structures.

A rich picture for a library system is included as Fig. 3.1. It also includes a 'Beady Eye' representing the Library Sub-Committee who wish to ensure that they get good value for their money. There are no agreed standards for drawing rich pictures and you may wish to add other symbols and ideas that you feel are particularly appropriate for a certain set of circumstances. This is valuable until the picture becomes so complicated that the essential structures and processes are obscured. At this point rich pictures begin to have more in common with art than information system design.

3.2.2   Management by objectives — the effective computer

A more pragmatic, and perhaps more accessible, approach is suggested by Grindley and Humble in their 1973 text, *The Effective Computer*. Their book was written in response to observation of many projects where the computer failed to satisfy the expectations of managers, a failure that still exists over a decade later. In it they suggest that

'The only valid objective for computers is to assist in achieving defined business improvements which would be impossible or uneconomic without the computer.'

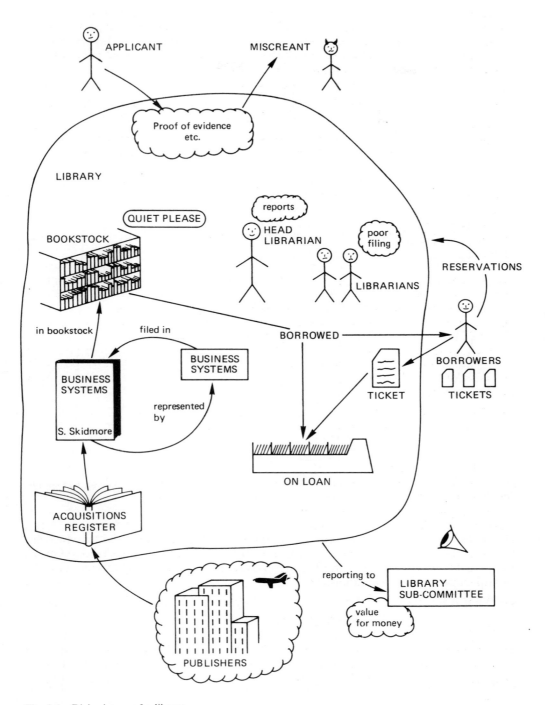

Fig. 3.1 Rich picture of a library

Thus the computer is seen to aid the *doers* and *makers* of an organisation to achieve their profit or service objectives. Benefits are of two fundamental types — getting more for the things that are provided or sold (selling more, selling at a higher price) or reducing the costs of making and selling them (carrying less stock, making production more efficient). However, as the authors note

'Those who run the computer do not usually have the responsibility for selling, pricing, or production efficiency. It is not open to them to obtain benefits directly. Their role, therefore, must be to help those who can achieve benefits.'

Their proposed effective computer approach takes a business approach to computerisation. It consists of six stages, illustrated in Fig. 3.2 and described below.

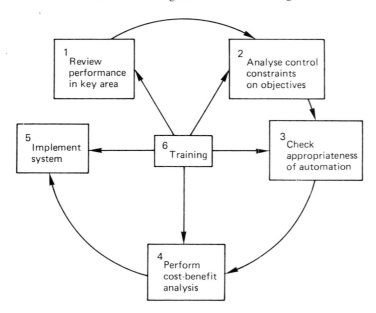

Fig 3.2   The effective computer — a six stage approach (Adopted from K Grindley and J Humble, *The Effective Computer*, Courtesy of McGraw-Hill Ltd)

1   Review performance in key area.
The first step is to identify the key areas of the business; five or six activities which are crucial to the organisation's success. This is so that improvements are suggested in the areas that critically affect profits or service. Three sets of questions aid the identification of these key areas.

● What is our purpose? Why do we exist? What needs or markets are we trying to satisfy? What major changes would we wish to bring about in the next three to five years?

● What is the present situation of the firm? What are our internal strengths and weaknesses? What external threats are posed by governments or competitors?

● Given our present situation, what are the vital activities that will help us fulfill our plans and purpose?

These questions are not easy to answer but they do force a therapeutic self-diagnosis which can lead to a clearer vision of the organisation's present position and future aspirations.

2   Analyse control constraints on objectives

Having established a particular key area it is now necessary to set a realistic target for objectives and to examine what control factors may prevent their achievement. In doing so the contribution of the computer to achieving each objective will also be considered.

Grindley and Humble give a series of examples of which two are repeated below.

Corporation   Aircraft spares
Key area   Market share
Objective   To increase sales volume by 40% by. . .
Contribution To install an on-line terminal in customer's premises showing our stock and delivery position and price.

Corporation   Carton manufacturer
Key area   Productivity
Objective   To reduce waste on box manufacture by 8%
Contribution To implement an order analysis system for determining optimum width and run size for corrugated paper.

It is important that the objectives are quantified. This forces realistic target setting and agreed measures of success. An objective to 'reduce inventory holding' is successfully achieved if only one less item is carried! However, an objective to reduce inventory by 5% by January 1987 makes the criteria of success more specific.

3   Check appropriateness of automation

This is to examine whether a possible area of computerisation will create unacceptable jobs or cause unnecessary customer difficulties. Seven major areas repay investigation.

- Is an apparently irrelevant duplication of work actually propping up the present system?
- Does the new system threaten an important application of human judgement or local knowledge?
- Will unacceptable jobs be created?
- Will automation remove a necessary human contact?
- Does the present system rely on bending rather than following rules? Has this been recognised and planned for?
- Will a proposed change create inflexibility which may hinder future adaptation to changing requirements?
- Will automation destroy the motivation of humans involved in the system?

4   Perform cost-benefit analysis

Cost-benefit analysis will be examined in a later section of this chapter. Grindley and Humble suggest that benefits should be listed before costs and that *all* benefits and costs associated with the project should be included. This will include operational costs required to achieve the objective that have nothing to do with computerisation. For example, a press release, a new administrative structure, a mailshot. They suggest that any attempt to identify the *computer's* contribution to an objective will not be possible or worthwhile.

5 and 6   System implementation and training

Implementation and training will be considered in Part 5.

The strength of The Effective Computer approach is its view of the computer as an aid to achieving some new business objective, one that would be difficult, costly or impossible to achieve without computerisation. Grindley and Humble make the important point that

'this approach differs from those which simply attempt to perform some existing system better (cheaper, faster, more accurately, etc.)'

Thus two distinct approaches have been introduced. They both have much to offer and both repay further investigation. What they have in common is their attempt to prevent inappropriately simplistic responses to complex organisational problems.

3.3   Triggers of change

An important factor to consider early on in a systems study is the motivation behind the desire to computerise. What has triggered off the organisation's need for change? Three types of trigger may be identified.

3.3.1   Positive trigger

'I spend a lot of my time compiling figures, producing and revising forecasts and then presenting reports and plans based on these figures. Surely the computer can help me in some way.'

In such instances the problems of the present system have been identified by those who run and use the system. The computer is seen as a possible way of getting system improvements. There is a positive commitment to computerisation — the system's user is on the analyst's side.

3.3.2   Negative trigger

'We have had problems with stores ever since I became a director. It's time we computerised it and got up with the times. That will sort them out down there!'

In many instances the decision to consider computerisation is taken by the system's user, not those who actually operate the system. In such circumstances the perception of the present system's performance is unlikely to be shared by all those concerned with running the system. Indeed the operators of the system may see any investigation as a criticism of their present performance and the systems that they have created.

In the example represented in the above quote, the company's managers had 'lost control' of stores. They had been looking for an excuse to impose new controls for some time and computerisation presented that opportunity. All the members of the stores section resisted the computerisation plans. They felt that management did not understand what happened in the stores section and staff morale was low. They were aggrieved that the systems that had been developed over many years were now deemed to be inadequate by people who, they believed, did not understand them.

Both sides had valid points, but pity the poor analyst stuck in the middle! In such projects the chance of failure is much greater because many of the key personnel in the system are actually willing that failure. In these circumstances the climate of implementation, the timescales and the level of ambition are all very different to projects undertaken in response to positive triggers. The analyst has to tread more carefully, take more time and be less ambitous in the proposed changes.

Such projects are very common. The problems they present are too fundamental to be solved by rational argument or advisory meetings and presentations. The analyst has no option but to get on with the system under conditions and constraints that may, at some time, seem to be intolerable. In such instances the computer is being used as a substitute for management and the analyst must recognise this and plan accordingly.

3.3.3 Neutral triggers

'The insistence of the auditors that we improve our controls and reporting systems finally convinced us of our need to computerise.'

Neutral triggers are events that are outside the scope and control of the system. These may be as a result of government instructions (a need to present accounts in a certain way), legal requirements or the advice of external agencies such as professional associations or auditors. Such triggers have little positive or negative effect on the project in hand.

The reasons behind making the large, and sometimes traumatic, step to computerisation undoubtedly affect the rest of the project. Thus we need to probe and understand these reasons to help guage the climate of the project and to adjust timescales and objectives accordingly.

3.4 Feasibility study

Once a preliminary area of application has been established it may then be subjected to a more rigorous examination in a **feasibility study**. The analyst will, of course, already have formed some ideas about the application from the preliminary investigation. The feasibility study represents an opportunity to 'firm up' knowledge of the system and to form ideas about the scope and costs of possible solutions. In many respects the feasibility study is a quick mini-systems analysis with the analyst being concerned with many of the issues and using many of the techniques required in later detailed work. Feasibility studies are usually undertaken within tight time constraints (3 months is typical) and normally culminate in a written and oral feasibility report. The content and recommendations of such a study will be used as a basis for deciding whether to proceed, postpone or cancel the project. Thus, as the feasibility study may lead to the commitment of huge resources, it is important that it is conducted competently and that no fundamental errors of judgement are made. This is easier said than done!

Perhaps the best way of illustrating what might be undertaken in a feasibility study is to examine the possible contents of a feasibility report. The structure given below is based upon one suggested by Collins and Blay (see Further reading).

Introduction

Terms of reference This is likely to include reference back to the preliminary analysis and an explanation of how the system under discussion was selected as a candidate for investigation. It will also include details about the scope, resources and timescale of the study.

Existing system A description of the relevant system(s) currently operating in the organisation. These will have been investigated using the fact finding techniques described in the next chapter and documented and presented using appropriate methods such as flowcharts and dataflow diagrams.

System requirements   These will be derived from the existing system (outputs currently produced may still be required when the system is replaced) and from discussion with system users and operators who have identified requirements that are not currently fulfilled. Critical performance factors must also be covered (e.g. the need to produce 5000 invoices per day, to process transactions in less than five seconds) because these will have an important bearing on the hardware selection. Audit, security and data protection implications may also be discussed.

Proposed systems   An outline *logical* system design may be presented, together with sketchy definitions of inputs and outputs. These will be described more in their content than their layout and display.

The differences and advantages of the proposed system over its predecessor will be highlighted, together with its effect on other systems currently operating in the organisation. The new system may impose certain constraints in operation (e.g. all input documents must be submitted by 4 p.m.) and these should be clearly described and discussed.

The possible effects on staff must be identified and a strategy for staff training, reduction or redeployment suggested.

The equipment and software requirements of the system must be described. The extent to which this can be done depends upon the current resources of the organisation. If the firm already has a large computer then the extra hardware is likely to be additional terminals, more secondary storage, perhaps more memory. It is likely that these will not be required until the system becomes operational and so such requirements may be altered as detailed analysis and development clarifies the nature of the system.

In contrast, large projects and organisations without significant computing resources will have to invest in hardware before development can get under way. As a result there are significant pressures to select and purchase hardware very early in the project's life, before many of the detailed implications of the systems have been discovered.

Plans will also have to be made for security and disaster recovery. For example, the purchase or two machines may be considered so that if one fails the other can be brought swiftly into operation.

Development plan   Suggested project plan (see Part 5) and suggestions for phasing in the project and managing the transition from the present to the proposed system.

Costs and benefits   These are discussed more fully when economic feasibility is considered (3.4.1).

Alternatives considered   In the process of arriving at a suggested system the analyst usually considers and rejects a number of alternatives. It is important to record these considerations for two main reasons. Firstly, it may nip a number of time-consuming 'have you considered. . .' discussions in the bud. Secondly, it permits the sponsor of the study to examine the legitimacy of the reasons for rejection. For example, the analyst may have rejected a certain option because, in impressions gained from the preliminary analysis, it appeared to be too costly. However, the information contained in the study may now persuade the sponsor to change his mind about the level of ambition of the project and so the option rejected by the analyst may become feasible. This alteration would be unlikely if details of rejected alternatives were not included.

Conclusions and recommendations
Appendices

3.4.1 Three types of feasibility
In the conduct of the feasibility study the analyst will consider three distinct, but inter-related types of feasibility.
Technical feasibility
This is concerned with specifying equipment and software that successfully support the tasks required. The technical needs of systems will vary considerably, but might include the following.

- The facility to produce outputs in a given time scale — e.g. 20 000 examination certificates in three weeks.

- The ability to provide certain response times under certain conditions — e.g. no more than two second response time at each terminal when there are four terminals being used simultaneously.

- The facility to input a large number of documents in a limited time scale — e.g. 400 000 gas readings in one day.

- The ability to process a certain volume of transactions at a certain speed — e.g. to report and record airline reservations without a significant delay to the passenger.

- The facility to communicate data to distant locations — e.g. regional sales figures transmitted to an American head office.

In examining technical feasibility it is the **configuration** of the system that is intially more important than the actual *hardware make*. The configuration should show the system's requirements: how many workstations are provided, how these units should be able to operate and communicate, what input and output speeds should be achieved and at what quality etc. This can be used as a basis for the tender document against which dealers and manufacturers can bid (see Part 5). Specific hardware products are then evaluated in the context of these logical needs.

At the feasibility stage it is possible that two or three different configurations will be pursued which satisfy the key technical requirements but which represent different levels of ambition and cost. Investigation of these technical alternatives can be aided by approaching a range of suppliers for preliminary discussions. The technical performance and costs of rejected alternatives should be documented in the feasibility study.

Operational feasibility
Operational feasibility is concerned with human, organisational and political aspects. General impressions of these factors will have been gained during the preliminary analysis and through consideration of the system trigger. Amongst the issues examined are the following.

- What job changes will the system bring? Most people react unfavourably to change. Planned job changes must be carefully handled so that those affected are seen to gain in a way that they feel is acceptable. This may be through job enrichment or through raising wages.

- What organisational structures are disturbed? The suggested system may cut across accepted organisational relationships and threaten the status of individuals and their promotional expectations.

- What new skills will be required? Do the current employees possess these skills? If not, can they learn them? How long will they take to learn?

It is unlikely that a project will be rejected solely on the grounds of operational infeasibility but such considerations are likely to affect critically the nature and scope of the eventual recommendations.

It should also be recognised that although the computer brings significant alterations to an organisation it is not the only source of change. The way that an organisation manages and implements changes in other areas must be considered when computer related changes are planned. Agreed procedures for discussing proposals — staff consultative committee, trade union agreements, staff forums etc. — should be identified and adhered to.

Economic feasibility
Many organisations and projects are evaluated on a financial basis. For this reason, management tend to give more weight to economic feasibility than to technical and operational considerations. A number of approaches to costing solutions have been suggested. Options include the following.

Least cost   This is based on the observation that costs are easier to control and identify than revenues. Thus it assumes that there is no income change caused by the implementation of a new system. In such an evaluation only the costs are listed and the option with the lowest cost is selected.

The costs listed will include

Capital costs
Hardware
Software
Communication facilities
Furniture
Cost of converting the data from present to proposed system
Staff retraining

Operating costs
Hardware maintenance
Software maintenance
Operating expenses
Consumables
Salaries
Staff training

Time to payback   The 'time to payback' method of economic evaluation is an attempt to answer the question 'how long will it be until we get our money back on this investment in systems?'. This requires data on both costs and benefits. However, benefits are typically more difficult to quantify than costs. There are several reasons for this.

● Uncertainty about the timing and amount.

● Problems of expressing certain benefits in direct monetary terms. What is the value of not having to apologise for as many order errors? Many benefits will often appear as 'intangibles' — better management information, improved management controls etc.

● The benefit is often due to a joint effort of a number of departments in the organisation. In such cases it is very difficult to assess the computer's contribution. You will recall that Grindley and Humble explicitly recognised this by suggesting *all* costs and benefits incurred in a system project should be included.

These difficulties will have to be faced if benefits are to be included in any type of evaluation.

In the 'time to payback' method, the alternative which repays the initial investment the quickest is selected. This is illustrated in the example given in Table 3.1.

Table 3.1 Illustration of the 'Time to Payoff' method

Years from now	Costs Alternative		Benefits Alternative		Net difference alternative	
	A	B	A	B	A	B
0	20	30	0	0	−20	−30
1	40	50	0	0	−40	−50
2	80	75	0	0	−80	−75
Investment	140	155	0	0	−140	−155
3	30	30	40	40	+10	+10
4	20	20	50	45	+30	+25
5	20	20	60	65	+40	+45
6	20	20	65	70	+45	+50
7	20	20	50	60	+30	+40
8	20	20	40	45	+20	+25
9	20	20	40	45	+20	+25
10	20	20	40	40	+20	+20
Income	170	170	385	410	+215	+240

Calculation of 'Time to payback'

Average annual = Operational / No. of
difference   difference / years.

$$\begin{array}{lll} & = A & B \\ & =215/8 & 240/8 \\ & = 26.875 & 30.00 \end{array}$$

'Time to payback' = investment/average annual difference = 140/26.875   155/30.00

$$\begin{array}{ll} = 5.21 & 5.16 \end{array}$$

plus the two years of investment

$$\begin{array}{ll} = 7.21 & 7.16 \end{array}$$

option B is selcted because it 'pays back' sooner

This method of evaluation has two significant disadvantages.

- It only considers the return on the original investment and ignores the system's long term profitability. Thus alternatives that are more profitable *in the long run* are not selected.

- It does not recognise the time value of money. Benefits in options that accrue in the distant future are not worth as much as benefits in projects which occur more quickly. The 'time to payback' method fails to recognise this.

Net present value This is a well defined and practised method of economic evaluation. It builds in an allowance for the 'time' value of money, represented by the **present value factor**. In this method the net benefits are discounted in value by applying this factor, reducing the value of a benefit to its present worth. Hence benefits of £30 000 planned for ten years time will actually be worth only £4 800 if a present value factor of 20% is selected. Thus benefits that appear late in the project's life span contribute little to its economic feasibility. The application of net present value is shown in Table 3.2.

Table 3.2   Illustration of net present value

Year	Cash flows (from Table 3.1) Alternative A	B	Present value factor at 10%	Net present value Alternative A	B
0	−20	−30	1.000	−20.00	−30.00
1	−40	−50	0.909	−36.36	−45.45
2	−80	−75	0.826	−66.08	−61.95
3	+10	+10	0.751	+ 7.51	+ 7.51
4	+30	+25	0.683	+20.49	+17.08
5	+40	+45	0.621	+24.84	+27.95
6	+45	+50	0.564	+25.38	+28.20
7	+30	+40	0.513	+15.39	+20.52
8	+20	+25	0.467	+ 9.34	+10.60
9	+20	+25	0.424	+ 8.48	+ 8.48
10	+20	+20	0.386	+ 7.72	+ 7.72
				− 3.29	− 9.34

Option A is chosen but note that more money could be earned by placing money in bank (assuming 10% interest).

Although the evaluation of alternatives using this method is reasonably well accepted it must be recognised that the technique is rather conservative. In most computer projects the costs arrive early, while most benefits accrue in the later years. As a result these are heavily discounted and consequently projects which produce benefits earlier are favoured. There is also the problem of selecting a suitable present value factor. Often the interest rate is chosen because it represents how much could be earned by placing the money in the bank rather than investing it in computer systems.

Breakeven analysis   This is a technique that does not require the selection of an interest rate because it has no concern for the time value of money. It is particularly useful where the system is subject to varying workloads.

Breakeven analysis distinguishes between fixed and variable costs and fixed and variable benefits. The data is plotted on a graph where the vertical axis is the amount of cost or benefit, and the horizontal axis is the level of the workload. The fixed costs are plotted first with the variable costs plotted above them to show the increase in total costs as the workload increases. The same is done for the benefits. The crossing point of the total benefits line with the total costs line indicates the breakeven point. Workloads to the left of this point do not justify the use of the system, while workloads to the right of the breakeven point do. Breakeven analysis does not give the full picture needed for the economic evaluation of systems, but its emphasis on the operational phases can be useful.

In conclusion, there are a variety of methods which may be used in economic evaluation. These methods may give contradictory advice and none of them enjoys universal acceptance. However, it has to be accepted that many organisations will expect projects to be justified financially usually using the organisation's standard method for project evaluation.

3.4.2   The feasibility compromise

The three ways of approaching feasibility are likely to conflict. In general, 'better' technical solutions cost more money while robust, helpful, user-friendly software is time consuming to write and hence development costs are high. Such software may also mean larger programs and so the system has to carry a much larger software overhead and this may begin to conflict with performance requirements. In many instances technical and economic factors become paramount — 'the system must have a two second response time and return its investment in three years' — and so it is the operational factors that become devalued. This often has unfortunate consequences.

The feasibility study differs from analysis 'proper' in its level of detail. It is difficult to give general advice on what constitutes an acceptable depth of analysis because this will vary with the organisation and the application. There is always the nagging doubt that the detailed analysis work will uncover a hitherto overlooked fact that now makes the project infeasible. This is further complicated by the difficulty of reconciling the three feasibility criteria, particularly with the insistence of many organisations on an economic cost benefit analysis. The restricted timescale of a feasibility study also makes it difficult to evaluate comprehensively and offer sufficient alternative options at different levels of cost and ambition.

The microcomputer market has special difficulties in conducting feasibility studies. In large organisations the task may be given to a senior analyst, but in a firm computerising for the first time there is no equivalent person. Thus the firm is very dependent upon its own resources and the integrity of possible suppliers. In most instances the suppliers of microcomputers will not have the necessary resources, skill or time to perform a proper feasibility study. It is difficult to justify even one day of analysis on a job with a likely profit margin of less than £1000. Thus the preparation for computerisation may be less than ideal.

3.5   Summary

This chapter has given a brief review of some of the preliminary issues that will be encountered in a systems project. It began by recognising that problems may be difficult to identify and suggested that a rich picture might be an effective way of exploring the problem setting. Once possible systems have been identified, they may be placed in priority order using the approach suggested by Grindley and Humble. These possible areas of application can then be subjected to a feasibility study. Three important criteria must be considered — technical, operational and economic — and a reasonable compromise suggested. The feasibility study will culminate in the feasibility report which will be presented to management for approval. If this approval is forthcoming then detailed analysis and design will commence.

Further reading

Chapin N, 'Economic Evaluation in Systems Analysis and Design', in *Systems Analysis and Design — A Foundation for the 1980s*, Cotterman et al (ed) W, North Holland (1981)

Considers financial feasibility in more detail.

Checkland P, *Systems Theory: Systems Practice*, Wiley (1981)

The definitive textbook on 'soft systems' analysis. The first part of the book gives a historical perspective, while the second part examines a series of case studies in the context of Checkland's suggested framework. Even if every nuance of academic argument is not understood, the case studies provide stimulating and interesting reading.

Collins G and Blay G, *Structured Systems Development Techniques — Strategic Planning to System Testing*, Pitman (1982)

The source of the feasibility study content discussed in this chapter.

Grindley K and Humble J, *The Effective Computer*, McGraw-Hill (1973)

Excellent introduction to strategic business computing within a management by objectives framework. Many interesting and relevant case study examples.

Isshiki K, *Small Business Computers*, Prentice-Hall (1982)

Includes relevant sections on the economic evaluation of systems.

Wood-Harper A T, Antill L and Avison D E, *Information Systems Definition — The Multiview Approach* Blackwell (1985)

The Multiview approach includes an accessible approach to problem formulation in the spirit of Checkland. Useful case study example runs as a thread through the book.

4
Systems analysis

4.1 Introduction

The detailed analysis of systems and their user's and operator's needs and requirements may begin once the go ahead for a project has been received.

Analysis is primarily concerned with three aspects: *finding facts* that will support
our understanding of the present system and aid the design of any successor; *mastering
fact-finding techniques* that will enable us to find these facts; *organising* the facts into a
rigorous set of documentation.

A selection of fact-finding techniques will be considered before examining how and
where they can be used.

4.2 Fact-finding techniques

4.2.1 Interviewing
Interviews are formal meetings where the analyst can obtain information about the
operation of the present systems and statements of needs and requirements for any
proposed replacements. It is likely that a series of inteviews will be held with users and
operators and these will change in nature as the project progresses. Early meetings
will mainly be concerned with the analyst feeling the way, trying to understand the
operations and terminology of the present system. Later meetings are more likely to
be concerned with specific issues in the design of a new system — for example, the
content and layout of an aged debtors report.

In many respects the first few interviews in a project are the most difficult. They are
often undertaken at a time when the user feels vulnerable and there has been little
opportunity for the development of mutual trust between the participants. It is
particularly important that the analyst follows principles of good practice in these
preliminary discussions (see Further reading) — conforming to certain dress requirements is an example. Effective communication is difficult enough without erecting
avoidable barriers.

The analyst should prepare a **checklist** of points to cover during the interview.
However, this should not be slavishly adhered to as it may lose the opportunity of
discovering vital information not connected with the interview plan. Permitting the
user to develop certain themes (e.g. his/her views on the future of the stores
department) may give useful insights into inter-departmental tensions and personalities and this may ultimately prove more vital than a piece of operational information
such as the movement of the second copy of the GRN after the goods have been
despatched. Information will be provided at varying degrees of detail, bias and
significance — 'facts' will not emerge in neat parcels!

During an interview there will be certain types of inadequate response which the
analyst should attempt to identify.

- Non-response. The interviewee refuses to answer a question. The very act of refusal may give an important insight. An accountant's refusal to discuss his relationship with the marketing department may indicate certain inter-departmental conflict.

- Inaccurate response. This may occur through deliberate or accidental distortion. It is very common to find that two or three members or an organisation give slightly different descriptions of how certain operations are undertaken. There is often a distinction between how a manager *thinks* something is carried out and how it *actually* is. All responses should be cross-checked.

- Irrelevant response. The interviewee does not give an answer to the question asked. This tends to be a waste of time but is little more than an irritation if the information can be elicited from the next, more carefully phrased, question.

- Inappropriate question. The interviewee lacks the necessary information to frame an adequate response. This gives some ideas about the organisational boundaries. Incorrect information about part of a certain system may suggest that the interviewee has little direct connection or involvement in that particular operation.

- Partial response. A relevant but incomplete description is given. This is particularly dangerous as the analyst must be able to design a system that covers all forseeable possibilities.

4.2.2 Questionnaires

Questionnaires are a more structured and formal method of collecting data. They may be used by an interviewer to give a very controlled interview or, more commonly, they may be mailed to the respondent who returns the questionnaire after completion. This may be the only viable option where there are a large number of dispersed users. The mailed questionnaire has a number of advantages over interviews.

- It is relatively cheap, particularly the system concerns a scattered group of users and operators.

- It is free of interviewer distortion and error.

- It permits time to refer to documents and documentation. Questions which concern detailed factual data — e.g. how many customers live in the South West are suited to questionnaire collection.

- It may be possible to ask more personal and controversial questions particularly if the response is to be anonymous.

However, a number of disadvantages can also be identified.

- The questions have to be relatively simple and straightforward.

- The answers given on the questionnaires are final and so there is no chance to probe beyond the answer or to clarify ambiguities unless a follow-up visit or phone call is made. This is not only expensive but impossible in surveys where questionnaires have not asked for name and address so permitting the respondent to be anonymous.

- The mailed questionnaire does not give the opportunity for the analyst to observe the user's workplace and work practices.

- There are likely to be difficulties in achieving a sufficient number of responses. It is not just the *number* of returned questionnaires that is important but, more seriously, running the risk that non-respondents differ significantly from those who have returned their questionnaires. If this is the case then conclusions based on those who have replied may be erroneous.

A fuller discussion on the relative merits of interviews and questionnaires is given in Moser and Kalton (see Further reading).

4.2.3 Special purpose records

A possible method of collecting information about certain aspects of a system is to establish special records and recording procedures. For example, in a stock control system there were worries about the time it took to 'pick' a customer's order. The stock staff themselves thought it took a 'fair amount of time due to the conditions in which we work' but they could not fully explain the factors which led to picking delays. As a result special records were established where the 'Picker' entered the order number, quantity and the time of commencing and completing the order. The data was collected for three representative months and then analysed. The results led to a number of new working procedures being included in the proposed computer system.

However, in general, special purpose records should be avoided where possible because they are likely to impose additional administration on the operators of the system.

4.2.4 Observation

This is concerned with watching and recording certain events as they occur. In some systems it may be the only feasible method of data collection. For example, in a system to control and plan reservoir levels, the pattern and volume of water inflow had to be observed and measured — it is very difficult to interview a river!

In more conventional administrative systems the analyst will constantly be observing features of a business operation (shop floor layout, relative position of senior officer's offices) usually in an informal way. There is also the opportunity to make this more formal by, for instance, working at a desk in the user's office so as to observe the 'way that customer queries are dealt with at first hand'. This may be useful but should be treated with some caution. It has repeatedly been shown that people who know that they are being observed tend to change their normal patterns of behaviour, so reducing the value and validity of information gathered in this way.

4.2.5 Listening

Listening is an important but neglected skill. Sperry (now Unisys) attached such importance to this that they developed a company wide programme to improve the art of good listening. In their advertising they made the points that

'Most of us spend about half our business hours listening. . . research studies show that on average we listen at a 25% level of efficiency.' 'With more than 22 million workers in Britain a simple £5 listening mistake by each of them would cost £110 million.'
(Reproduced here with the kind permission of Unisys)

4.2.6 Document analysis

Documents are very important because they represent the formal flows of data in the present system. Most of these flows were initiated for a good reason, even if no-one can remember it! The analyst should collect specimens of all documents — input forms, output analyses, reports, invoices, delivery notes, customer statements etc. in an effort to build up a picture of how data is passed and used in the current administrative systems.

Document analysis should also include an assessment of the clarity of the form and how well it satisfies its purpose. The analyst is particularly looking for ambiguity or obsolescence — e.g. column headings that do not correctly indicate the data entered under that item. The volume of documents produced or received is also significant. Any new system must be able to cope with the amount of data passing through it including seasonal peaks or other variations. A simple average measure is of little use in these circumstances as a system built around averages will under-perform for almost half of the time! The growth rate of document use is also important. If the number of documents (say invoices) is increasing by 12% per annum then it would be inappropriate to tailor the system around current volumes.

Documents may also be copied — or be multi-part in the first place — with copies going to different people or departments. Each copy must be traced, its purpose ascertained and the filing sequence noted as this is likely to indicate how old copies are currently retrieved. For example, if copy invoices are filed in date order then it is very likely that their retrieval will be based on date of invoice, not on any other data item on the invoice such as customer name. This information may be of importance in the subsequent design of files on any proposed computer system. We may decide to *index* on date of order as well as on more likely fields such as customer name or account number.

4.3   Organising the facts

During the fact-finding stage it is important to organise and record the collected facts in some standard way. This is usually as prescribed in a set of data processing standards developed or adopted by the systems section of the organisation. One of the most widespread sets of standards used in the UK is that suggested by the National Computing Centre (NCC). Two examples are included illustrating aspects introduced in Section 4.2 Fig. 4.1 is a record of an interview (meeting) and Fig. 4.2 permits the documentation of a clerical document.

Standards have a wider use than just documentation. They should aid analysis and design by prompting the analyst to pose certain questions so that parts of the documentation may be completed. The clerical documentation specification requires the analyst to insert the maximum and minimum number of the documents passing through the present system. Thus the analyst must obtain that data and include the question in an interview with the relevant user. In this way documentation provides *prompts* for action not just a *record* of actions.

Standards also represent a method of controlling projects. The head of the systems section can effectively control the way that all system projects are developed by insisting upon completion and adherence to certain standards. This may be very useful because, as Daniels and Yeates (see Further reading) once wrote, 'until the system is implemented the only tangible evidence that the analyst has done any work is his documentation'.

Finally, standards usually include modelling tools such as flowcharts which permit the communication of facts between the analyst and the users and between the analyst and colleagues and managers.

Thus standards are primarily concerned with *aiding* analysis and design, *documenting* the results of analysis and *communicating* these results to other people. To achieve these aims the standards will use a number of diagrammatical models and techniques — flowcharts, dataflow diagrams, Structured English — and the variety and scope of such methods has been amply demonstrated in Martin's recent book (see Further reading). Clearly a thorough treatment is beyond this text and so only one

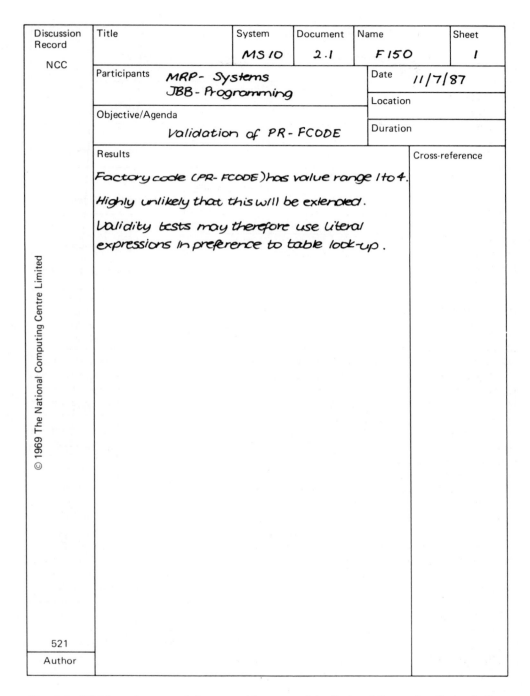

Discussion Record NCC	Title		System MS 10	Document 2.1	Name F 150		Sheet 1
	Participants MRP- Systems JBB- Programming				Date 11/7/87		
					Location		
	Objective/Agenda Validation of PR- FCODE				Duration		
	Results Factory code (PR- FCODE) has value range 1 to 4. Highly unlikely that this will be extended. Validity tests may therefore use literal expressions in preference to table look-up.					Cross-reference	

521

Author

Fig. 4.1 NCC Interview record document (Courtesy of the National Computing Centre Ltd)

Clerical Document Specification NCC	Document description	System	Document	Name	Sheet
	Factory Order Ledger	SOP	4.1	OLED	1

Stationery ref.	Size	Number of parts	Method of preparation
SCL 10	A4	1	Handwritten

Filing sequence	Medium	Prepared/maintained by
Page no.	Loose-leaf ring binder	Factory office clerks

Frequency of preparation/update	Retention period	Location
Daily / as required	6 months after despatch	All branch offices

Weekly receipts VOLUME	Minimum	Maximum	Av/Abs	Growth rate/fluctuations
1.	314	555	375	Long-term trend unknown
2.	275	484	336	
3.	145	259	178	Seasonal variations with orders
Total	734	1298	889	

Users/recipients	Purpose	Frequency of use
Factory office clerk (FOC)	To record orders received	daily
	To record completed despatches	daily
	To check that orders are despatched on time	weekly

Ref	Item	Picture	Occurrence	Value range	Source of data
1	Page (number)	9(5)	1 per page	10,000 - 99,999	FOC
2	Date (order received at factory)	99 AAA 99	1 per order, 41 per page	Valid date	FOC
3	SCL order number (SALEON)	9(6)	as ref 2	100,000 - 999,999	4.1 / ORDES
4	Customer name		as ref 2.		4.1 / ORDES.
5	Due (date)	99 AAA 99	as ref 2.	Valid date	4.1 / ORDES
6	Actual (date despatch completed)	99 AAA 99	as ref 2.	Valid date	4.1 / ADCONS (copy s)

Notes	Ref 4 : Customer name is usually first line of delivery or invoice name and address whichever is more meaningful to factory office clerk.
S41	

Author	Issue Date	

Fig. 4.2 NCC Clerical document description form (Courtesy of the National Computing Centre Ltd)

modelling method has been chosen to illustrate each general *type* of fact that must be collected. Readers who wish to extend their knowledge to include other models in the analyst's toolkit are encouraged to read James Martin's text.

4.4   What facts must be collected

The following are types of facts that should be of interest to us.

4.4.1   Physical resources

The analyst requires a clear understanding of the work processes undertaken in an organisation. Grindley and Humble asserted that the computer should be used to help the 'doers and makers' of an enterprise. Clearly this is only possible if the making and doing processes are thoroughly understood by the analyst. Thus models of, for example, the sequence of processes in garment manufacture or the machine layout in a foundry, can be used to aid understanding of the physical processes to which the system will be expected to contribute. The model will also illustrate environmental constraints such as available space, immovable objects and general conditions of cleanliness, atmosphere and light. These may again affect the siting and configuration of any eventual computer solution. Finally, the model of the physical layout will be useful in communicating ideas to people unfamiliar with the system, such as a computer manufacturer's representative, as well as providing a focus for otherwise abstract discussions with current employees of the company.

There is no standard method of modelling the physical resources and processes — a rough sketch, scale diagram, narrative, pictures and named symbols may all be appropriate. Possible examples arc given in Figs. 4.3 and 4.4. The first diagram identifies some of the physical boundaries of the company — the yarn store, the knitting room, the geographical dispersion of the make up factories. The second diagram presents the detail of the knitting room and provides a number of prompts for further analysis. For example

What is the temporary yarn store? How large is it?
How are reject rolls identified and dealt with?
How close are the machines? Will this cause problems?
What is the difference between an Orizio and an Interlock machine? Does it matter?

In fact the modelling of the knitting room led to two early project decisions. Firstly, the closeness of the machines ruled out the data collection method originally envisaged by the management. They had seen a possible system running at an exhibition but had failed to realise that it required more space than was available in their rather cramped knitting room. Secondly, the project had started due to 'production problems' and it was expected that most of the systems work would be concerned with the actual processes of production. However, a discussion of the layout of the knitting room with senior management, led to queries about the temporary yarn store — 'no such thing' said one. In fact this store was an unofficial repository maintained by the employees so that they were not slowed down by delays in requisitioning yarns from stores. This led to an investigation of stores and stocking procedures where numerous inefficiencies were uncovered. Many of the production difficulties were actually symptoms of poor stores procedures. This illustrates again the problem of knowing what the problem *is*! The model of the physical resources led to an earlier investigation of stores than may have otherwise occurred.

Finally, the physical model gives important clues to document flow in an organisation. Usually each physical flow, process or activity is recorded in some way. For

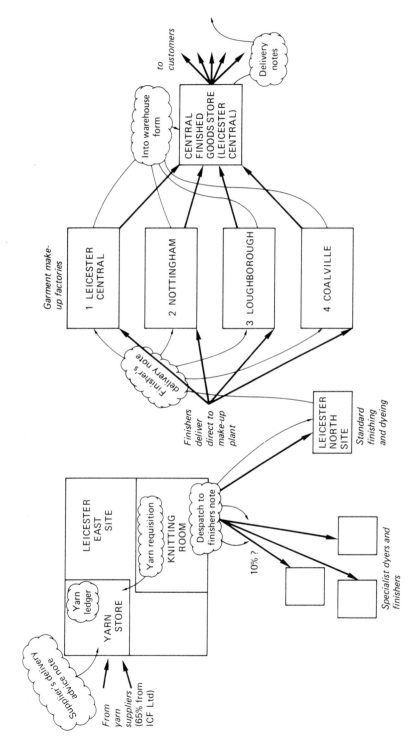

Fig. 4.3 Knitwear company — overview. 'Flows of information' represented by fine lines have been superimposed on the physical layout model

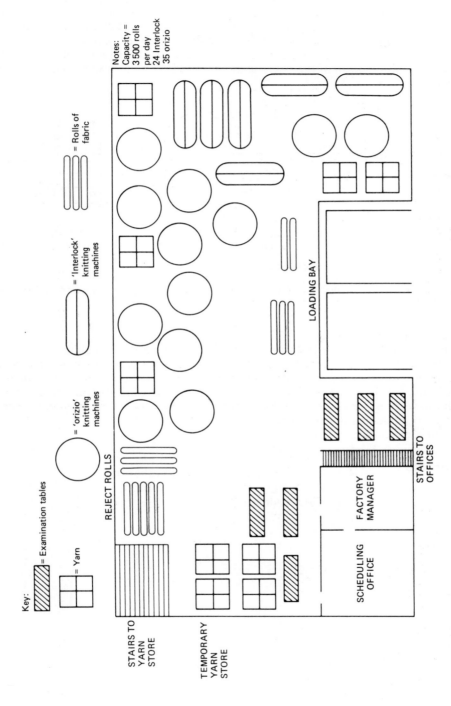

Fig .4.4 Knitting company — knitting room. Flows of information have not yet been added to this model

example, the activity 'send finished goods to customers' has an associated document called a delivery note; the breakdown of a machine prompts the completion of a downtime notification. Parkin (see Further reading) makes a useful distinction between the *object* system, the physical events that occur, and the *message* system which describes, regulates, coordinates and controls the object system. His example of the relationship between the object and the message system is repeated in Fig. 4.5. In this way a consideration of the physical model may lead naturally on to a model of document flow.

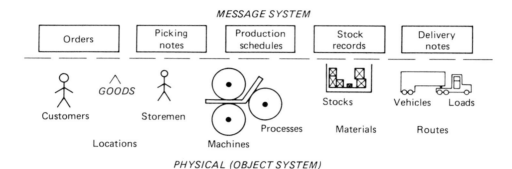

Fig. 4.5   The relationship between the message and the physical system (from A Parkin, *Systems Analysis*, Edward Arnold)

4.4.2   Document flow

The importance of the present document flow in the system was highlighted in the short discussion of document analysis in Section 4.2. It is not only necessary to collect and record details about reports and forms; it is also important to show their *sequence* and *interaction*. This is because any new system is likely to affect and change such flows and so we must be sure that they are properly understood. The system flowchart is one way of modelling document flow.

A system flowchart uses five basic symbols.

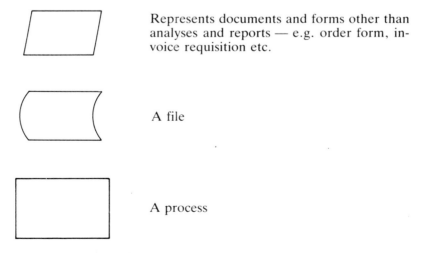

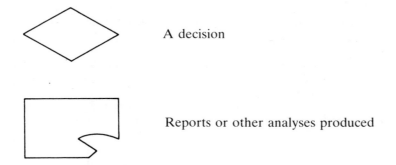

A decision

Reports or other analyses produced

The flowcharts are **columnar** in that they are drawn in such a way that the columns are used to represent different sections, departments, factories or personnel. This simplifies the modelling of flows and illustrates the passage of a document through an organisation at a glance.

Five things should be borne in mind when drawing up a system flowchart.

- It will begin as a scribble and it will be incorrect first time round.

- Sort out the column headings before drawing the flowchart — do not keep adding them as you go along.

- Try to show flows moving from top to bottom and from left to right.

- There is no 'one best way' of representing most systems. A number of flowcharts, correct in logic but different in detail, are likely to be equally valid.

- Try to keep the flow continuous and self-explanatory. This may require the addition of explanatory processes which help illustrate the timing of subsequent actions. To show this the system flowcharts given in Fig. 4.6 are accompanied by the original narrative. Certain physical events and assumptions have had to be built into the flowchart to preserve continuity.

4.4.3 Modelling processes and procedures

Most administrative systems include examples of alternative actions where the option taken depends upon the value of some variable. The discount rate given to customers is a typical illustration. In such an example a discount of 10% may be given if the order value exceeds £200, but it is raised to 12% if the order value is greater than £300. This may be represented by the programming type structures introduced in the Part 1.

```
IF Order Value > £300 THEN Discount = 12%
   ELSE
   IF Order Value > £200 THEN Discount = 10%
      ELSE
      Discount = 0%
   END IF
END IF
```

We have already recognised that programming languages support decision taking and that this is an important part of the programming task. It is the role of the analyst to

- identify all *decisions* made in the system

- find all the *conditions* that affect the decision

- list all the *actions* associated with a condition or combination of conditions.

A bakery operates the following system for its cash sales from vans direct to housewives.

Each driver places a daily order in triplicate with the sales department for the following day.

The sales department consolidates the orders and advises the bakery for production that night. The sales department passes two copies of each van driver's orders to the despatch department.

One copy of the order is passed to the van driver when the van is loaded the following morning. The second copy, signed by the van driver and marked 'executed' is passed by the despatch department to the accounts department.

Any stock unsold is returned by the van driver who then receives a credit slip. The driver and the despatch manager both sign a copy of this credit slip which is passed to the accounts department.

The van driver pays his daily takings to the cashier and receives a receipt for it. The cashier passes a copy of each receipt to the accounts department.

The accounts department prepares a weekly report in cash terms for the sales department, for sales and cash control purposes, showing the performance of each driver. A daily report of any cash discrepancy in excess of £2 in respect of any one driver is also made to the sales department.

Fig. 4.6   System flowchart — narrative

This narrative was given as an illustrative question by the Certified Accountants Educational Trust. The flowcharted answer is mine and reflects my assumptions and interpretations. Notice the inclusion of physical activities to permit continuity. The chart is also well balanced Every piece of paper ends up somewhere and can be cross checked. For example, the account's records can be compared with the vans driver's so that any dispute can be resolved.

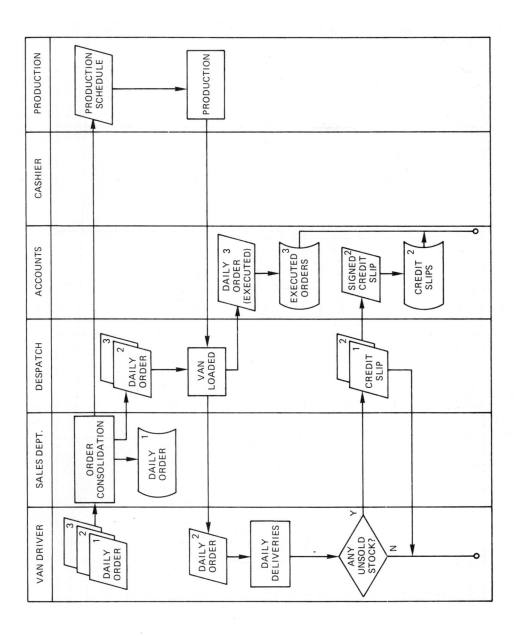

56   *Systems analysis*

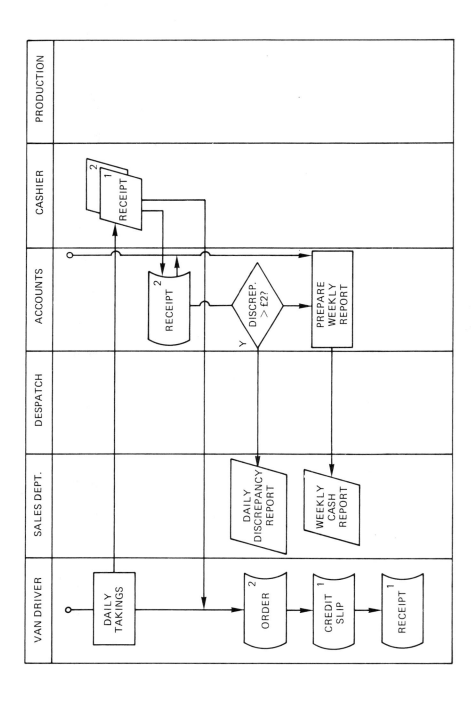

Decisions are clearly an important and critical part of a system and the analyst should strive to fully understand them. A model to help is the **decision table**.

Decision tables are grid like diagrams which show the action to be taken given a set of conditions. An example is given in Fig. 4.7. The table has four sections.

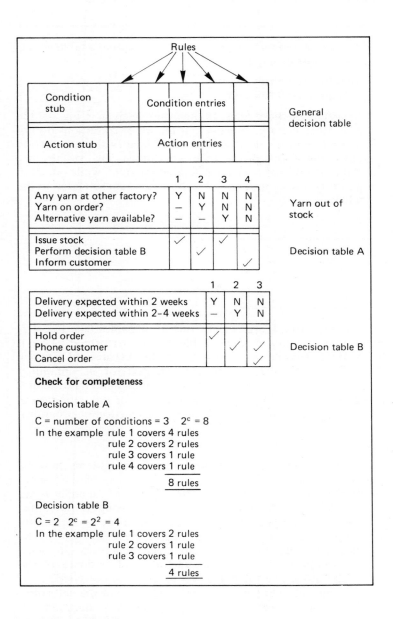

Check for completeness

Decision table A

C = number of conditions = 3 2^c = 8
In the example rule 1 covers 4 rules
                rule 2 covers 2 rules
                rule 3 covers 1 rule
                rule 4 covers 1 rule
                            8 rules

Decision table B

C = 2 $2^c = 2^2 = 4$
In the example rule 1 covers 2 rules
                rule 2 covers 1 rule
                rule 3 covers 1 rule
                            4 rules

Fig. 4.7 Decision table

Condition stub	A set of conditions which affect the resultant actions. In the limited entry decision table — the only type covered here — the conditions are phrased so that they may be answered Yes or No (Y or N).
Action stub	A set of actions that result from different combinations of conditions.
Condition entries	Each column represents a rule which shows
Action entries	the action required given a certain combination of conditions.

The table can be checked for completeness by using the simple rule that a table with C conditions should have 2^c rules. For example

a table with 2 conditions should have 4 rules
a table with 3 conditions should have 8 rules etc.

It is not always necessary to specify all these rules. In the example given in Fig. 4.7 the Yes response to 'any yarn at other factory?' means that the other conditions do not have to be investigated. If yarn is available from the other factory then the action 'issue stock' is taken whatever the status of the other conditions. Two dashes in a condition entry means that four rules have been consolidated into one, while one dash represents the consolidation of two rules into one. The four rules consolidated in the yarn example are given below.

Any yarn at other factory?	Y	Y	Y	Y
Yarn on order?	Y	N	Y	N
Alternative available?	Y	Y	N	N
Issue stock	✓	✓	✓	✓

The decision table may be set into a hierarchical structure of tables (see Fig. 4.7) with an action statement that requires a lower table to be performed. This is particularly useful if the main table has more than five conditions because if C=6 then there are 64 rules! The decision table is sometimes criticised for its unfamiliar representation which makes it confusing to users who do not understand its structure. However, its self-checking logic means that it is a powerful tool for the definition of computer procedures and it may be used for the automatic production of programs.

4.4.4 Personnel and jobs
Systems analysis is a political occupation. The failure of many systems may be attributed to a pre-occupation with technical factors at the expense of time spent studying and understanding the users and operators of the system. More analysts are trying to involve affected employees in the analysis and design of computer systems, some out of expediency — such involvement will lead to a more successful system — others from compassion — believing that people have a right to be involved in the design of their new work procedures. Whatever the motivation such a move is a recognition of the importance of 'human factors' and evidence of the desirability of investigating and modelling the personnel involved in the system.

At the simplest level a valuable aid to understanding the structure of the enterprise is an organisation chart. In certain instances a formal organisation chart may be available but this should not be taken too literally. Indeed a valuable exercise is to contrast the *actual* (informal) organisation with the *theoretical* (formal) chart. This may give clues to working relationships (see Fig. 4.8).

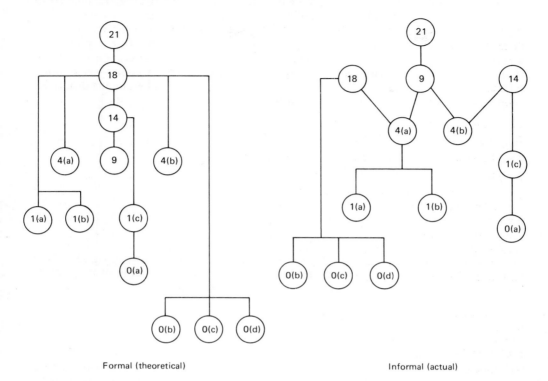

Formal (theoretical)   Informal (actual)

Fig. 4.8 Organisation chart showing the formal and informal arrangements for a department in a large company. The numbers represent grades and illustrate relative incomes with 21 at the top of the scale and 0 at the bottom. The relative importance of the grade 9 employee could be overlooked if the formal chart is used.

Documenting job responsibilities may help identify such facts as

- Who is responsible for filling in the requisition advice?
- Who checks the goods delivery note?
- Who has to authorise the cancellation of an order?

Finding out who does what may be quite eye opening. It is not uncommon to find quite lowly paid junior staff effectively running departments.

Job descriptions should be collected, compiled and compared. Inconsistencies and overlaps should be noted for possible action. Value judgements, such as 'I am overworked', should be qualified by at least one of the following:

- quantitative analysis of responsibilities — e.g. how many invoices are compiled in one day?
- qualitative judgement by employee's managers and peers
- efficiency of work procedures. Is the 'overwork' due to the inherent inefficiencies of the present system?

These qualifying statements are necessary because few would claim that they were underworked!

The analyst must constantly be picking up information about the general climate of the organisation — attitude to management, expectations of employees, promotion prospects, stability, general level of education and training. The analyst may introduce systems that change long held notions and expectations. It is important to identify the effect of the system on employees and to predict their response to these changes. A strategy can then be formulated to cope with such responses — regrading, retraining, redeployment or redundancy. The analyst has to manage change otherwise change will manage him or her, often with dire and unexpected results.

Thus the organisation has now been modelled from four different perspectives designed to highlight different aspects of the enterprise:

- physical resources
- document flow
- decisions and processes
- people and jobs.

The final perspective is slightly different because it is concerned with logical rather than physical activities. It provides a link between our understanding of the *present system* and our *design of a successor*. It is the modelling of data.

4.4.5 Modelling data

Dataflow diagrams show the passage of data through a system *irrespective* of current departmental structures and administrative control procedures. In this way they focus attention upon the logical events required by the system and not the present arrangements for executing those events. There is no reason why such administrative structures should necessarily survive the transition from manual to computerised systems. The fact that many do is probably testament to the reluctance or inability of organisations to grasp the full strategic possibilities of computerisation. There is a tendency to play safe and to produce 'computerised manual systems' whose very scope limits their chance of success. The point is put most eloquently by Stafford Beer (see Further reading).

'The departments or section of a firm. . . are there and are identifiable because of the limited capacity of the human brain. The methods they use and the very tasks they undertake exist in this form because of the limitations of eye, hand and the capacity for human communication. . . Our systems are tailored to these limits. What idiocy then to slap these limits on a computer, a machine devised by the wit of man precisely to circumvent them. What anthropomorphism to cut down these machines to the size of human frailty, and to enshrine the inadequacies of men in steel and wire and semiconductors.'

The analyst needs tools which separate the logical tasks of an organisation from their administrative trappings. The dataflow diagram is such a tool.

The passage of data through a system is shown using four basic symbols.

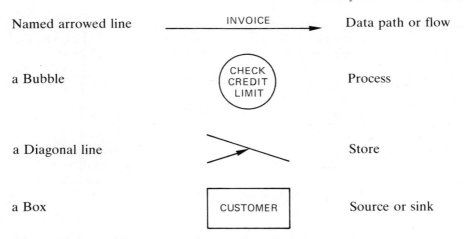

Named arrowed line — INVOICE → Data path or flow

a Bubble — CHECK CREDIT LIMIT — Process

a Diagonal line — Store

a Box — CUSTOMER — Source or sink

A data path or flow can be viewed as a route which enables packets of data to travel from one point to another. If it helps, you can imagine the path as a road with busloads of data passing along it at certain intervals. Data may flow from a source to a process, or to and from a data store or process.

Data flows must be named, preferably with titles which clearly describe the flows, and no two items should have the same name. The data flows moving in and out of stores do not require names, the store name being sufficient to describe them.

Processes represent transformations, changing incoming data flows into outgoing data flows. Processes must also be named using descriptions which convey an impression of what happens to the data as it passes through the process.

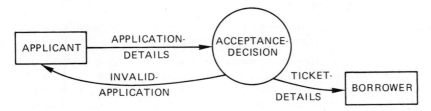

The store is a repository of data. It may be a card index, a dBASE III file or a wastepaper basket. The physical representation is again irrelevant, it is the logical requirement that is important. Stores should also be given convenient descriptive names.

A store may be used in the checking of data. For example, in the diagram shown below the process ACCEPTANCE DECISION requires access to data which permits this decision. The data items required to carry out this process correctly must be available in that store. In the diagram the arrow is single headed and points towards the process. This is to signify that the process does not alter the contents of the store; it only uses the data available. However, if the contents of the store are altered by the process, as well as being read, then the diagram uses a double headed arrow.

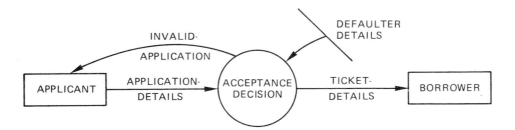

In this way a single headed arrow shows **read** (looking at the data only) or **write** (changing data only) operations. In circumstances where the data is both examined and changed (read and write) then a double headed arrow is used.

A source or sink is a person or organisation which enters or receives data from the system but is considered to be outside the context of the dataflow model.

Five hints for drawing dataflow diagrams are as follows.

- Do not be worried by detail. Tom de Marco (see Further reading) quotes Gerry Weinberg's Lump Law:

  'If we want to learn anything, we musn't try to learn everything.'

- Start with an obvious input from a source or output to a sink and concentrate on the dataflows. Place a bubble where a process is required to transform one flow into another. Bubbles can be named later.

- For all data outputs consider whether you have enough data flowing into the process (from stores and flows) to perform the stated transformation and to produce the required output. This self-checking nature of dataflow diagrams can help identify extra data items that were not obvious from a narrative or verbal description.

- The first dataflow diagram you draw of a system is bound to be wrong. Start again and modify until you are satisfied.

- Do not worry about absolute correctness. Even wrong (not dramatically wrong!) diagrams have much to contribute to understanding.

A dataflow diagram of the narrative introduced earlier in this chapter is shown in Fig. 4.9. You may like to compare it with the system flowchart of Fig. 4.6.

The dataflow diagram gives a good impression of the flow of data but it fails to record it in sufficient detail for the subsequent design stage. This may be remedied by providing **data dictionary** entries for all the major elements of the diagram. A data dictionary is simply a record of data about data and using it forces further consideration of properties of the data. Two illustrative data dictionary entries are given as Figs. 4.10 and 4.11. The actual structure of the entry is adapted from Gane and Sarson (see Further reading) where a comprehensive treatment may be found. The data dictionary may be physically maintained in a variety of ways, ranging from a loose leaf folder to a fully integrated software package.

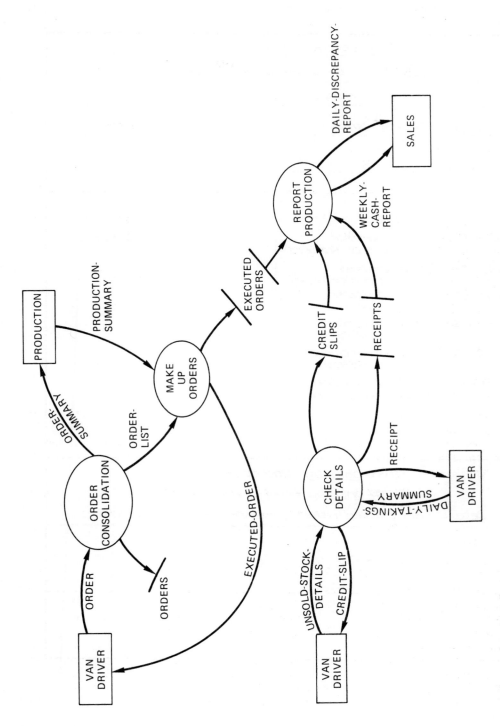

Fig. 4.9 Dataflow diagram

DATA ELEMENT NAME: *COURSE - TITLE*

SHORT DESCRIPTION *Title of the course as defined in the*
Prospectus

ALIASES *COURSE - NAME*   TYPE *Character*

FORMAT *XXX XXX*

──────────── VALUES ────────────

DISCRETE	CONTINUOUS
BSC CSH : BSc Computer Science (Honours)	*NOT APPLICABLE*
BSC CSO : BSc Computer Science (Ordinary)	
HND CSC : HND Computer Science	
HND CSS : HND Computer Studies	
HND ITE : HND Information Technology	
BSC ITH : BSc Information Technology (Honours)	

SECURITY *Created only by Head of Department*
Deleted only by Head of Department
Details only created/deleted/amended by Course Leader

EDITING
NOT APPLICABLE

COMMENTS
NONE

Fig. 4.10   Data dictionary entry: Data element

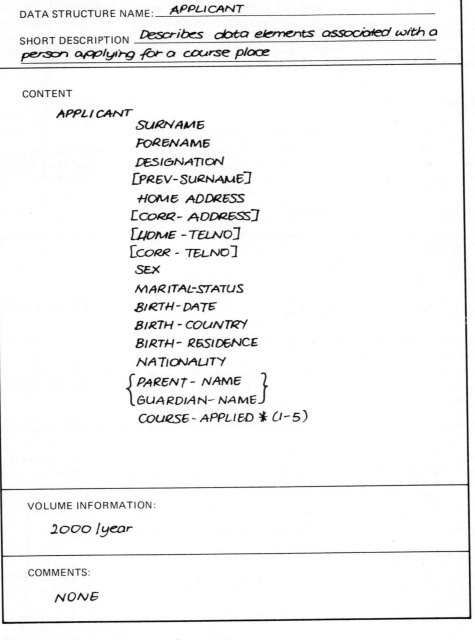

DATA STRUCTURE NAME: _APPLICANT_

SHORT DESCRIPTION _Describes data elements associated with a person applying for a course place_

CONTENT

APPLICANT

        SURNAME
        FORENAME
        DESIGNATION
        [PREV-SURNAME]
        HOME ADDRESS
        [CORR-ADDRESS]
        [HOME-TELNO]
        [CORR-TELNO]
        SEX
        MARITAL-STATUS
        BIRTH-DATE
        BIRTH-COUNTRY
        BIRTH-RESIDENCE
        NATIONALITY
        { PARENT-NAME
         GUARDIAN-NAME }
        COURSE-APPLIED * (1-5)

VOLUME INFORMATION:

   2000 /year

COMMENTS:

   NONE

Fig. 4.11 Data dictionary entry: Data structure

4.5   Summary

This chapter has examined facts to collect, fact-finding techniques and fact organisation. It ended with a method of drawing a logical model of a system. Dataflow diagrams are simple and useful and their consideration of the flow of data irrespective of the physical environment makes them particularly helpful in spanning the bridge between analysis and design. Chapter 5 picks up the structure of the dataflow model and examines its usefulness in design.

Further reading

Beer S, 'Love and the Computer', *METRA* paper, **111**, 1, 1964

The quotation is taken directly from the paper referenced above. It is unlikely that this paper is still available, but parts of it may be found in 'The Manager', October 1963 and November 1963 editions. Stafford Beer is a visionary writer. All of his books — *Brain of the Firm, Heart of the Enterprise* etc. — are worth reading for their vision and clarity.

Daniels A and Yeates D, *Basic Systems Analysis*, Pitman (1984)

A conventional introduction to systems analysis. The quotation is taken from an earlier book *Basic Training in Systems Analysis*, NCC (1971)

deMarco T, *Structured Analysis and System Specification,* Prentice-Hall (1979)
Gane C and Sarson T, *Structured Systems Analysis*, Prentice-Hall (1979)

Two seminal books on structured analysis and design. Both include a detailed consideration of dataflow diagrams and data dictionaries.

Martin J and McClure M, *Diagramming Techniques for Analysts and Programmers*, Prentice-Hall (1985)

A large survey of most of the models available to the analyst. This chapter has chosen *one* model in each fact-finding area. A dip into Martin and McClure will give an indication of the range of models that are actually available.

Moser C and Kalton G, *Survey Methods in Social Investigation* (Second Edition) Heinemann (1971)

Most practising analysts do not study the wealth of knowledge already available in other professions concerned with fact-finding. Moser and Kalton's classic text gives important insights into interviewing and questionnaire design.

NCC, *Student Notes on NCC Data Processing Documentation Standards*, NCC (1978)

A physically reduced set of NCC standards specifically for the student market.

Parkin A, *Systems Analysis*, Edward Arnold (1980)

A less conventional systems analysis text that includes a useful distinction (with examples) between the object and message systems. The structure of NCC documentation is discussed and completed examples are given.

Part 3
Systems Design

This part looks at some of the issues faced in taking a logical system through to the delivery of a computer-based replacement. Chapter 5 examines some of the aspects that arise in the design of a replacement system. This takes the logical model of the operations — defined at the end of the analysis stage — into a physical design that can be implemented using a computer. Input, output, file and process design are considered in turn, examining, where appropriate, both the technology (e.g. Optical Character Recognition) and the design objectives.

Chapter 6 looks at the tasks involved in system implementation. These broadly cover practical issues, implementation strategies and the principle of prototyping. This latter aspect is particularly important at present, because the emergence of fourth generation languages has presented new development opportunities.

5
Systems design

5.1 Introduction

Before embarking on a consideration of some of the issues of system design it is worthwhile re-stating the main concerns of the previous chapter. It concentrated upon establishing the *operations of the current system* and the *user and operator* requirements of its successor. The results of these investigations were summarised in a number of models, including a logical model of the required system illustrated by a dataflow diagram. This chapter examines some of the issues that must be faced in taking this *logical* model to a *physical design* that can be implemented on a computer. In doing so it must constantly be borne in mind that there is no clear cut distinction between analysis and design. Some of the issues discussed in this chapter may be considered early in a project, while others will only be significant nearer the end of systems development.

The logical model described three areas of design.

- Data flows. These will be *inputs* and *outputs* in the proposed system.
- Data stores. These become possible *files* in the new system.
- Processes. These describe *clerical procedures* or *programs*.

We shall also wish to consider the design of controls.

5.2 Data flows — input design

5.2.1 General considerations
Input design is concerned with collecting data for the system. It is possible to identify five main tasks in such data capture.

- Data describing significant events is recorded by the data provider. This could be a visit by a Health Visitor to an old age pensioner recorded on a statistical form.
- The collected data is conveyed to a place of processing. The Health Visitor sends his/her summary statistical report through the internal mail to the computer centre.
- The data is scrutinised for obvious omissions and errors.
- Data is transcribed from 'human readable' to 'machine readable' form. In doing so **transcription errors** may occur and so, in some instances, the data is transcribed again and differences between first and second transcriptions are investigated. This is the process of **verification**.
- Data items are entered into the main computer system and checked for logical correctness by a **data validation** program. Detected errors are listed out for appropriate action.

Thus **data capture** is concerned with

- methods of recording data

- methods of communicating data

- locating errors in data so that incorrect data are not processed and erroneous results produced.

The general objective of data capture is to collect and convert the data into machine readable form with the minimum delay, minimum introduction of errors and at minimum cost.

It is inevitable that these three goals will conflict and their relative importance will depend upon the circumstances. In some instances absolute accuracy must be achieved at whatever cost, whilst in other circumstances economic considerations are paramount. The designer will be looking for an acceptable compromise between cost, speed and accuracy. In such circumstances a number of different hardware and software opportunities will exist. General guidelines for data capture may aid the evaluation of these alternatives.

5.2.2   Design guidelines

Seek to minimise data transcription
Every time data is transcribed or copied the chance of error and delay is increased. Data preparation staff transcribing data from a survey form (human readable) to magnetic disk (machine readable) incur cost and delay. There will also be transcription errors as the data is copied and so procedures will have to be designed to locate these errors. This leads to further expense and delay.

To reduce transcription errors the designer should attempt to minimise the number of times the data is transcribed and look for opportunities to capture data as close as possible to the form in which it is generated. It may be possible to justify expenditure on devices which permit entry of data directly into the computer system, while in other instances it may be fruitful to pay special attention to the procedures followed by the 'data provider'. Every effort should be made to make data capture as unobtrusive as possible, a by-product of the data provider's normal activity rather than an irritating distraction from 'real work'.

Attempt to minimise data transmission or communication
In data capture procedures each transmission, whether by word of mouth, post or telephone line, incurs cost, delay and an increased chance of error. The cost of transmitting data along telephone lines may be an important consideration in the design of a computer-based system. If the cost is significant it may be advantageous to place processors at a number of locations with only limited interaction between these local processors and the organisation's main computer. For example, summaries of stock transactions may be despatched weekly rather than posting individual transactions to a geographically remote computer. Placing data processing near the point of data recording is a claimed advantage of **distributed systems**. These systems provide smaller processors near the users of the computer in preference to large centralised computers.

Strive to minimise the amount of data recorded
Designers should use their prior knowledge of the characteristics of the system to reduce the burden placed on the data provider. A request, for example, for payment of water rates can print or code data about the user's name, address, postal code,

property reference and payment required. The data provider's only action is to pay the bill! The same principle applies to a bank cheque transaction where the data concerning branch, account and cheque number is already recorded in a sequence of codes and the only data collection required is the amount of the cheques — the only variable data. The opportunity to code or print known data items varies from system to system but the designer should seek such opportunities because every additional data item required from the data provider increases the chance of error in the collected data.

5.2.3   Input technologies
Certain input devices will be used in the design of the data capture procedures. These devices fall into two distinct categories. One uses **keyboard transcription** where data is transfered from human readable to machine readable form by some form of keyboard input, the other is concerned with **direct input** into the computer.

Keyboard transcription
This includes the traditional task of data preparation where the operator takes clerical documents and transcribes data onto a suitable computer medium. This medium is usually some kind of secondary storage — tape, disk or cards. Data entered in this way must be subjected to some kind of verification and validation. Verification is usually achieved by transcribing the data twice and investigating any discrepancies. Validation is likely to be the task of a specially written data validation program that examines incoming data and rejects entries that do not conform to an expected value range or format. These checks may be very simple — e.g. ensuring that the data is entered in a DD/MM/YY format — whilst others may be a little more sophisticated. For example, if Reason for Resignation = Maternity check that Sex = Female. The checks made in a data validation program may be very sophisticated and demand a thorough understanding of the characteristics of the data. The data dictionary will be a valuable source of such information.

   Data validation assumes greater importance where there is no opportunity for double entry verification. This is usually where data is not entered onto some intermediate secondary storage but is keyed directly into the main computer system. In such a system the data entered via the keyboard is validated by a program run on the main computer and detected errors are shown on the screen. It is possible to use quite complex software to ease the problems of data entry for the relatively inexperienced or casual user. This may take the form of a series of **prompts** and the keyboard operator effectively enters into a conversation or **dialogue** with the computer. The design of such dialogues is becoming increasingly important and merits a section of its own (Section 5.5).

   Terminals **on-line** to the main computer permit fast data entry with sophisticated data validation facilities provided by the software. However, this is achieved at the expense of increased cost due to central processor time, communication facilities and software development overheads. Processor time is precious and it cannot remain idle waiting for the keyboard operator to enter data; it must be engaged on another job. This requires a successful and efficient **operating system**.

   The type of keyboard transcription method used will again be critically affected by the nature of the data that is being considered. Data such as Health Visitor statistical returns may be collated, batched and entered on to some intermediate medium before being transmitted to the main computer system at a convenient time. In this instance the data capture and data preparation does not tie up the resources of the main computer and clearly in such circumstances an on-line facility would be wasteful and not reflect the needs of the system. On the other hand fast data capture facilities may be required in a system monitoring patient health. Information concerning drugs administered by one clinician on a ward round must be entered quickly into the system so that the patient's profile is quickly updated. This prevents a second clinician ordering treatment incompatible with the administered drugs. Slow data entry via an intermediate media would be unacceptable in these circumstances.

Direct input into the computer

Devices which permit direct entry of data into the computer eliminate transcription errors completely. Perhaps the most exciting and desirable method of achieving direct input is speech — talking directly to the computer. Speech recognition is still in its infancy and current systems are limited to 'understanding' single words or short utterances, but important commercial applications do exist. Research in this area is pursued enthusiastically, particularly by the Japanese whose language structure is more suited to voice than keyboard input.

Human script has almost as many idiosyncracies as speech but devices are available that can read a range of printed characters. The principle of reading written data directly into the computer system is that of **optical character recognition** (OCR). The technique is widely used in insurance premium notices, public utility billing and hire purchase agreements. Many systems have an associated screen and keyboard where unrecognised characters may be displayed and re-entered. For example, an unclosed nine (9) is rejected by the OCR reader and displayed on the operator's screen. The operator can then check the figure and use the keyboard to enter the valid nine if it is correct. OCR is particularly useful where the data can be pre-coded in a font that is recognised by the OCR reader and so is a possible design option where much of the input can be anticipated by the designer. In general, the cost of entering each document is well below that of any system involving keying but to be economically viable the volume of data must be high and the time allowed for data input relatively short.

A more specialised form of character recognition is **magnetic ink character recognition** (MICR) used mainly in the banking industry with the characteristic font found in every cheque book. MICR readers magnetise, recognise and interpret the ferrite impregnated ink and this reliance on magnetic qualities makes it less vulnerable than OCR to damaged or folded documents. However, MICR has been little used outside banking because few other applications have to guard so rigorously against fraudulent data entry and hence cannot justify the considerable expense of the MICR equipment.

Optical mark recognition (OMR) readers recognise hand or machine printed marks on forms. Current devices are not limited to pencil marks but can interpret any dense mark: biro, typewriter etc. Examples of OMR applications are given in Fig. 5.1. In all these examples the appropriate lozenges have to be filled in. Difficulties occur with OMR where a large amount of data has to be collected or where the details of the system change quickly (e.g. fashion stores, record shops) demanding uneconomic alterations of the OMR form. Optical mark recognition is probably best used in a stable environment where there is a large number of short numeric records.

There are numerous badges, tags, cards and similar devices which may be used for specialised data capture requirements. Two examples must suffice.

Bar coding   It is possible to code all items in, for example, a library or supermarket and record sales of goods or books withdrawn or returned, by passing the item in front of a reader.

Kimball tags   This is a small tag used extensively in the garment trade on which details about size, colour, style and price are recorded. The label is attached to the

Parts Used Data

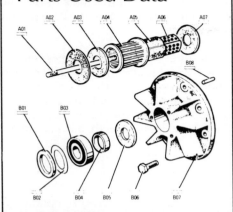

Multiple Choice Answer Sheets

1	⊏A⊐ ⊏B⊐ ⊏C⊐ ⊏D⊐ ⊏E⊐	11	⊏A⊐ ⊏B⊐ ⊏C⊐ ⊏D⊐ ⊏E⊐
2	⊏A⊐ ⊏B⊐ ⊏C⊐ ⊏D⊐ ⊏E⊐	12	⊏A⊐ ⊏B⊐ ⊏C⊐ ⊏D⊐ ⊏E⊐
3	⊏A⊐ ⊏B⊐ ⊏C⊐ ⊏D⊐ ⊏E⊐	13	⊏A⊐ ⊏B⊐ ⊏C⊐ ⊏D⊐ ⊏E⊐
4	⊏A⊐ ⊏B⊐ ⊏C⊐ ⊏D⊐ ⊏E⊐	14	⊏A⊐ ⊏B⊐ ⊏C⊐ ⊏D⊐ ⊏E⊐
5	⊏A⊐ ⊏B⊐ ⊏C⊐ ⊏D⊐ ⊏E⊐	15	⊏A⊐ ⊏B⊐ ⊏C⊐ ⊏D⊐ ⊏E⊐
6	⊏A⊐ ⊏B⊐ ⊏C⊐ ⊏D⊐ ⊏E⊐	16	⊏A⊐ ⊏B⊐ ⊏C⊐ ⊏D⊐ ⊏E⊐
7	⊏A⊐ ⊏B⊐ ⊏C⊐ ⊏D⊐ ⊏E⊐	17	⊏A⊐ ⊏B⊐ ⊏C⊐ ⊏D⊐ ⊏E⊐
8	⊏A⊐ ⊏B⊐ ⊏C⊐ ⊏D⊐ ⊏E⊐	18	⊏A⊐ ⊏B⊐ ⊏C⊐ ⊏D⊐ ⊏E⊐
9	⊏A⊐ ⊏B⊐ ⊏C⊐ ⊏D⊐ ⊏E⊐	19	⊏A⊐ ⊏B⊐ ⊏C⊐ ⊏D⊐ ⊏E⊐
10	⊏A⊐ ⊏B⊐ ⊏C⊐ ⊏D⊐ ⊏E⊐	20	⊏A⊐ ⊏B⊐ ⊏C⊐ ⊏D⊐ ⊏E⊐

Capturing Numeric Data

ACCOUNT NUMBER			PACK SIZE	TOTAL NO. REQUIRED	
Territory	Type	Disc. Gp.	Full case	⊏1⊐ ⊏2⊐ ⊏3⊐ ⊏4⊐ ⊏5⊐ ⊏6⊐	
			Half case	⊏7⊐ ⊏8⊐ ⊏9⊐ ⊏10⊐ ⊏11⊐ ⊏12⊐	
⊏8⊐ ⊏8⊐ ⊏8⊐	⊏8⊐ ⊏8⊐ ⊏8⊐	⊏8⊐ ⊏8⊐ ⊏8⊐	Singles	⊏13⊐ ⊏14⊐ ⊏15⊐ ⊏16⊐ ⊏17⊐ ⊏18⊐	
⊏4⊐ ⊏4⊐ ⊏4⊐	⊏4⊐ ⊏4⊐ ⊏4⊐	⊏4⊐ ⊏4⊐ ⊏4⊐			
⊏2⊐ ⊏2⊐ ⊏2⊐	⊏2⊐ ⊏2⊐ ⊏2⊐	⊏2⊐ ⊏2⊐ ⊏2⊐			
⊏1⊐ ⊏1⊐ ⊏1⊐	⊏1⊐ ⊏1⊐ ⊏1⊐	⊏1⊐ ⊏1⊐ ⊏1⊐			

EMPLOYEE NO.	HOURS WORKED	QUANTITY ORDERED	COST		DATE		
			£	p	Day	Month	Year

EMPLOYEE NO.: 0 0 0 0 0 0 / 1 1 1 1 1 1 / 2 2 2 2 2 2 / 3 3 3 3 3 3 / 4 4 4 4 4 4 / 5 5 5 5 5 5 / 6 6 6 6 6 6 / 7 7 7 7 7 7 / 8 8 8 8 8 8 / 9 9 9 9 9 9

HOURS WORKED: 0 0 / 1 1 ¼ / 2 2 / 3 3 ½ / 4 4 / 5 5 ¾ / 6 6 / 7 7 / 8 8 / 9 9

QUANTITY ORDERED: 0 0 0 / 1 1 1 / 2 2 2 / 3 3 3 / 4 4 4 / 5 5 5 / 6 6 6 / 7 7 7 / 8 8 8 / 9 9 9

COST: 0 0 0 0 / 1 1 1 1 / 2 2 2 2 / 3 3 3 3 ½ / 4 4 4 4 / 5 5 5 5 / 6 6 6 6 / 7 7 7 7 / 8 8 8 8 / 9 9 9 9

DATE: Day 0 0 / 1 1 / 2 2 / 3 3 | Month Jan Feb Mar Apr May Jun Jul Aug Sep Oct Nov Dec | Year 82 83 84 85 / 4 / 5 / 6 / 7 / 8 / 9

Recording Subjective Data

ATTITUDES TO OPEN PLAN

The list of statements below consists of comments made by teachers about open plan schooling. Please indicate your reaction to each of these bearing your present unit in mind by marking **one box** on each line.

In my unit:–	Strongly agree	Agree	No opinion	Disagree	Strongly disagree
1. There is plenty of space to do things	⊏⊐	⊏⊐	⊏⊐	⊏⊐	⊏⊐
2. Noise spreads from one group to another	⊏⊐	⊏⊐	⊏⊐	⊏⊐	⊏⊐
3. A lot of organisation is required	⊏⊐	⊏⊐	⊏⊐	⊏⊐	⊏⊐
4. There are excessive demands on teachers' attention	⊏⊐	⊏⊐	⊏⊐	⊏⊐	⊏⊐

Fig. 5.1 OMR form (Courtesy of DRS Data and Research Services Ltd)

garment and, on sale of the item, the tag is detached and details read by a ticket reader. This provides automatic capture of sales data, updating of stock records, sales statistics and product planning information. This technique requires most of the data to be pre-recorded and as a result is most applicable to systems where the designer has virtually complete knowledge of the data requirements.

The relative expense and specialist nature of the direct entry technologies and the problems of keyboard dexterity have led to other possible options designed to ease interaction with the computer. These include **touch screens** where the operator selects the required option by touching it with a finger, **joysticks** where a handle is used to move the screen cursor in an appropriate direction, or a pointing device known as a **mouse**. These small control units may be used to 'draw' input directly onto the screen as well as being used as a selection pointer.

5.2.4 Input — summary

Thus input design is concerned with the following.

- Determining the content of input documents and displays in terms of data items. This will be derived from the logical model and its associated data dictionary entries.

- Selecting an appropriate technology to permit data entry. This will take place within the framework of the three important design guides, outlined in Section 5.2.2.

- Performing detailed design work on those selected options. This will include form and dialogue design.

A bewildering number of options are available to the designer of the data capture system. However, many designers seem loathe to explore fully the potential of many of the devices or to spend adequate time analysing and designing the data capture requirements and procedures.

5.3 Output considerations

Some of the devices used to enter data may also be used to display output. The most popular methods of presenting results are **visual display units** (VDUs) and a variety of printers which produce printed paper copies of the data (so called 'hardcopy' to distinguish it from the transitory images presented on the VDU).

A general distinction can be made between **impact** printers which operate in a similar way to the conventional typewriter where the character strikes an inked ribbon to leave the image on the paper, and **non-impact** printers which use a variety of techniques to produce an image without physically contacting the paper. An example of this latter group is an electro-thermal printer which uses a specially coated paper and small heating elements in the printing head. Non-impact printers tend to be faster but more expensive than impact devices and can usually only be justified in systems which require a substantial amount of hardcopy printing at low noise levels.

The choice of suitable impact printer will be guided by the *quality* and *speed* required. **Dot matrix** printers form their letters by printing an appropriate pattern of dots and this tends to produce an image of less clarity than those of the fully formed embossed character set of **daisywheel** printers. However, daisywheel printers are generally slower and more expensive than their dot matrix competitors. The designer should again be guided by the demands of the system. A computer used mainly for word processing may dictate the purchase of a relatively sophisticated daisywheel printer. In other circumstances — printing out laboratory figures, drafting reports — a dot matrix printer will suffice. A dot matrix printer will also be required if simple graphical presentations are required. Such graphs may be quite limited (many machines print pie charts that are lozenge shaped), but may be sufficient for the purpose in hand. Graphs of better quality and sophistication require dedicated graph plotters. In many respects the flexibility of printers has been enhanced by their ability to work in two modes. Thus a dot matrix printer may be switched to a slower near letter quality (NLQ) feature that provides acceptable output.

In circumstances where the output is to be used as subsequent input the data may be produced in a format suitable for direct entry. This may be in a human readable form (OCR font, kimball tag) or in a medium only suitable for machine reading (magnetic tape, paper tape). Organisations which need to store a considerable amount of data (libraries, hospitals etc.) may use **computer output onto microfilm** (COM) devices which convert computer output into characters on rolls of microfilm. A sheet of microfilm, microfiche, can be selected as required and viewed through a microfiche viewer. COM devices are best used in applications with a large number of records where each record is accessed relatively infrequently. Clearly the capital cost of the image processor and viewers has to be justified but the COM technique is an invaluable method of reducing the problems of record storage.

Understanding the demands and requirements of the system is as important in designing output procedures as it is in selecting data capture techniques. The range of options is not as large partly due to the fact that a considerable amount of the output is destined for human users. Design of output documents (pay slips, mail order coupons, reports) requires as much detailed consideration as input documents and many of the guidelines of good practice still hold true. Unfortunately such documents rarely receive adequate attention, particularly reports to management which are often little more than sheets of printer paper stapled together.

Thus, in summary, output design is concerned with the following.

- Determining the data items required on the output documents. This will come from a combination of the data flow model and the data dictionary.

- Selecting a technology to display or communicate these data items.

- Performing detailed design of output screen and documents.

5.4   Input and output in two example systems

5.4.1   A library

Each member of the library is issued with a membership card which includes a photograph and a bar code. Each copy of a book held in the library also has a bar code. When a book is taken out the librarian runs a light pen over the bar code on the membership card and over the bar code in each book. The bar code reader interprets the bar code and the data on the borrower and the books on loan are automatically stored in the computer system. A limited number of books may be borrowed at any one time. When a member reaches that limit a message is displayed on a screen warning the librarian that no more books must be lent to this borrower.

Bar codes are ideal because the elements of the data capture system — borrowers and books — may be easily identified and their details pre-coded. The data is not subject to frequent change and there is no volume data. The library may hold three copies of *Data Analysis for Data Base Design* but these have three different codes as *copies*, not *books*, are of interest. The data collection point is in a calm, clean environment and may be controlled in that there are only as many data collection points as bar code readers available. Thus the system minimises transcription (through direct input to the computer using bar codes) and precodes most of the data required by the system. The only additional information concerns the links between copies and borrowers. The maintenance of this link provides immediate error detection.

Little output is required from the system — the most significant being an overdue loan reminder, which involves only a relatively small number of borrowers.

5.4.2 A large shoe manufacturer

A large shoe manufacturer can pre-code data about the shoes he sells. This is achieved by printing a label which contains a description of the shoe, price, size and style. This label is attached to each box containing a pair of shoes. When these shoes are sold in retail stores a part of the label is torn off and returned to the data processing department. An OCR reader is used to interpret the stylised characters on the returned slip and hence the sale is recorded in the computer system. This data is subsequently used for supplying information for sales analysis, accounting, branch performance measurement and stock and production planning.

The only data capture required in the system is the detaching and return of the slip. The use of OCR for data entry avoids the need for data transcription. The information is not needed on-line because the decisions made on the data do not require 'up to the minute' information. Hence the delay incurred by returning the slips through the company's internal mail system is quite acceptable.

The large number of shoes produced demanded the purchase of a fast laser printer for label production as it is crucial that the despatch of goods is not delayed by the unavailability of labels. The printer is also used to produce the label that is stuck to the side of the shoe box, using its facilities to draw a facsimilie of the shoe style to aid easy recognition in the retail store.

5.5 Dialogue design

The design of the dialogue, or conversation, between the computer and its operator has increased in significance in the last few years. This is mainly due to an increase in the direct use of computers by system users, so by-passing traditional intermediaries such as the data processing and data preparation departments. The inherent unfriend-liness of many computer systems could be tolerated by trained staff and indeed it formed much of the mythology of computing. However, such interfaces were largely unacceptable to the variety of staff who now found themselves directly in contact with a computer, whether it be a terminal linked to a mainframe or a single user microcomputer.

5.5.1 Conversation structuring

The designer has a number of ways of *structuring* the conversation between computer and user.

Menus
The actions open to a user are displayed on the screen together with the user responses required for each action. Letter or numerical responses may be used. The former tend to be easier to use particularly if the response can be made to be the first letter of the action. For example

E — Edit a record

Clearly this requires unique action letters and prevents the use of the following option in the same menu.

> E — Exit to operating system

This may be overcome by the slightly contrived

> X — eXit to operating system

Menus are usually organised in a **hierarchical form** with an option in a higher menu, say:

> R — Reports

leading to a further menu giving the different type of reports available:

> D — Daily value report
> M — Monthly analysis
> A — Audit report

It is important to build **links** between the strata of the menu so that the user can easily return to higher level menus. This permits, amongst other things, the easy correction of errors where the operator has inadvertently chosen the wrong branch of the menu. An option

> R — Return to main menu

may be all that is needed.

The hierarchical structure also permits the restriction of the number of options available at each menu level. The main menu of an early SAGE Accounts Software release (now superceded) — see Fig. 5.2 — presented too many options for the user to be comfortable. Seven or eight actions is probably a realistic maximum, both from the point of view of user comprehension and of neatness of screen presentation.

```
                         SAGE ACCOUNTS

   1)  INITIALISATION ROUTINE

       DATA ENTRY ROUTINES

   02)  Sales Invoices            11)  CREATE LEDGERS
   03)  Sales Credit Notes        12)  SALES/PURCHASE REPORTS
   04)  Sales Receipts            13)  STATEMENT ROUTINES
                                  14)  ACCOUNTS REPORTS
   05)  Purchase Invoices
   06)  Purchase Credit Notes
   07)  Purchase Payments

   08)  Cash Book Receipts        15)  Information Trail
   09)  Cash Book Payments        16)  RECONFIGURATION
   10)  Journal Entries           17)  Exit from program

   Which Option : >—
```

Fig. 5.2 Early version of SAGE Accounts — main menu (Courtesy of SAGESOFT Ltd)

Form fill
In this method the designer lays the screen out as if it were a form and the operator makes entries in a similar way to a hand compiled example. The SAGE Accounts package uses this method for the input of invoices — see Fig 5.3. This method is

ACCOUNT CODE	ACCOUNT NAME	INVOICE DATE	INVOICE NUMBER	NOMINAL CODE	NOMINAL ACCOUNT	DETAILS	NETT	VAT CODE	VAT	INVOICE TOTAL
1	076	Galaxy Catering	170184	7621	102	Software Sales	Accounts Package	375.00	1	56.25	431.25
2	068	Delvin Electronics	170184	7622	102	Software Sales	Accounts Package	375.00	1	56.25	431.25
3	096	Riverside Rentals	180184	7623	101	System Sales	Osborne + Printer	1785.00	1	267.75	2052.75
4										
5										
6										
7										
8										
9										
10										
11										
12										
13										
14										
15									2585.00	—	380.25	2915.25

Fig. 5.3 Sales invoices — clerical batching document

particularly suitable for fast data entry, although a number of rules should be followed.

- The completion of a field entry should be unambiguous. It may be wise to insist on a carriage return after each entry so demanding a positive action to skip to a subsequent field. Some form fill systems also skip fields after the current field has been completely filled. This may be useful in some circumstances but can lead to an increasesd number of errors for the unwary or infrequent operator.

- Error correction should be made easy. The SAGE form fill example uses a coordinate system where the user specifies the column and row intersection of the entry that he/she wishes to change.

Question and answer
This is a sequence of actions where the user reacts to prompts from the computer.

Computer:	Type of Field?
User:	Character
Computer:	Length of field?
User:	15
Computer:	Name of field?
User:	Forename

Such a staccato dialogue quickly becomes tiresome but may be useful in certain circumstances — for example suggesting and confirming the backup of disks.

In practice the designer will probably make use of all three of the structures outlined above. The type and level used will reflect both the task and the user's experience and expectations. Alternatives may be offered — for example entering data by form fill or question and answer — which may reflect different preferences or expertise. The dialogue may be simplified as the user becomes confident and begins to feel irritated by a friendly but time consuming menu selection.

5.5.2 Dialogue design — other factors
A number of other factors should also be considered in dialogue design. Briefly, these are as follows.

Consistency of presentation
The SAGE Accounts system uses the same general format for entering details of all accounting transactions. This means that skills learnt in one part of the system are directly transferable to other parts. Format, entry and error correction are instantly familiar.

Consistency of operation
For example, the option R is made available in each menu to return the user to a menu one stratum higher, whilst X always exits to the operating system. Use of different symbols for the same operation in different menus is unnecessarily confusing. A lack of consistency in the use of the carriage return key may also cause difficulties. If it is required in some instances but not in others then the user tends to become both confused and anxious.

Provision of HELP facilities
A screen giving an explanation of the current operation being attempted by the user, together with a reference to an appropriate manual where further help can be found. Such HELP facilities may also be displayed automatically on the input screen with the

option to turn them off when the user feels he or she has gained sufficient competence in the use of the system.

An abort facility

The facility to **escape** from the system without making any permanent changes. This is particularly useful when the user is completely confused and fearful of making an entry that will possibly wreck the system. The provision of an abort routine permits them to start again secure in the knowledge that no irretrievable changes have been made to the system.

Default values

Data entry may be speeded up by placing values in certain fields. If this **default** value is relevant to the record being entered then no direct entry is required and the value can be accepted by keying, say, a carriage return. This may also force the user into a positive response in certain circumstances. For example:

> Delete all files (Y/N): N

The default response is **No**. The user has to take the positive action of entering a **Yes** for all the files to be deleted.

In general the system should be easy to use and understand. If the user makes an error then the messages displayed by the system should be both explanatory

> The Trial Balance does not balance

and suggest a course of action

> Post £2.31 to the Sundries account

Above all, the dialogue should reflect the expertise and vocabulary of the users so that it stands a chance of achieving a balance between being patronising or bewildering.

5.6   Design of data stores (files)

The logical data flow model helps determine the *content* of the data stores in terms of data elements. These data elements are documented and explained in the data dictionary. They now need grouping into files.

Unfortunately a rigorous approach to file design is well beyond the scope of this book and interested readers are referred to the texts recommended in the further reading. However, a rough intuitive approach can be outlined, together with comments on some of the issues that should be considered in design.

5.6.1   Content of files

The data store information will provide the basis for this. The file will be made up of logical records where a record consists of a number of associated data elements. Thus a customer record may consist of such elements as

Customer number
Customer name
Delivery to address
Invoice to address
Telephone number
etc.

These records may be collected together into a logical file. There are a number of possibilities.

- Place all customers in one large customer file.

- Integrate the customer record into a large mailshot file which includes *potential* as well as *actual* customers. This would represent the merging of two logical types of records — customers and prospects.

- Split the logical file on the basis of the activity on the file. For example, there may be a case for splitting off *active* customers from *inactive* ones (i.e. those who have not placed an order for one year) on the assumption that most orders and queries will take place on the active customers.

Organising the file in this last way utilises the concept of a 'hit group'. A hit group consists of those records which are accessed the most often — for example, in a product catalogue 80% of the orders may be for only 20% of the products. These popular products constitute a hit group and are perhaps stored in a file split away from the more slow moving goods. A related concept is the 'hit ratio' which measures the activity on a file in a particular run or period of time.

$$\frac{\text{Number of records accessed}}{\text{Number of records on file}}$$

This is usually expressed as a percentage — for example customer orders in one day hit 15% of the product file. Hit ratios and groups may be used as a guide to file organisation and processing. However, some of the rules of thumb used by data processing professionals have been shown to be unfounded (see Waters — Further reading).

5.6.2 Sequence of files

This concerns the order of records in the file. A number of possibilities are again available with the nature of the system and processing determining the most appropriate. Options include the following.

- The processing may have to be done in a certain sequence and organising the file in that sequence may save on processing time. For example, the issueing of overdue loan reminders in a library system may benefit from a file organised in date due rather than borrower number order.

- The output is required in a certain sequence. For example, the payslips of an organisation may be required in department/section order to save on time consuming manual sorting. Consequently, the file could benefit from being organised in this sequence.

- Input may be in a certain order — for example, house number/street — and this may be an appropriate sequence for the file, thus saving initial sorting runs.

- The size of the file may be affected by its sequence.

- The file sequence may be determined by the activity on the data. For example, a customer file may be ordered in sequence of number of orders so that the most regular customers are placed together at the beginning of the file. Most of the activity — i.e. processing of orders and customer queries — will take place on those customers and so seeks between customer accesses should be reduced.

5.6.3 Access methods of files

There are three basic choices (described in Part 1) — search, index and algorithm. A consideration of these alternatives leads to a design in which the files have been defined in terms of *content, sequence* and *access method*. Subsequent design is now affected by an understanding of the processes in the system.

It is also helpful to make a distinction between **master files** holding basic data which changes little over time, such as customer name, address etc. and **transaction files** which hold temporary data. Many systems have such characteristics. For example, in a personnel records system there will be a master file holding basic information about employees and a number of transaction files such as leavers and joiners, absences, holidays etc. holding such transactions over a period of time. These will be run against the master file to update the details of the employees. Transaction files will be associated with certain types of processes identified on the dataflow diagram — update, amend, delete — and programs will have to be written to perform these operations correctly and successfully.

5.6.4   Processing mode of files

Although each file will be ordered in a certain sequence it is likely that it will be processed by programs in a variety of ways. In general there are three distinct possibilities, although other hybrid options exist.

Serial

The whole file is processed in its *physical* sequence. This is the only processing mode possible if a **serial access device** is chosen. A file with associated indexes or algorithms can be processed serially although this really only makes sense if the process needs to access every record.

Sequential

The entire file is processed in its *logical* sequence — that is, the order of its key values. Thus a file organised in ascending customer number sequence will be processed in this order even though the records may be physically scattered around the disk.

Random

Records are processed in neither serial nor sequential order. Indexed and algorithmic files can be randomly processed but, in general, other types of file cannot. Random processing is usually necessary in systems which require quick response times, because the other two methods incur unacceptable overheads associated with processing irrelevant records.

5.6.5   Device allocation

The logical system is then implemented onto selected or given hardware, allocating files and programs to storage devices to produce a physical system. The device should obviously meet the chosen access method. Thus indexed or algorithmic files should be assigned to a random or direct access devices (see Part 1) while large serially processed files may be more suitable for tape storage. Small, frequently accessed files may be held in primary storage. For example, in a customer order system it is likely that the price of goods ordered will be automatically retrieved from a price list file. If this file is held on disk this will mean multiple accesses during the input operation and this is likely to cause unacceptable slowness. A possible alternative is to hold the file in primary store so using the fast access nature of this type of storage and hence avoiding time consuming disk searching.

5.7   Design of processes

The processes of the dataflow model use data items from flows (inputs) and stores (files) to produce further flows (outputs). The processes are only defined in a logical way and so it is up to the designer to decide *how* these activities will be carried out in the implemented system. Three broad alternatives are available.

5.7.1   Human

The process is carried out by a human being. This is usually reserved for decisions which require important subjective judgements, or are sufficiently 'one-off' that they do not justify data collection and interpretation.

5.7.2   Human/computer

The process is carried out by some combination of human being and computer. For example, the process allocate-priority may describe the allocation of priorities to customers by a customer services manager. He or she may undertake this task by supplementing subjective observations of the firm with buying pattern data provided by a computer system. In reality, many management processes fall into this category.

5.7.3   Computer

The process is carried out completely by computer. This is possible when it is feasible to predict completely the states and actions of the system. The computer is a *rule following* machine. Therefore it may be used only in circumstances where those rules may be identified and completely defined. Grindley and Humble (see Further reading) identified four main areas where the computer appeared to contribute to success. Briefly, these were as follows.

Improved performance in repetitive tasks
   If a task can be found that is essentially predictable and repetitive then it can almost certainly be carried out more successfully by using a computer. This is because the rule following nature of the machine will cause it to consistently and tirelessly carry out the specified tasks. In contrast, few human beings are rule following, preferring wilfully to choose different paths and alternatives so as to keep control over the activities of the work system. In addition the human being may become tired, forgetful, inaccurate and inconsistent.

Increased volume of repetitive tasks
   Even if clerks are cajoled into performing repetitive tasks the inherent lack of job satisfaction leads to the need to seek compensation in the form of raised salaries. The result is that firms with large processing requirements cannot afford to maintain an 'army of clerks' and so turn to the computer to perform the required volume of processes.

Humans released for discretionary tasks
Relieving human beings of routine rule following work leaves them more time to perform the more discretionary tasks of management. This is essentially what has happened to accounting in the last two decades — losing the overhead of book-keeping to the computer has left time for budget management, corporate strategy and financial planning.

Improved control method
This is concerned with cases where a decision, once solely made by human judgement, may be improved by the contribution of some rule following data processing. This

often covers circumstances where the rules have been too complicated or the volume of data too great to make it practically possible for human beings to do.

Thus the designer is concerned with *allocating* the process to a suitable medium — human, human/computer, computer — and then specifying the process in some way. In certain instances this will be a clerical procedures document; in others it will be a specification for a computer program.

5.8   Summary

This chapter has attempted to raise some of the issues faced in moving from a logical to a physical specification of the system. The design phase may end by the production and eventual agreement of a system specification document, describing in narrative and diagrams the system that the designer intends to deliver to the client. This document will be supplemented by more detailed design documents for use by the programmers of the system. The system specification is essentially a paper version of the information system that will eventually be implemented and so both users and developers need a clear and agreed picture of the system. This may extend to a formal acceptance of the system by the client ('signing off the specification') whereby any subsequent changes required or demanded need to be formally agreed. There are inherent problems in this method of development (discussed in Chapter 6) but the contractual nature of the document is often required for both developer's and client's peace of mind. Selecting a suitable model for communicating the operations and procedures of the system may cause difficulties — although a number of standard methods have been proposed — and tales of misunderstandings abound.

Once a system specification has been agreed the task of converting it into an actual working system must commence. This requires the creation of files, writing of programs and the compilation of documentation. In a traditional data processing environment this often means the selection and organisation of a large programming team and writing a suite of programs in a conventional high level programming language such as PL/1 or COBOL. However, changes in technology and the market place have served to challenge this approach to system development and the nature of these changes is discussed both in Chapter 6 and in Part 4.

Whichever development strategy is adopted, the objective is to produce a working system that is faithful to the paper specification. This may take many months of painstaking programming culminating in a system which the developer feels is ready for testing and delivery to the client. The tasks involved in this latter phase are discussed in Chapter 6.

Further reading

Gaines B and Shaw M *The Art of Computer Conversation*, Prentice-Hall (1984)

A useful introduction to dialogue design, screen presentation and other aspects of the interface between the computer and the user. Includes examples of less conventional interfaces and culminates in a suggested list of proverbs of good design.

It is very difficult to cover file design satisfactorily in an introductory textbook, as Parkin has demonstrated in his article

Data Analysis and Systems Design by Entity-Relationship modelling: A Practical Example; *The Computer Journal*, **25**, 4, pp 401–9, Nov. 1982.

In this book I have briefly introduced the framework established by Waters (see below), but serious students of design should read all of the three books listed directly below to appreciate three complementary approaches to the design of files and data bases. Data analysis is a much sounder approach to file content design than 'intuition' or 'rules of thumb', whilst Hansen's speciality is the detailed performance of different file arrangements. The referenced text gives a good introduction to his work.

Hansen O, *Essentials of Computer Data Files*, Pitman (1985)
Howe D, *Data Analysis for Data Base Design*, Edward Arnold (1983)
Waters S, *An Introduction to Computer Systems Design*, NCC (1974)

The input and output section is based (as mentioned in the Preface) on unpublished lecture notes of Frank Land. Readers interested in finding out more about the technologies are guided to

Hirschheim R, *Office Automation: Concepts, Technologies and Issues*, Addison-Wesley (1985)

6
System implementation

6.1 Introduction

Once the system has been developed it must be delivered and implemented. This chapter examines three aspects of this implementation. The first looks at the practical tasks that must be completed — testing, conversion, documentation and training. The second is a consideration of the different implementation strategies that could be adopted — parallel running, pilot implementation and direct changeover. Finally, the advantages of prototyping are discussed and examples of prototyping software are given.

6.2 Practical tasks

6.2.1 Testing

During the programming stage each programmer or programming team will perform their own program testing to the specifications laid down by the designer. The completed programs are then passed to the designer for further testing. He or she will be anxious not only to examine the delivered programs but also to prove their interfaces with the rest of the system. Testing will be performed both by **desk checking** — comparing the program flowcharts with the original specifications — and by **running** the programs using **test data**.

Test data should be taken from the existing system and results produced by the computer compared with manually compiled examples. So, for example, in a system designed to produce and print examination certificates, a sample of students should be taken and entered into the new computer system. The certificates can then be compared with their clerically produced counterparts and discrepancies investigated.

It is also important that the system correctly identifies errors and omissions and testing for these is especially critical. The same can be said for validating outputs, particularly those which are a little unusual, such as the nil statement and the multi-page invoice. Testing is a vital but time consuming activity. It is inevitable that errors will be found. These may be due to incorrect programming, misunderstanding of specifications or simply omissions in the original design. The amendments required must be coded by the programmer and the programs and system retested. This retesting is very important because the amendments may have caused unwanted side effects and so new errors and problems may appear.

It is also at the system testing stage that the *timing* aspects of the system become clearer. Required response times (maximum of ten seconds for retrieval of patient data), processing times (all employee records updated in two hours) and output schedules (all examination certificates produced in one week) must all be checked. Problems that are due to inefficient programming or misspecified files may be tackled by the designer. Problems due to hardware not achieving its claimed specification must be taken up with the supplier.

Testing represents the last opportunity for preparing the system before its exposure to users and the harshness of the real world. From now on any errors or idiosyncracies will become public knowledge.

6.2.2 File conversion

Most systems require an established set of files if they are to be immediately operational. Thus an order entry system will need such files as customer data, outstanding orders, products etc. This data has to be transferred from the current operational systems thus creating a large, one-off data entry or data conversion task. This leads to both programming and management tasks.

The designer may be able to use the data input routines of the proposed system for entering current information into the computer. However, it is more likely that a certain amount of historical data will also be required and this facility will not be available in the normal input routine. A simple example will illustrate this.

A system for maintaining mail order customers required the recording of the date of last order. This was not entered on the input screen as it could be picked up automatically from the operating system. Consequently, the proposed input screen could not be used for entering established customers as their date of last order could have been any time within the last decade. A special file creation program had to be written to capture date of last order together with other historical data required by the system.

In general, the designer will have to specify a suite of file creation programs. These will have to be specified, written and tested with the same care as those produced for the proposed operational system. It is likely that a certain amount of re-routing of input data will also be required. For example, the user may be asked for customer details which are then used to create two or three complete or partial files. Validation and verification are vital in file creation programs. It is at this stage that the users begin to lose their established filing methods for something that is less tangible. Errors are pounced upon and confidence may quickly ebb away.

The task of *organising* the creation of files must also be approached in meticulous detail. Entering 50 000 customer records is a daunting, not to say tedious, task. The clerical resources of the department may not be sufficient or willing to undertake such activities on top of their daily work. The employment of temporary staff or the use of computer bureau facilities must be considered. It may be possible to phase the file creation by entering established records over a period of time, in parallel with the running of the operational system. This requires a certain discipline to ensure that the completion of data entry does not stretch too far into the future and, in addition, it has the disadvantage of the system operating for some considerable time with incomplete files.

In summary, file conversion creates important technical and operational requirements which have to be planned for by the designer. Poor planning may lead to delayed or erroneous file creation.

6.2.3 Preparation of documentation

Documentation should be a constant task in system development. Implementation provides the opportunity to complete and tidy up documentation associated with the maintenance of the system — programs, file specifications, input and output formats. A number of documents are also required for the implementation itself. These include user manuals, security and recovery procedures, clerical advice documents, notices and wall charts. Procedures will also have to be established for requesting advice, hardware maintenance and system amendments.

The writing of user manuals will be a lengthy but vital task. Such manuals will need to reflect the expertise and vocabulary of the variety of users involved in the system and it is preferable to write a series of documents aimed at different *types* of user rather than to produce one all encompassing manual whose weight ensures that it will never be used! Manuals should concentrate on the issues that concern users the most — **functions** (how to do something — create a customer, delete a product type) and **errors**. These manuals will be the user's main point of reference when the system is operational and so possible problems should be anticipated and documentated. This can save unwanted time consuming phone calls after the system has been implemented. Manuals will also supplement and consolidate the information given in formal training sessions.

6.2.4   Training

Training will cover the retraining of current staff and the recruitment of new personnel. The latter will involve job specifications, advertising, salary advice and interviewing. Retraining will require planning and coordination. Unfortunately too much training is poorly planned and presented at the wrong level, failing to take the expertise and expectations of staff into consideration. To compound this, management are often reluctant to give training sessions the time or resources they require. This often manifests itself in under-funding training or not releasing staff for sufficient time from their daily duties. As a result, many systems are implemented with users and operators who do not fully understand their tasks and roles. This greatly reduces the chance of a successful implementation.

It should be clear that the tasks of implementation — system testing, file conversion, documentation and training — all require careful planning and coordination. Certain tasks must not be left too late (rushed user manuals are usually unimpressive), done too early (operator training months before the system will go live) or in the wrong sequence. Implementation is a *project* in its own right and will benefit from controls that are applicable to any project. Some of these are considered in Part 5. There is sometimes a tendency to relax during implementation believing that all the hard work is done. This is false confidence; lack of control and planning in implementation can undo months of good system and programming work.

6.3   Implementation strategies

The changeover from old to new system can be arranged once the computer system is tested and approved. Three possible strategies are available.

6.3.1   Parallel running

In this method the old and new systems are run simultaneously for an agreed period of time and results from the two systems are compared. Once the user has complete confidence in the system the old system is abandoned and transactions are only passed through the new one. Parallel running places a large administrative overhead on the user department because every transaction has to be effectively done twice — once through the established procedures and then again through the new computer system. Results have to be cross-checked and the source of errors located. This will lead to system modifications if problems are discovered in the computer system.

This method does have the advantage of having a 'fail-safe' system to fall back on should the new system crash for some reason. System problems can then be sorted out and the parallel run resumed. However, the duplication of effort can be something of a mixed blessing. Many operators and users still tend to rely on the established system and so some problems never appear until this has been abandoned. In addition, it may be difficult to justify a parallel run for the whole cycle of processing. Problems may only appear, say, the end of the financial year, months after the 'fail-safe' manual system had been phased out.

In summary, it could be claimed that parallel running is perhaps the safest, costliest and most time consuming way of implementing a system.

6.3.2 Pilot implementation

Two different possibilities exist. The first may be seen as a sort of retrospective parallel running. This takes historical data, say the last three months invoices, and the output produced is then compared with the known results. This is only, in effect, a large set of test data, and although this is not a bad thing in itself it does not really give the users and operators the experience and urgency of live processing.

The second type of pilot implementation does use live operations. Instead of *all* the transactions being passed through the new system, as in parallel running, only a limited number are entered into the computer system. This may be on a sample basis (say 1 in every 10) if this still facilitates cross-checking or, perhaps more realistically, by entering only certain sections, departments or accounts. This gives practice in live processing and reduces the overheads of duplicated entry. It is less rigorous in its testing than parallel running because only a limited set of transactions are used. Murphy's Law suggests that the transaction that causes the system to crash is in the other nine or in another department; a fact that is only found out when the existing system is abandoned and full live running commences.

6.3.3 Direct changeover

The final strategy is to implement the new system completely and withdraw the old without any sort of parallel running at all. Thus manual processing may end on a Friday night and all transactions pass through the new computer system from Monday morning onwards. There is no 'fail-safe' system at all. Direct changeover has none of the cost and time overheads of the previous two methods. Neither does it permit the old loyalty to the replaced system to be reflected in the relative performance of the two systems. It clearly demands very thorough testing and well planned file creation and training strategies. All operations of the system must be understood at the moment of going live because the opportunity for gradual training and further testing does not exist. Thus direct changeover is the quickest and most complete of our three implementation strategies but it is probably the riskiest.

In certain instances there is no real alternative to this method. This tends to happen when

- there is little similarity between the old and the replacement system so that cross checking is not possible
- the cost of parallel running is so prohibitive that it is cheaper to pay for the mistakes of a direct changeover.

Where possible, direct changeovers should occur in slack periods and take advantage of natural breaks in the operations of the organisation, such as industrial holidays.

6.4 Prototypes

The sequential nature of the narrative of Parts 2 and 3 may misleadingly suggest a series of discrete events; analysis, design and implementation, in that order. Such a clear sequence will not exist in a project unless it is imposed. It is likely that analysis will be *preoccupation* of the early part of the project while implementation will usually be near the end, but otherwise the tasks of the systems project will be jumbled up. For example, it may be possible to produce parts of a working system quite early in the project permitting users to gain working experience of a section of the system. This is part of the philosopy of **prototyping**.

In some respects prototyping is a reaction against a once fashionable school of thought that did try to partition the analysis, design and programming of systems. There are still numerous textbooks suggesting that programming must not start until user requirements are agreed. This would often be after the agreement of a monolithic System Specification document describing a system which would effectively remain frozen until delivery. Thus changes that may occur in user needs and the operating environment in the time between specification agreement and system delivery are not taken into consideration. The result is often the delivery of the 'system we needed two years ago'.

A further problem associated with the specification approach is that it presumes that the users and operators are able to state their requirements in advance. This seems rather optimistic. In many instances it is unclear to a user how a system may help, either because the role of the computer is not understood or because the information needs are unclear. Most users cope with this uncertainty by 'asking for everything' so that amongst the data the system eventually produces are the nuggets of information that they actually required. It is difficult for most users to really envisage what they want and how they can use it until they are able to experiment with a tangible system. A simple prototype designed to accomodate the user's broad needs, together with possibilities suggested by the designer using experience gained in other projects, may be used to refine requirements more accurately. It has been suggested that the use of a prototype system in this way changes the user's perceptions of what is possible, increases his insights into his own environment, and indeed often changes that environment itself.

6.4.1 Prototype philosophy
The prototype is a *live, working system* not just a paper based design. Thus users do not have to imagine how it might appear during operation; they can actually experience its operations. This is a much more effective and reliable method of communicating a design than a written description.

The prototype may become the actual replacement system. It is sensible to build a prototype system without, for example all the bells and whistles of data validation. However, if the prototype is greeted enthusiastically then it is possible to add the finishing design touches fairly quickly. In other circumstances the prototype may be discarded.

It is essential that the prototype is created *quickly*. This requires software tools that permit the creation of quick, dirty, first shot systems. Conventional high level programming languages are not suited for this type of development. Prototyping requires powerful software tools of the type described in Section 6.4.2. These are needed if the prototype is to be relatively inexpensive to build.

Finally, it must be stressed that prototyping is an **iterative process**. The first system is built around the user's basic requirements and refined in the light of comments and difficulties. Thus the prototype passes through a number of iterations until it becomes an accurate reflection of the user's requirements. At this stage the designer has three options.

- Refine the prototype into a final running system. This may require some development of error trapping and recovery routines.

- Re-code certain sections of the prototype to make them more efficient.

- Re-code the entire system. For example the prototype may have been developed with the prime aim of refining user requirements. The software used to do this may turn out to be completely inadequate over a certain volume of transactions. Thus re-coding is required to permit the phasing out of the prototype.

6.4.2 Prototype tools

The tool(s) chosen for prototype development must, above all, permit the quick development of working systems.

Application packages

The concept and growth of application packages is examined in Part 4. It may be possible to develop a demonstrator system using an appropriate package and let the user identify problems, possibilities and opportunities using the package as a yardstick. It is often easier to say what is inadequate about, say, a production control package, than it is to define requirements in the abstract.

Program generators

Program generators have been around for a number of years and a variety of different types may be identified. One sort uses a question and answer English dialogue to produce the program logic which it then encodes in a high level language such as BASIC or COBOL. A different type adopts a screen based approach where the designer effectively *paints* the screen by typing directly onto it. Once satisfied with the display, the program generator is invoked to automatically write the code needed to produce that screen. It may also produce validation routines, stopping only to request what type and range of data is required in a certain field and what error message should appear when the user makes a mistake. These may be produced directly if the program generator has access to a data dictionary.

Reusable code

Many systems are conceptually similar. Tasks appear over and over again — menu design, password protection, print routines, date checking etc. It is possible to build up a library of well proven, well documented routines which may be plugged together to make up a system. The *content* not the logic will require changing and some patching will be required to make a complete system. However, access to a store of well tested, standard parts should ease development and maintenance.

Application generators or Fourth Generation Languages

These go beyond the scope of program generators. Such products are likely to include a fully integrated data dictionary, a data base management system, a simple query language, a procedural language and report and program generators. All system development can be achieved within the software.

The development of such powerful and flexible tools merits closer inspection. Interested readers are referred to the product range listed under Further reading. As an example of the sort of facilities offered by these products Fig. 6.1 highlights details of three of them — MIMER, EASYTRIEVE and NOMAD2 — taken from their advertising literature.

6.5 Summary

This chapter has looked at the tasks associated with system implementation. Once the system is running it must be subject to review and modification. Some errors may not

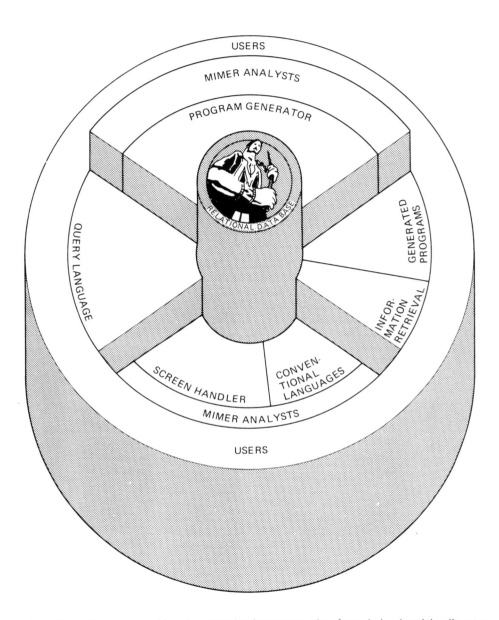

Fig. 6.1   Three illustrations of fourth generation languages taken from their advertising literature.

Fig. 6.1   (a) MIMER shows the possible scope of a fourth generation language. The MIMER system was created at Uppsala Data Centre in Sweden where its maintenance and development continue to be based. Development began in 1976 with the first international marketing in 1982 (Courtesy of Savant Enterprises)

```
> from accounts select monthpaid = &nav

> list from accounts by acct amount_due subtotal past_due —
> extract match from customer custno custname salesrep —
> title 'accounts with payments overdue' fold 'as of the month of september' —
> footing 'please contact your customers and remind them of our 30 day policy'

PAGE 1

                              ACCOUNTS WITH PAYMENTS OVERDUE
                                 AS OF THE MONTH OF SEPTEMBER

CUSTOMER        TOTAL       MONTHS
ACCOUNT        AMOUNT        OVER        CUSTOMER               MARKETING
 NUMBER          DUE         DUE           NAME                    REP
 1498          $12.76         5         REITORO INC.           WELLES, GIDEON
 1512         $605.40         6         PARKER EQUIPMENT       HOOKER, THOMAS
              $309.86         3         PARKER EQUIPMENT       HOOKER, THOMAS

   *          $915.26

 2032         $133.33         8         BURNES INTERNATIONAL   FOSTER, LAFAYETTE
              $198.63         4         BURNES INTERNATIONAL   FOSTER, LAFAYETTE

   *          $331.96

 2080         $111.12         5         BRADBURY INC           HOOKER, THOMAS
              $111.12         3         BRADBURY INC           HOOKER, THOMAS

   *          $222.24

 2112          $82.14         3         DEERING COMPANY        FOSTER, LAFAYETTE

 3412          $73.84         6         SPENCER ASSOCIATES     CRANDELL, PRUDENCE

PLEASE CONTACT YOUR  CUSTOMERS AND REMIND THEM OF OUR 30 DAY POLICY
```

Fig. 6.1 (b) NOMAD2 illustrates report construction with simple data retrieval criteria. The relational operators of NOMAD2 are used in this example to combine data from two different sources. Customer number (custno) is used to match data from accounts and customer. The fields custname and salesrep are brought over from customer. Note the insertion of title and footing lines in the report (Courtesy of PANSOPHIC SYSTEMS Ltd)

..with EASYTRIEVE®

```
FILE FILEA
DEPARTMENT 98 3 N NAME 17 20 A EMPL# 9 5 N
SEX 127 1 A NET 90 4 P2 GROSS 94 4 2 9999
IF DEPARTMENT = 911, 914
SORT DEPARTMENT
CONTROL DEPARTMENT
T1PAYROLL FOR DEPARTMENTS 911, 914
LIST DETAIL DEPARTMENT NAME 'EMPLOYEE,NAME' EMPL# 'EMPLOYEE,NUMBER' MORE
SEX NET 'NET,PAY' GROSS 'GROSS,PAY'
```

...with COBOL

```
00001   IDENTIFICATION DIVISION.
00002   PROGRAM-10. REPORT 1.
00003   ENVIRONMENT DIVISION.
00004   CONFIGURATION SECTION.
00005   SOURCE-COMPUTER. 1BM-370.
00006   OBJECT-COMPUTER. 1BM-370.
00007   INPUT-OUTPUT SECTION.
00008   FILE-CONTROL.
00009       SELECT INFILE ASSIGN TO UT-S-INFILE.
00010       SELECT REPORT-FILE ASSIGN TO UT-S-PANPRINT.
00011       SELECT SORT-FILE ASSIGN TO UT-S-SORTWORK.
00012       SELECT OUTFILE ASSIGN TO UT-S-OUTFILE.
00013   DATA DIVISION.
00014   FILE SECTION.
00015   SO  SORT-FILE DATA RECORD IS SORT-RECORD.
00016   01  SORT-RECORD.
00017       05   FILLER PICTURE A(6).
00018       05   EMPL-S PICTURE 9(5).
00019       05   FILLER PICTURE A(3).
00020       05   NAME-S PICTURE A(20).
00021       05   FILLER PICTURE A(53).
00022       05   NET-S PICTURE S99999V99 COMPUTATIONAL-3.
00023       05   GROSS-S PICTURE S99999V99 COMPUTATIONAL-3.
00024       05   DEPT-S PICTURE 999.
00025       05   FILLER PICTURE A(26).
00026       05   SEX-S PICTURE A.
00027       05   FILLER PICTURE A(23).
00028   FD  INFILE
00029       LABEL RECORDS ARE STANDARD
00030       BLOCK CONTAINS 0 RECORDS
00031       DATA RECORD IS INPUT-RECORD.
00032   01  INPUT-RECORD PICTURE A(150).
00033   FD  REPORT-FILE
00034       LABEL RECORDS ARE STANDARD
00035       REPORT IS PAYROLL-REPORT.
00036   FD  OUTFILE
00037       LABEL RECORDS ARE STANDARD
00038       DATA RECORD IS OUTPUT-RECORD.
00039   01  OUTPUT-RECORD PICTURE A(150).
00040   REPORT SECTION.
00041   RD  PAYROLL-REPORT
00042       CONTROL IS DEPT-S
00043       PAGE LIMIT IS 59 LINES
00044       HEADING 1
00045       FIRST DETAIL 6
00046       LAST DETAIL 56.
00047   01  TYPE IS PAGE HEADING.
00048       05   LINE NUMBER IS 1
00049            COLUMN IS 47
00050            PICTURE IS A(39)
00051            VALUE IS
00052   'PAYROLL REPORT FOR DEPARTMENTS 911, 914'.
00053       05   LINE IS 3.
00054            10   COLUMN IS 46
00055                 PICTURE IS A(8)
00056                 VALUE IS 'EMPLOYEE'.
00057            10   COLUMN IS 62
00058                 PICTURE IS A(8)
00059                 VALUE IS 'EMPLOYEE'.
00060            10   COLUMN IS 79
00061                 PICTURE IS A(3)
00062                 VALUE IS 'NET'.
00063            10   COLUMN IS 91
00064                 PICTURE IS A(5)
00065                 VALUE IS 'GROSS'.
00066       05   LINE IS 4.
00067            10   COLUMN IS 28
00068                 PICTURE IS A(10)
00069                 VALUE IS 'DEPARTMENT'.
00070            10   COLUMN IS 48
00071                 PICTURE IS A(4)
00072                 VALUE IS 'NAME'.
00073            10   COLUMN IS 63
00074                 PICTURE IS A(6)
00075                 VALUE IS 'NUMBER'
00076            10   COLUMN IS 71
00077                 PICTURE IS A(3)
00078                 VALUE IS 'SEX'.
00079            10   COLUMN IS 79
00080                 PICTURE IS A(3)
00081                 VALUE IS 'PAY'.
00082            10   COLUMN IS 92
00083                 PICTURE IS A(3)
00084                 VALUE IS 'PAY'.
00085   01  DETAIL-LINE TYPE IS DETAIL LINE NUMBER IS PLUS 1.
00086       05   COLUMN IS 31
00087            PICTURE IS 999
00088            SOURCE IS DEPT-S.
00089       05   COLUMN IS 40
00090            PICTURE IS A(20)
00091            SOURCE IS NAME-S.
00092       05   COLUMN IS 63
00093            PICTURE IS 9(5)
00094            SOURCE IS EMPL-S.
00095       05   COLUMN IS 72
00096            PICTURE IS A
00097            SOURCE IS SEX-S.
00098       05   COLUMN IS 76
00099            PICTURE IS ZZ.ZZZ.99
00100            SOURCE IS NET-S.
00101       05   COLUMN IS 89
00102            PICTURE IS ZZ.ZZZ.99
00103            SOURCE IS GROSS-S.
00104   01  TYPE IS CONTROL FOOTING DEPT-S
00105       LINE PLUS 1 NEXT GROUP PLUS 2.
00106       05   COLUMN IS 27
00107            PICTURE IS A(16)
00108            VALUE IS 'DEPARTMENT TOTAL'.
00109       05   NET COLUMN IS 76
00110            PICTURE IS ZZ.ZZZ.99
00111            SUM NET-S.
00112       05   GROSS COLUMN IS 89
00113            PICTURE IS ZZ.ZZZ.99
00114            SUM GROSS-S.
00115   01  TYPE IS CONTROL FOOTING FINAL LINE PLUS 2.
00116       05   COLUMN IS 76
00117            PICTURE IS ZZ.ZZZ.99
00118            SUM NET.
00119       05   COLUMN IS 89
00120            PICTURE IS ZZ.ZZZ.99
00121            SUM GROSS.
00122   PROCEDURE DIVISION.
00123       SORT SORT-FILE
00124           ASCENDING KEY DEPT-S
00125           INPUT PROCEDURE IS READ-INPUT
00126           OUTPUT PROCEDURE IS PRINT-REPORT.
00127       STOP RUN.
00128   PRINT-REPORT SECTION.
00129       OPEN OUTPUT OUTFILE OUTPUT REPORT-FILE.
00130       INITIATE PAYROLL-REPORT.
00131   LOOP2.
00132       RETURN SORT-FILE RECORD AT END GO TO ENDER.
00133       WRITE OUTPUT-RECORD FROM SORT-RECORD
00134       GENERATE DETAIL-LINE.
00135       GO TO LOOP2.
00136   ENDER.
00137       TERMINATE PAYROLL-REPORT.
00138       CLOSE OUTFILE REPOR" FILE.
00139   BACK-TO-SORT.
00140       EXIT.
00141   READ-INPUT SECTION.
00142       OPEN INPUT INFILE.
00143   LOOP1.
00144       READ INFILE RECORD INTO SORT-RECORD AT END GO TO END-READ
00145       IF DEPT-S = 911 OR 914
00146           RELEASE SORT-RECORD.
00147       GO TO LOOP1.
00148   END-READ.
00149       CLOSE INFILE.
00150   BACK.
00151       EXIT.
```

Fig. 6.1(c) EASYTREVE gives a comparison with Third Generation Language code (Courtesy of D & B Computing Services)

appear until well into the life of the system — for example a failure of an end of year report. The passing of time will bring new circumstances, new users and new technology. Modifications eventually become counter-productive. The obsolescence of the system itself becomes a trigger for a new phase of system development. A new project rises from the ashes of the old.

Further reading

Daniels A and Yeates D, *Practical Systems Design* Pitman (1984)

Lobell R.F, *Application Program Generators: A State of the Art Survey*, NCC (1984)

I am not aware of any one text that exhaustively reviews the practice and theory of prototyping so a number of accessible reference papers are given.

Naumann J D and Jenkins A M, 'Prototyping: The New Paradigm for System   Development' *MIS Quarterly*, September 1982
Boehm B et al, 'Prototyping versus Specifying: A Multiproject Experiment', *IEEE   Transactions on Software Engineering*, **SE – 10**, 3, May 1984
Dearnley P and Mayhew P, 'In favour of System Prototypes and their integration in to   the System Development Cycle,' *Computer Journal*, **26**, 1 1983

Products which claim to be Fourth generation languages may be identified from Lobell (see above) or from

Martin J, *Fourth Generation Languages* Volumes 1 and 2, Prentice-Hall (1985)

Part 4
Business Systems

Part 4 examines some of the operational systems of an enterprise, particularly those which are suitable for computerisation. Chapter 7 gives a brief overview of the scope of business activities and illustrates how they may all be viewed at three levels:

Physical   the movement and supply of goods.
Information data is recorded about the physical transactions.
Financial   movement and supply of goods incurs costs and generates income.

Two important non-financial systems are then considered — order entry and inventory control.

Chapter 8 is devoted to financial systems and illustrates the inter-relationship between the purchase, sales and nominal ledgers. The payroll system is also examined in the latter part of this chapter.

Chapter 9 looks at three important 'generalised' application packages and gives examples of each of these. The three areas — spreadsheets, data management and word processing — are common microcomputer applications and have made significant contributions to the large sales of these smaller machines.

Chapter 10 suggests an approach to software selection that recognises the recent technical and economic changes that have affected the computer system marketplace. It suggests that conventional programming should be a last resort and that more resources should be devoted to package identification and evaluation.

7
The business enterprise

In Part 2 it was stressed that the computer should be seen as a way of helping the organisation achieve its defined objectives. Clearly different organisations have different aims and objectives depending on, amongst other things, such factors as their function, ownership, size, marketplace and geographical position. Consequently it is difficult to be specific about systems that will contribute to successful business acitivity. In some cases it might be an innovative patient care system, in others a real time production control package.

It is important to gain an appreciation of some of the principal operational activities of organisations and the computer systems that support them. These functions are largely common to organisations of different sizes and sectors — for example, stock control systems are required in manufacturing, hospitals, retailing and education. The 'stock' being controlled will vary but the principles remain the same. A selection of these fundamental financial and non-financial operational systems is examined in this part. Chapter 9 also considers software to support more tactical and strategic management decisions.

7.1 Business activities — a brief review

It is useful to review the basic activities of an enterprise and to identify some of the systems needed to support its main needs and objectives. For illustrative purposes a manufacturing example will be taken and the chain of events caused by the placement of a customer order will be considered.

Two elements of the order have to be checked — the goods ordered and the customer placing the order. If this is the first order received from a particular organisation then it may be necessary to request bank and business references before supplying the goods. These references will also be used to establish the credit limit for that account. However, if the order has been placed by an established customer, it will be necessary to check the current credit standing of that account showing goods supplied but not yet paid for. If the customer already exceeds the allocated credit limit then it may be prudent to request the payment of certain outstanding invoices before supplying the goods. Thus systems are required to support the activities outlined in Fig. 7.1.
The other aspect of the order that requires checking is the goods being requested. Firstly, are the goods on the order form actually supplied by our organisation or has there been an ordering error or product misunderstanding? Such orders must be identified and appropriate enquiries made. If the goods are available from us then we

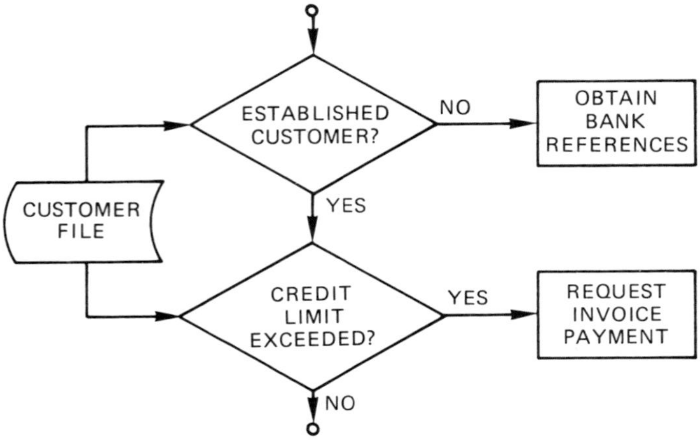

Fig. 7.1   Part of a customer enquiry process

need to examine a number of issues. Can the order be fulfilled immediately? If not, can part of the order be supplied and is it meaningful to do so? If all or part of the order cannot be fulfilled, when will it be possible to undertake or complete delivery?

Organisations vary in how they respond to requests for goods. Most firms supply from stock so that orders can be fulfilled very quickly. This means that most of the manufacturing in that organisation will be to *stock* not to *order*. The implications of this will be examined a little later. In other organisations it is not feasible to produce stock and all manufacturing is done to order. An example of this is the building of airliners. An order for six A-300 airbuses is unlikely to be met overnight. The overhead costs of building up such stocks would be prohibitive and in any case would not fit in with the long term planning of the airlines themselves. The time taken to allocate routes and plan schedules means that the airlines can estimate their aircraft needs well in advance and place orders accordingly. The same economic pressures affect industries such as shipbuilding where it is unlikely that a shipyard would build, say, 20 frigates to stock, on the off-chance that a navy will place an urgent order for ships of that particular specification. The advantage of manufacturing to order is that the firm can be sure of selling what it is making. The same cannot be said of manufacturing to stock. However, the competitive disadvantage and manufacturing overhead of making goods to order make it inappropriate in many spheres of economic activity.

If the firm intends to supply all orders from stock then it must be able to forecast the demand for a product in a certain period so that enough stock is carried. This is the task of sales forecasting. Such forecasts will be based on both qualitative and quantitative data. The latter might include past sales, trends, seasonal fluctuations and produce statistical forecasts using an appropriate mathematical technique. This will be supplemented by qualitative factors such as sales promotions, new market entries, discounts and special offers. These may be used as the basis for a subjective modification of the statistical forecasts. The result is a profile of the demand for a product over a given period of time. The effect of this demand on the stock position is calculated and this leads to the manufacturing requirement. A simple example for a consumer product is given in Table 7.1. This example illustrates the basic concept of manufacturing to stock. Production is not geared to *actual* orders but to what the orders are *expected* to be. This demonstrates the importance of the accuracy of the sales forecast. If it is incorrect then goods may be overstocked (leading to price reductions to clear them), understocked (causing expensive panic manufacture or lost orders) or even to the complete destruction of perishable goods. A system to support good forecasting is obviously very useful.

Production to stock also has important implications for at least two other aspects of the organisation's activity. The first is production itself. In the example given in Table 7.1 the order values are passed weekly to the Production Planner and are used to help plot the production schedule for the period ahead. This will have implications for the planning of staff shifts and the order of raw materials. This latter factor is the other aspect affected by the decision to manufacture to stock. If the production planner has to manufacture a given amount of goods in the next week then the raw materials required for that production must be readily available. Thus the stores section is not only concerned with holding stocks of the products *made* by the firm but also raw materials and goods needed to *make* those products. In both instances it needs to be supported by a system that permits a balance between the costs of holding stocks (storage charges, handling costs, security etc.) and the costs of not holding them (high cost panic buying, production disruption, lost orders).

There will also have to be arrangements for dealing with orders which can only be partially fulfilled. A number of alternative responses are available:

- supplying similar substitute goods at a discount price

- supplying from another source

- informing customers of a delay while goods are produced.

In the last instance it may be possible to supply part of the order and to give a further delivery date for the outstanding items. This is only possible when supplying the part order is feasible: providing 350 of the 500 World Cup tee shirts is

Table 7.1

| | Period (weeks) | | | | | | |
	1	2	3	4	5	6	7
Opening stock	500	1220	1310				
Order forecast	100	300	200	250	300	450	300
Sales forecast	200	210	230	250	230	270	300
Closing stock	400	1310	1280				
Cover forecast	1.82	4.36					
Required cover	4.00	4.00					
Order change	820	0					

In this simple example order forecasts are made at the start of the year; Sales forecasts are modified monthly. Orders are 'placed' with depots around the country. The aim of the system is to have a required cover period (4 weeks in the example above) which defines how much stock should be held. In period 1 in the example given above they are holding 1.82 weeks stock $\frac{210 + 230}{400}$ and this is deemed insufficient (4.00 weeks is required). Thus an order change is sanctioned which increases the production requirement at depots. In the actual example that this was based on the required cover had tolerances (eg 3.6 weeks was acceptable) so that order changes did not occur every week.

viable; supplying two thirds of a car is not. If part orders are supported then the adminstration of the rest of the order must be carried out efficiently. The residue of part orders (back orders) must be fulfilled as soon as the goods become available and the Production Planner should be notified of such backlogs so that the schedule includes plans for their supply.

The stores activity itself may be seen as two distinct functions. The first is concerned with the *administration* of stock — maintenance of records, stock issue, returns etc; and the second with the *purchase* of stock. This latter aspect may often be delegated to a separate purchasing department. It is the overall task of purchasing to establish favourable and reliable deals with suppliers. This will not only include the negotiation of contractual terms of supply, prices and discounts but also delivery arrangements, distance and an assessment of supplier reliability. It will be essential to order sufficient stock to avoid the need for expensive small quantity panic purchases from occasional suppliers. Such orders will increase the unit cost of manufacture and so make finished goods less profitable.

The monitoring of purchasing may be very useful. At the start of the year the *cost* of the sales forecast may be calculated by applying a standard production cost to each product. This standard production cost is usually a combination of the labour cost and the cost of the raw material. Thus standard costs for each raw material and good used in product production have to be provided by the purchasing section. For example:

GHT Controller System
Sales forecast: 1200
Forecast unit production cost: Labour: $3.00
                                Materials: $6.50

Cost of sales forecast: 1200 × $9.50 = $11 400.00

Costing of the sales forecast is necessary to produce the estimated profit for the coming year. For example

GHT Controller System
Sales forecast: 1200

Selling price: $11.50

Estimated income: $13 800.00
Estimated cost: $11 400.00

Estimated profit: $2 400.00

Unit costs may critically affect pricing policies. In the example given above senior management may not consider the product to have a sufficient profit margin at the forecast volumes. As a result a price increase is recommended.

However, it must be recalled that the unit costs given above are estimates provided for budgetary purposes. If these costs are not adhered to then profit margins begin to rise or fall. This may not be a problem if the suggested costs turn out to be overestimates, although the effect of such external factors on recorded profits should be understood. However, the serious consequences of under-estimating costs lead to a requirement for continual monitoring. Action will be needed (sack Purchasing Manager, seek new suppliers, increase product prices) if profitability is to be maintained.

Once the goods have been manufactured they have to be checked (quality control), stored and then packaged and delivered. Planning distribution may be yet another candidate activity for improvement.

7.2   Business activities — three levels of system

Figure 7.2 attempts to summarise and extend the inter- relationships that exist between different functions within the overall business activity. It also tries to demonstrate the three levels of a system's operation. Two of these levels — the physical and message systems — were introduced in Part 3. The third level is the financial expenditure and income associated with every activity. Each action has a cost (labour, materials, stationery, insurance, heating, lighting etc.) and these all have to be

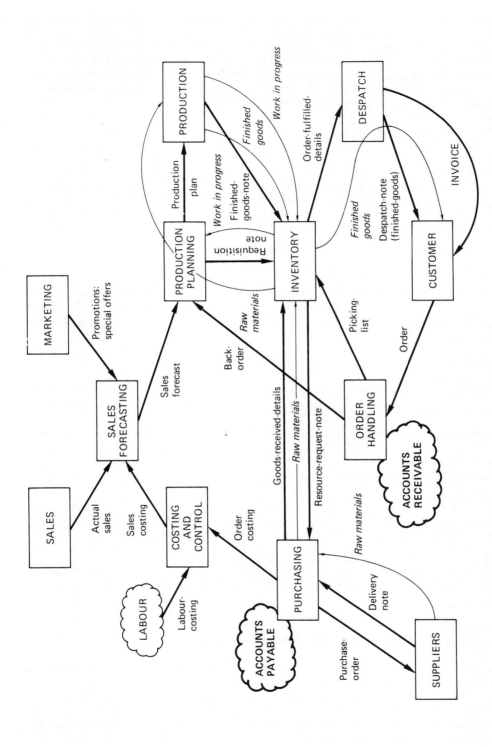

Fig. 7.2 Interaction of business systems — an example

accounted for and built into the price of a product. The **budgetary system** attempts to predict these costs and the **accounting ledgers** record the actual costs as they are incurred. Many of the **message** and **financial** systems are suitable for computerisation. A brief review of six of these areas is given in the rest of this chapter and in Chapter 8. It should be stressed that these represent possible not recommended areas for computerisation. The decision to implement in one of these areas in a particular organisation should be taken in the context of that firm's overall business objectives.

7.3   Order entry

7.3.1   Introduction
Order entry is concerned with the handling of sales orders from customers. It must validate both goods ordered (is this item supplied by the organisation?) and the credit status of the customer ordering the goods. Back orders must be identified and raised. Customers may place an order for several different items on the same order form.

7.3.2   System characteristics

Outputs
Back order   Created from the items on the sales order that cannot be satisfied immediately. It is likely that a back order report will be available which shows all back orders chronologically within product. This may be used to help plan production schedules.

Invoices   Raising an invoice to be sent to customers.

Picking list   This is a summary of the demand for each product in a batch of invoices. These may be arranged into bin number sequence to help picking in the stores.

Sales data   For onward transmission to the sales and nominal ledgers.

Inputs
Sales order   from the customer identifying:

Customer number
Items required
Quantity of each item
Date of order

Goods received notes (GRNs)   A note of damaged or incorrectly supplied goods which accompanies the return of those goods.

Files
Customer file
Inventory file   Covering all *product* information
Satisfied order file
Back order file
Price list

Processes
Programs to retrieve correct customer and item descriptions given valid customer and item codes.

Routines to compare order requirements with the stock amounts recorded in the inventory file and to create back orders if necessary. This is clearly linked to the stock control system discussed in Section 7.4.

Programs to create invoices and picking lists. Posting of details to the appropriate ledgers (see Chapter 8).

7.3.3 Other issues

The order entry system is fairly straightforward. Many of the issues that it has to deal with have already been introduced in Section 7.2. It is primarily concerned with money (Fig. 7.3 shows a typical invoice) and stock (a stock report for the warehouse is illustrated in Fig. 7.4). It benefits from the following.

- Integration with the financial ledgers. Raised invoices are passed directly to the accounts receivable system (the sales ledger).

- Integration with inventory control. Sales orders from customers is one of the major inputs required by the stock control system (see Section 7.4).

- A fast and flexible enquiry system. It is common for an organisation to receive many queries concerning the status of particular orders. Good customer relations dictates that it is necessary to quickly locate information about the current position of an order.

- Order data is very important to an organisation because it reflects the fruits of its activities. Thus the ability to request information about the pattern of orders may aid marketing and product strategy. Typical queries might be:

'How many TRG Accelerators were ordered by companies in North Wales?'
'Did any small companies place orders for the new GHT Activator in the month after our appearance at the Small Firm Business Venture Show?'

Order volumes may be used to evaluate sales promotions and marketing initiatives. They may also be used to modify the sales forecasts discussed earlier in this chapter.

7.4 Inventory (stock) control

7.4.1 Introduction

The fundamental purpose of an inventory control system is to establish stock records and to maintain these against:

purchase orders placed with suppliers (stock on order)
receipt of stock from suppliers
sales orders from customers (see Section 7.3).

7.4.2 System characteristics

Outputs
Inventory control systems are primarily concerned with the production of reports for management action. The scope of these reports will vary from system to system. Typical outputs might include the following.

Stock out report   Reporting all items where the stock level has reached zero.

Reorder level report   Showing all items which have reached their recommended reorder levels. The suggested reorder quantities may also be printed if required (see Fig. 7.5).

SALES INVOICE

No. A999999   19-JAN-87

From:

PAXTON COMPUTERS LTD.
28 New St.
St. Neots
Huntingdon
Cambs. PE19 1AJ

Vat Reg. No.

Invoice to:

Attila Videos
3, Woodland Avenue
Conistone
Leicester

Delivered to:

YOUR REFERENCE

Order no.   C11000
Order date   19-JAN-87

OUR REFERENCE

Account   ATT01

Quantity	Part No.	Description	Price	Per	Discount	Nett
1	DE1002	Business Desk Issue Discs On Sirius Disc Format	35.00	1		35.00
1	DE3001	Business Desk User Guide	15.00	1		15.00
1	DE2001	Business Desk Module Credit	150.00	1		150.00

VAT ANALYSIS

Code	Goods	Rate	VAT
1	185.00	15.00%	27.75
2	15.00	0.00%	0.00

Total Goods	200.00
Total VAT	27.75
AMOUNT DUE	227.75

Fig. 7.3 An example invoice. Note the VAT analysis to distinguish between different rated items (Taken from the Paxton Business Desk System, courtesy of Paxton Computers Ltd)

Multisoft Systems Company AA	Stock Recording Multi-balance Stock Report					Batch 001/ Sample Date 1.07.87			Page 1 Time 09:00	
Prod	Description	Units	Group	Bin	Balance	On order	Reserved	Allocated	Free	Orders
A001	Acme Carpet Tiles (1ft sq)	BOX-36	TC	36A	236		120	21	95	141
A002	Dulux White Gloss, 2.5L	EACH	PD1		5	244	56	5	188	61
B001	Magicote White Gloss, 1L	EACH	PM1	20C	189			28	161	28
B004	Ajax Ceramic Tiles -- Red	BOX-50	TA	47A	18				18	
B005	Ajax Ceramic Tiles — Blue	BOX-50	TA	47A	11			41		28
B006	Ajax Ceramic Tiles -- White	BOX-50	TA	47A		50	12		38	12
B104	Nuvo Ceramic Tiles -- Red	BOX-50	TA	48R	73			6	67	6
B105	Nuvo Ceramic Tiles — Sky blue	BOX-50	TA	48B	38			12	26	12
B106	Nuvo Ceramic Tiles — White	BOX-50	TA	48B	5	100	32	5	68	83
C001	Crown Vymura Wall Covering	ROLL	WV1	12A	283			37	246	37
C101	Novomura Wallpaper-Prepasted	ROLL	WV1	13A	82		20		62	20
C102	Novomura Wallpaper	ROLL	WV2	16C	12				12	
C900	Novo Super Paste — Normal	BOX-24	WP	10A	18	50	28	11	29	39
C901	Novo Super Paste — Economy	BOX-24	WP	10A	72			3	69	3
H001	Acme Builders Hammer	DOZEN	HAM	73R	2	5			7	
H002	Acme Carpenters Hammer	DOZEN	HAM	74R	7				7	
ML05P	Suffolk Puncher Petrol Mower	EACH	MOW	8A	3				3	
ML05E	Suffolk Puncher Electric Mower	EACH	MOW	8A		1			1	
MR001	Surform Lawnraker — 15'' Blades	EACH	MOW	9A	5	5		1	9	1

Fig. 7.4 A multi-balance stock report. Note the alphanumeric code (some packages offer only numerical codes) and the facility to provide data and time stamps (Produced by the Multisoft Inventory Control package, Courtesy of Multisoft Systems Ltd)

Multisoft Systems Company AA	Stock Recording Stock Valuation & Warning Report						Batch 001/ Sample Date 1.07.87				Page 1 Time 09:00	
Prod	Description	Units	Group	Bin	Balance	Value	On order	Min	Roq	Rec	Max	Over
A001	Acme Carpet Tiles (1ft sq)	BOX-36	TC	36A	236	2655.00						
A002	Dulux White Gloss, 2.5L	EACH	PD1		5	9.60	244					
B001	Magicote White Gloss, 1 L	EACH	PM1	20C	189	209.79						
B004	Ajax Ceramic Tiles — Red	BOX-50	TA	47A	18	115.74		50	20	40		
B005	Ajax Ceramic Tiles — Blue	BOX-50	TA	47A	11	57.87		50	20	50		
B006	Ajax Ceramic Tiles — White	BOX-50	TA	47A			50					
B104	Nuvo Ceramic Tiles — Red	BOX-50	TA	48R	73	429.97						
B105	Nuvo Ceramic Tiles — Sky blue	BOX-50	TA	48B	38	223.82						
B106	Nuvo Ceramic Tiles — White	BOX-50	TA	48B	5	29.45	100					
C001	Crown Vymura Wall Covering	ROLL	WV1	12A	283	877.30					200	83
C101	Novomura Wallpaper-Prepasted	ROLL	WV1	13A	82	254.20						
C102	Novomura Wallpaper	ROLL	WV2	16C	12	34.20		60	50	50		
C900	Novo Super Paste — Normal	BOX-24	WP	10A	18	171.00	50					
C901	Novo Super Paste — Economy	BOX-24	WP	10A	72	829.44					50	22
H001	Acme Builders Hammer	DOZEN	HAM	73R	2	96.52	5					
H002	Acme Carpenters Hammer	DOZEN	HAM	74R	7	316.82						
ML05P	Suffolk Puncher Petrol Mower	EACH	MOW	8A	3	520.83						
ML05E	Suffolk Puncher Electric Mower	EACH	MOW	8A			1	2	1	1		
MR001	Surform Lawnraker — 15'' Blades	EACH	MOW	9A	5	162.45	5					
	Total Stock					6994.10						

Fig. 7.5 Re-order level report. Items that have fallen below their minimum level are shown on the right hand side with information about reorder quqantity (ROQ) etc. Items above their maximum levels are also identified together with the amount by which the balance exceeds this level (produced by the Multisoft Inventory Control system, courtesy of Multisoft Systems Ltd)

Stock quantity and value The stock balances on each item and the financial value of these balances.

Slow moving stock It may be valuable to identify slow moving goods which may then become the subject of a 'special offer'.

Purchase order reports Showing goods ordered, or on order, and the cost of these goods.

Price variance report   Compares the cost of goods ordered with the notional unit costs allocated in the budget. This may be used to monitor the effectiveness of the purchasing section as well as permitting the re-setting of profit forecasts.

Inputs
Sales orders from customers   Reduces the amount in stock by the amount ordered.

Purchase orders from suppliers   Increases the amount in stock by the number received.

Stock adjustments   Usually made after a physical stockcheck.

Item prices and notional unit prices.

Files
Inventory file   Storing data on *all* items used by the company, not just products. The inventory file will include fields which permit links to the order entry system (for example back order references). A history file may be relevant in certain circumstances but it may be that a year-to-date field in the main file definition will provide sufficient historical data.
Price list

Processes
Programs will be primarily concerned with the correct calculation and manipulation of the stock figures. The mathematical sophistication of the package will vary considerably. Some may simply maintain stock receipts and issues while, in contrast, others provide suggested economic order quantities and other inventory *management* information. References for further reading on economic order quantity calculation and interpretation are given at the end of the chapter.

7.4.3   Other issues
Order entry is concerned with satisfying orders from stock. The manufacturing process requires goods and raw materials to be supplied from stock so that it can make the products that the company offers for sale. These represent the **stock issues** of the inventory control system. The **stock receipts** come primarily from purchases from suppliers. The issue of purchase orders and the checking and recording of the receipt of stock is not covered in this text. It is, however, conceptually similar to the order processing system described in Section 7.3, except that stock in hand will now be *increased* and accounts *payable* (not receiveable) updated.

7.5   Summary

It is important to recognise the inter-relationships of business systems and to see how they combine together to further the objectives of the organisation. This chapter has given a brief overview of the types of activity that are likely to be undertaken in a company. It has concluded with an examination of two significant operational systems — order entry and inventory control. These have certain financial implications — it costs money to buy stock, we sell goods at certain prices — and so Chapter 8 switches attention to the financial systems of the organisation.

Further reading

Anderson R G, *Business Systems*, M&E Handbooks (1977)

A good introduction to the inter-relationship of business systems. Computer related chapters of the book are weaker and there is a heavy bias towards organisation and methods terminology and modelling.

Best P, *Small Business Computer Systems*, Prentice-Hall (1980)

The details of the computerisation of small business systems are well explained in this text. Well written and plenty of practical examples and exercises.

Lucey T, *Quantitative Analysis*, DP Publications (1979)

Simple treatment of some of the mathematical foundations of inventory control.

8
Financial systems

The financial systems of an organisation broadly support two main areas of accounting. The first is concerned primarily with **stewardship** and the second with **management and planning**. Stewardship is reflected in basic book-keeping functions and systems designed to replace the manual compilation of accounts. This is usually achieved by installing an integrated package which automatically posts transactions between the purchase, sales and nominal ledgers. These systems deal with transactions in an agreed formalised way reflecting the established manual conventions. The automatic posting of transactions has greatly speeded up the book-keeping process and lessened the chance of error. Such systems have reduced the amount of time required to *maintain* the financial records, so presenting more opportunity to *manage* the financial resources of the organisation. This chapter considers four systems at the heart of financial stewardship.

- Accounts receivable. Money owed to the organisation for goods or services that it has provided. Details are maintained on the **sales ledger**.

- Accounts payable. Money owed to other organisations for goods and services they have provided to us. Details are maintained on the purchase ledger.

- **Payroll**. Paying for staff to make, distribute, market and sell the product.

- **Nominal ledger**. Summarising the financial position of the organisation and presenting the results in an agreed convention so that they may be inspected and interpreted. This may also be called the **general ledger**.

Management and planning will include the financial evaluation and implication of corporate plans, budget setting and the derivation of financial targets. Certain parts of the stewardship system will contribute to this and examples are given in the rest of the chapter. However, in many instances, corporate policy, assumptions and reporting structures will prevent the use of a specialised software package. This presents the opportunity to use a more generalised modelling tool to build customised software. The most popular software tool is the **spreadsheet** and this is discussed in some detail in Chapter 9.

8.1 Accounts receivable

Most organisations permit their customers to purchase goods on credit. Goods are usually supplied on an understanding that they will be paid for within a specified period, for example, 30 days. The accounts receivable system is designed to record all amounts of money owed to the organisation by its customers. An efficient accounts receivable system is required to ensure that the firm's generosity is not stretched too far and that slow payers are identified and chased for payment. In this way the accounts receivable system should aid the reduction of amounts owing to an organisation, hence improving its cash flow. It also maintains the credit limits and outstanding invoices and balances of all the firm's customers and regularly sends them details of their debts and payments. The details of debtors are maintained on a sales ledger.

There are three common types of accounts receivable systems.

- Balance only. This only maintains a record of the debtor's balance, not of individual invoices, remittances and credits. The statement produced for the debtor at the end of the month may only show

  previous month's balance
  amount due for current purchases
  net balance owing.

- Balance forward. This has an opening balance — the amount owed at the start of the month — a record of transactions in that month — showing the date, type and amount of each transaction — and a closing balance.

  This closing balance becomes the opening balance of the following month and subsequent statements do not show transactions prior to the current month, whether they have been settled or not. Thus queries on old invoices usually require the manual searching of filed statements.

  The balances are aged in a balance forward system. Thus the total closing balance is analysed, for example, into balances which are three months or more overdue, two months overdue and one month overdue. Remittances and credits issued during the month are usually applied against the oldest invoices. The age analysis of the balance is usually included on the debtor's statement.

  A report showing the ages of balances for all customers is also required. An example of such an aged debtor's analysis is shown in Fig. 8.1.

A/C	ACCOUNT DESCRIPTION	AGED DEBTORS ANALYSIS			BALANCES AS AT :310887		
		CURRENT	1 MONTH	2 MONTHS	3 MONTHS	OLDER	BALANCE
201	Adcal Services Ltd	94.21	0.00	0.00	0.00	0.00	94.21
220	D.W. Carroll & Son	520.00	789.14	18.40	0.00	0.00	1327.54
230	Devlin Electrics	112.47	1198.47	559.15	0.00	0.00	1870.09
240	Errington Reay & Co	36.90	81.60	0.00	0.00	0.00	118.50
260	Hoke International Ltd	110.00	906.03	0.00	0.00	0.00	1016.03
280	H. Irwin & Sons Ltd	0.00	125.60	129.20	0.00	0.00	254.80
295	Peakin Enterprises	0.00	1245.94	172.10	0.00	0.00	1418.04
310	Riverside Rentals	0.00	430.10	0.00	0.00	0.00	430.10
330	Searle & O'Rourke Ltd	275.00	57.60	325.00	0.00	0.00	657.60
370	Trident Products Ltd	196.00	0.00	0.00	0.00	0.00	196.00
		1344.58	4834.48	1203.85	0.00	0.00	7382.91

Fig. 8.1 Aged debtors analysis giving details of debts analysed by time since the issuing of the invoice, or from the posting of the invoice details into the sales ledger. The layout will vary from system to system with some giving six months and some 12 months figures (Produced by the SAGE Accounting system, courtesy of SAGESOFT Ltd)

- Open item. This is a more complicated system where details of each invoice are maintained and all remittances and credits relating *to that invoice* are recorded against it until it is paid off. The customer statement shown in Fig. 8.2 comes from a system which uses an open item approach. You will notice that specific invoices are detailed for payment. If this had been a balance forward system this

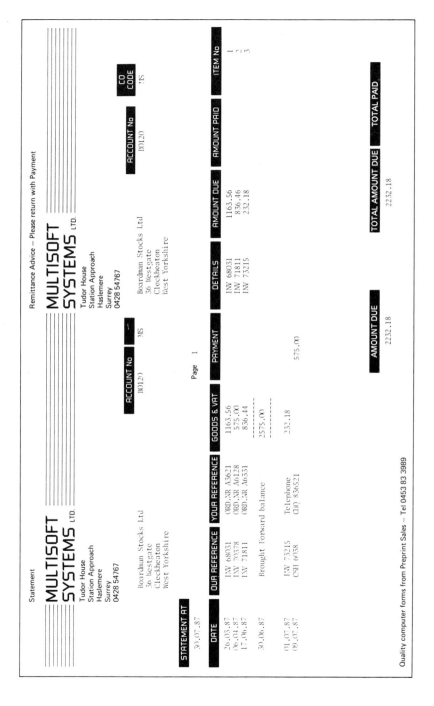

Fig. 8.2 Customer statement (Courtesy of Multisoft Systems Ltd)

information would have been missing and the statement would have started at the Brought Forward balance line.

It is easier to maintain an open item system when customers specify which transactions a certain remittance is supposed to cover. This is particularly crucial when one of the invoices is part-paid. If debtors fail to specify which invoices are covered by a remittance then the payment is usually credited against the oldest invoices.

8.1.1 Typical system characteristics

Outputs

Statements For each customer (see Fig. 8.2). A pre-statement listing is also helpful for internal control and validation. Clerical time can also be saved if the statements are produced in a layout directly suitable for inserting into a window envelope.

Aged analysis The aged analysis of a particular customer's balances may be included on the statement. An overall report will be required for credit control (see Fig. 8.1).

Management reports For example:

- Identification of dormant accounts. These may be used to target sales calls or mailshots.
- A list of all customers who have exceeded their credit limit.
- A list of customers who have exceeded certain volumes of trading. These may be accorded special offers or terms of payment.

  The scope of the reports offered by the system will vary from package to package and it is likely that the report facilities will be an important part of software selection. Figure 8.3 gives an illustrative list of the reports that are offered from Paxton's Business Desk accounts package.

Inputs

The following *types* of input should be supported.

Invoices
Credit notes
Debit adjustments
Credit adjustments
Receipts

The data recorded for each transaction type might include

Account number
Date of transaction
Amount Net
      Gross
      VAT (Usually calculated automatically from either gross or net values)
Transaction reference (e.g. invoice number)

Files and processes

The main files are likely to include information about the following.

Customers (debtors).
Receipts (a transaction file to be run against the customer master file).
Invoices (in an open item system).
Statements (in a balance forward system).

DEBTORS LIST	Produces a full aged debtors report for the selected accounts. The report shows the total outstanding and the aged balances for the current and previous three accounting periods together with any unallocated cash associated with each selected account.
CUSTOMER UNPAID INVOICE LIST	Produces a list for the selected range of accounts showing all currently outstanding invoices up to the specified date.
CUSTOMER STATEMENTS	Permits statements to be generated on request for all or a selective range of customers.
CUSTOMER STOP LIST	Generates a list of all customers who have been placed on stop via the Credit Control maintenance program.
CREDIT LIMIT LIST	Prints a report showing either all customers currently over their credit limit or all customers having a credit limit.
CUSTOMER TURNOVER LIST	Prints a report of the period to date and year to date turnover figures, exclusive of VAT, for selected customer accounts.
CUSTOMER RECORD CARD LIST	Generates a report for selected customer accounts showing the fixed data associated with each account.
CUSTOMER ADDRESS LIST	Used to print names and addresses. These may be printed either in label or report form.
STATEMENT ADDRESS LIST	Prints statement addresses, where applicable, for the selected range of customer accounts.

Fig. 8.3 Summary of reports available from Paxton Business Desk — sales ledger

Key programs will do the following

Validate entry details (a number of control checks will be required to ensure accurate recording).
Produce reports and statements.
Update customer master file details.
Post relevant data to the nominal ledger.

8.1.2 Other issues

There may be a requirement for periodic processing of certain transactions where, for example, a given amount is paid by a customer on the same day of every month. The facility to establish such transactions leads to their automatic generation and recording. Not all accounts receivable systems support this feature and so 'standing order' type of payments have to be entered individually every month.

A number of controls will be required to assist accurate data entry. A typical example is a hash total control (see Part 6) where certain figures are totalled prior to data input and compared with a total produced automatically by the software. Any discrepancies between the two totals must be investigated and corrected.

It may be desirable to extend the accounts receivable function to include sales handling and sales commissions. This permits the generation of sales analysis and salesman performance and commission reports.

It may also be desirable to integrate the accounts receivable system with the following.

● The nominal ledger. The adjustments on the nominal ledger will vary with the type of sales transaction. However, for simplicity, consider the processing of a sales invoice. This will debit the relevant sales account on the sales ledger by the gross amount (net price for the goods plus VAT). On the nominal ledger the debtor's control account (detailing how much we are owed by all our debtors) will be debited by the gross amount. This is balanced by the posting of credits to a sales nominal account (net amount) and to the VAT account (VAT amount).

- An order processing system. Information about invoices raised is passed automatically to the sales ledger.

The system should be able to cope with part payments. Part paid and unpaid postings should be clearly identified in sales ledger reports.

8.2   Accounts payable — the purchase ledger

The accounts receivable system discussed in Section 8.1 is concerned with the money owed to the organisation for the goods and services it has provided. In contrast, the *accounts payable* system monitors the money owed to other firms and organisations for goods and services they have supplied on credit. The accounts payable requires just as much management as the accounts receivable if the most effective use is to be made of the organisation's cash. In general, it is desirable to settle all accounts within the agreed credit terms, particularly if there are penalties for late settlement. However, balanced against this, bills should be paid no sooner than is necessary so that cash needed for payment may be released for as long as possible to earn interest through investment. Of course, payment may be deferred until after the agreed settlement date but this may endanger the goodwill which must exist between vendor and purchaser and indeed may lead to the removal of credit facilities. Discounts for prompt payment must also be identified, evaluated and exploited if the terms are favourable.

Like the sales system, the accounts payable usually allocates a numbered voucher to each invoice received by the organisation and this voucher number becomes the internal reference of a particular invoice. Details will also be recorded about amount due, settlement date and any discount values. At regular intervals, or on demand, the list of outstanding invoices may be printed out and certain invoices selected for payment. The selection of which invoices to pay will normally be made by a senior member of the accounts staff and will be based upon a number of factors. Some of these will be intangible — for example promptly paying large companies whose credit limits are tight and highly regulated at the expense of one-off purchases from small firms who can safely be made to 'wait for their money'. However, judgements about which accounts to settle will also be supplemented by factual information about the firm's projected cash flow. This may be provided by comparing the cash required to pay creditors (from the accounts payable system) with the expected receipts from debtors (from the accounts receivable system).

Details about the organisations owed money (our creditors) are maintained on a **purchase ledger**. Most purchase ledgers are open item systems whereby payments and part-payments are made against a specific invoice.

8.2.1   Typical system characteristics

Outputs
Outstanding invoices   Listing all invoices requiring payment.

Cash flow projection   To assist identification of invoices to pay.

Creditor's age analysis   Analysis of balances owing to creditors analysed by age of the balance. This is the equivalent of the aged debtors report from the accounts receivable system. This report may also help the accounts staff decide which invoices to pay.

Cheques

Remittance advice notes   To accompany the cheque identifying which invoice/invoices are being paid/part-paid (see Fig. 8.4).

```
***************************************************************
*       Quoin Demo Ltd      * REMITTANCE ADVICE :- 30/08/87       *
***************************************************************

Beat / Drummer Ltd                    Quoin Demo Ltd
Mews Road                             1a Arundel Road
Surbiton                              Chapeltown
Surrey SE1 4AE                        SHEFFIELD S30 4RB

                                      Cheque no         :  411334
                                      Remittance tr no  :    1272

                                      Remittance amount : 1604.38
                                      Discount          :   35.78
Account No : 2023
Tr no   Ref    Date      Gross Value   Amount Outstanding   Amount Paid

 999   35883  29/07/87     20.06           20.06               20.06
1005   35849  22/07/87      9.90            9.90                9.90
1018   36758  31/07/87     13.90           13.90               13.90
1000   36694  30/07/87    249.30          249.30              249.30
1001   36319  30/07/87     29.50           29.50               29.50
 998   36635  27/07/87    400.57          400.57              400.57
 984   36255  25/07/87     56.82           56.82               56.82
 980   36155  24/07/87     16.92           16.92               16.92
 978   36236  24/07/87     81.50           81.50               81.50
 969   36045  19/07/87    452.73          452.73              452.73
 975   35773  22/07/87    113.89          113.89              113.89
 979   36225  24/07/87     31.96           31.96               31.96
 968   35755  18/07/87      3.32            3.32                3.32
 967   36009  17/07/87      1.95            1.95                1.95
 966   35709  17/07/87      4.36            4.36                4.36
 964   35579  15/07/87     24.19           24.19               24.19
 878   35815  18/07/87     58.17           58.17               58.17
 876   34928  11/07/87      7.74            7.74                7.74
 877   34945  12/07/87      3.83            3.83                3.83
 818   34816  02/07/87     11.62           11.62               11.62
 814   34347  01/07/87     47.93           47.93               47.93

                                 Total amount debited    1640.16
                                 Discount claimed           35.78

                                 Amount remitted          1604.38
```

Fig. 8.4   Example of a remittance advice note (Courtesy of Quoin Computing Ltd)

Management reports   These will be similar to those available in the accounts receivable system.

Inputs

Approved invoices This requires some method of ensuring that the goods on an invoice submitted for payment have, in the first place, been ordered and secondly, that they have been satisfactorily received. Some software permits invoices for goods which are not satisfactory to be placed on 'Hold'.

Due dates Cheques may be produced automatically on their due date. However, there must be an option to over-ride this facility if payment is to be deferred for some reason — e.g. because the money is not available!

Approved vouchers Invoices cleared for payment.

Credits To reverse entries — for example when, for some reason, the cheque is void.

Manual entries A number of services are not normally invoiced — e.g. rent. There must also be a facility for entering cash payments.

Files and processes
The two main files will be

the creditors master file
creditor transactions to run against the master file.

The program tasks will be equivalent to those required for the accounts receivable system, with the aim of ensuring the integrity of creditor details. The need for selection of invoices to pay demands that the system makes a clear distinction between invoices requiring payment and those already paid. The selection of invoices to pay must also be supported by appropriate management reports — aged creditor analysis and cash flow projections. The latter requires access to the accounts receivable system.

8.2.2 Other issues
Just as in the accounts receivable system there may again be a requirement for the regular payment of 'standing orders'.
It may be desirable to have the option to place invoices on 'Hold' while they are queried or investigated. The facility to issue urgent one-off cheques is also essential.
There are generally two types of purchase.

● Purchase of fixed assets and services.

● Purchase to stock. The planning and budgeting of any activity requires certain assumptions to be made about stock costs. Standard costs of items are usually used in planning and costing proposed production. The accounts payable system records the *actual* cost of those stock items and so it may be desirable to keep details of these and compare them with the budgeted cost. Large variances between the standard cost of items and the amount paid for them may suggest a review of purchasing policies and planning assumptions.

Integrating the accounts payable with an order entry/purchasing system gives the opportunity to produce price variances and to take, where necessary, appropriate managerial action.
It may also be desirable to include budget information in the system and to allocate invoices or parts of invoices against specific cost centres. So, for example, every

department manager could be given a budget for the year and information regarding this could be stored on the system. Every item purchased by the employees in that department is then recorded against that budget. This permits the manager to monitor the department's expenditure and to make adjustments as necessary. It also permits corporate managers to request a cost centre report showing the cost structure of the whole company.

It may be desirable to integrate the accounts payable system with the nominal ledger. Consider the entry of a purchase invoice. This will debit the relevant purchase ledger account by the gross amount (net + VAT). The transaction will then be posted to the nominal ledger and cause the following adjustments. The creditor's control account (the total of what we owe other organisations) will be credited with the gross amount. To balance this the purchase nominal account will be debited with the net amount and the VAT account debited with the VAT amount.

8.3   Salaries and wages — the payroll system

The accounts payable system considers the payment for goods and services supplied by external organisations. Labour costs are the other large area of expenditure in most organisations and these are dealt with in the payroll system. The primary purpose of this latter system is the timely production of an accurate payslip for each employee, together with a cheque, a bank credit transfer or a coin analysis, as appropriate. Deductions have to be computed accurately and details sent with payment to the authorised recipient — government, trade union, pension fund etc.

Payroll systems have to be both accurate and flexible. This flexibility is particularly significant in two areas.

- Calculation of gross pay. The system will have to deal with different types and schedules of payment. For example

  full-time, part-time, seasonal
  paid monthly, weekly, bi-weekly
  overtime, double-time, night-rates, call-out rates
  sick pay, holiday pay, maternity pay.

- Calculation of deductions. These will include one-off deductions (to join the staff association?) as well as the regular deductions for income tax, superannuation, trade union subscription etc. These latter rates tend to change fairly frequently — for example tax bands usually change with every budget — and so regular updating is required.

Wages paid in cash are a particular problem because the wages section will need enough coins of the appropriate denomination to make up every wage packet correctly. It is not sufficient to draw the total wage bill amount from the bank because this will require the splitting of banknotes. Thus the payroll should provide a 'coin analysis' giving the total amount required, together with how this should be made up from the different denominations of currency. Factory wages are normally paid a week in arrears to allow sufficient time for the processing of time sheets, piecework tickets, down-time analysis etc.

8.3.1   Typical system characteristics

Outputs
Payslip (see Fig. 8.5)

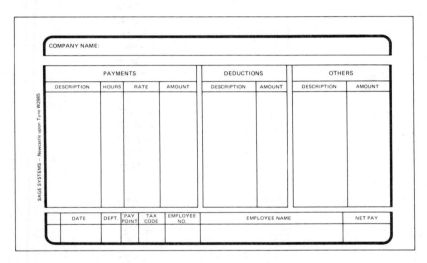

Fig. 8.5   (a) Payslip produced by the Leicestershire County Council mainframe system. Note the inclusion of a field for 'enquiries' (Courtesy of Leicestershire County Council) (b) Payslip provided for users of the microcomputer based SAGE payroll. Note the simpler 'general purpose' layout (Courtesy of SAGESOFT Ltd)

Cheques/bank credit transfers

Coin analysis

P – 60   A summary of the employee's annual earnings and deductions (see Fig. 8.6)

P – 45   A summary of the employee's earnings and deductions in the year to date, provided when an employee leaves employment during the year. It has to be given to any subsequent employer.

CERTIFICATE OF PAY, TAX DEDUCTED AND NATIONAL INSURANCE CONTRIBUTIONS

EMPLOYER'S NAME AND ADDRESS

LEICESTERSHIRE COUNTY COUNCIL,
COUNTY HALL,
GLENFIELD,
LEICESTER LE3 8RB

TAX DISTRICT: LEICESTER NO.1

DISTRICT REF.: L143

WORKS No., BRANCH, DEPT., CONTRACT, ETC.

YEAR TO 5th APRIL

EMPLOYEE'S NATIONAL INSURANCE NO.

EMPLOYEE'S SURNAME

FIRST TWO FORENAMES

FINAL TAX CODE

P.A.Y.E. TOTAL FOR YEAR

	PAY	TAX DEDUCTED
	£ 10312.92	£ 2190.90

PREVIOUS EMPLOYMENT

PAY	TAX DEDUCTED
£	£

THIS EMPLOYMENT

PAY	TAX DEDUCTED OR REFUNDED (IF REFUND MARK R)	REFUND
£ 10312.92	£ 2190.90	

NATIONAL INSURANCE CONTRIBUTIONS IN THIS EMPLOYMENT

TABLE LETTER	TOTAL OF EMPLOYEE'S & EMPLOYER'S CONTRIBUTIONS PAYABLE	EMPLOYEE'S CONTRIBUTIONS PAYABLE	Employees contributions at contracted out rate included in previous column
D	£ 1656.37	£ 783.73	£ 624.61

SUPERANNUATION CONTRIBUTIONS: £ 658.33

WIDOWS DEPEND 2ND % SUPN. CONTRIBUTIONS: £

UNDER NET PAY SCHEME

If week 53 Pay and Tax included above, complete these three boxes. See Employer's Guide.

Enter 'X' 54 or 56 in this box

PAY IN WEEK 53: £

TAX IN WEEK 53: £

DATE OF LEAVING IF BEFORE 5 APRIL (ENTER IN FIGURES): Day Month Year

AMOUNT OF STATUTORY SICK PAY INCLUDED IN THE 'PAY' SECTION OF THE 'THIS EMPLOYMENT' BOX ABOVE IS   £ 0.00

TO THE EMPLOYEE   DO NOT DESTROY

Keep this certificate. It will help you to check any Notice of Assessment which the Tax Office may send you in due course. You can also use it to check that your employer is deducting the right type of National Insurance Contributions for you and using your correct National Insurance number. If he is not, you should tell him. A duplicate form P60 cannot be supplied.

I/We certify that the particulars given above include the total amount of pay for Income Tax purposes (including overtime, bonus, commission, etc.) paid to you by me/us in the year ended 5th April last, and the total tax and National Insurance contributions deducted by me/us (less any refunds) in that year.

GROSS PAY (THIS EMPLOYMENT) = £ 10971.25

P60 Substitute

COUNTY TREASURER

Fig. 8.6 A P60 Form (Courtesy of Leicestershire County Council/HMSO)

Deduction reports A list showing who has paid deductions and how much. Inland Revenue requirements must also be fulfilled.

Other management reports These might include a report on overtime and sickness or an analysis of earnings

Other statutory reports and forms

Inputs
Documents showing hours worked Time sheets. Clocking on/off tickets.

Documents showing unproductive work-time For example, piecework employee cards detailing time that could not be worked due to machine breakdown.

Documents showing non-work-time Holidays, sickness certificates, paternity leave.

Deduction rate tables For calculating liability to income tax, national insurance etc.

Addition rate tables To permit calculation of bonus payments and commissions.

Joiners and leavers People who have left or who are leaving the company and those who have joined or are expected to join.

Files and processes
Files will include the following.

An employee master file.
Look-up files to permit the correct calculation of tax and other deductions and amendments.
Transaction files to show details of employee's work in the current payroll period.
A transaction file of leavers and joiners.

The main task of the programs in the payroll system is again to ensure the correct updating of the master file by the various transaction files recording the current period's activity.

Programs will also be required to output a series of important reports within a specified time. Achieving certain deadlines — e.g. all wage packets must be ready for collection by 4.00 p.m. Friday — places tighter time constraints on this system than any other that we have considered so far. This need for the fast processing of certain activities should be reflected in the system construction.

8.3.2 Other issues
Many organisations consider that the payroll contains their most confidential data. The system should reflect this, with secure internal and external controls and checks.

All of the methods of payment have a deadline. Failure to meet that deadline is likely to cause embarrassment, unrest and, perhaps, hardship. The payroll system should aid the easy achievement of payment deadlines but it can only do so if it is used within a planned framework of the other administrative tasks needed to produce salaries and wages.

The payroll system may be intergrated with the following.

• The nominal ledger.

• A personnel records system. The payroll may be viewed as a financial sub-set of a system that records all aspects of the individual's employment — for example join date, promotion date, review dates and results, previous employment, qualifications etc. Such a system becomes the basis for career planning, staff development schemes and staffing plans and budgets.

8.4   The nominal ledger

The nominal ledger (sometimes called general ledger) summarises the financial activity of an organisation in an accounting period. It is used to produce two important reports that communicate the financial status of an organisation. These are the **trading and profit and loss statement** and the **balance sheet**.

The nominal ledger uses the standard double entry book-keeping practice as described in numerous textbooks (see Further reading). The double entry method ensures that accounts are in balance by requiring each transaction to cause both a debit and a credit. The example transactions given in the accounts receivable and accounts payable sections demonstrated this. In both instances an account credit was balanced by an account or accounts debit.

The correctness of the balance is usually verified prior to report producton by the generation of a 'trial balance'. The structure of the nominal ledger will vary from company to company and should reflect the size, needs and operations of a particular organisation. For example, in a smaller company each company car might be a nominal heading, in contrast to a larger organisation where all company cars are dealt with together under one heading. The setting up of the nominal ledger codes critically affects the presentation and interpretation of the organisation's financial status and so assistance from a qualified accountant is suggested. It must be recalled that these financial statements significantly affect how external agencies and observers will judge the value of the company for loans, investment, credit and indeed for doing business in the first place.

Each nominal heading is given a code to which transactions may be posted. Some nominal codes — e.g. bank account, VAT, creditors control account and debtors control account — are already established and posting to these headings is performed automatically by the software. The nominal headings are, in turn, organised into a chart of accounts where accounts of a similar type are organised together. An example is given in Fig. 8.7.

8.4.1   Typical system characteristics

Outputs

Trial balance

Trading and profit and loss statement (see Fig. 8.8)

Balance sheet (see Fig. 8.9)

VAT return analysis

Trading Account			
1	Sales	101	104
6	Purchases	110	112
11	Subcontracted work	115	115
12	Labour	116	116
Profit & Loss Account			
1	Salaries	120	122
2	Rent & Rates	125	125
3	Electricity	127	127
4	Travel & Entertaining	129	129
5	Motor Expenses	131	132
6	Postage & Carriage	135	135
7	Telephone	136	137
8	Bank Charges & Interest	139	139
9	Sundry Expenses	141	141
14	Depreciation	145	145
15	H/P Interest	147	147
No entries for P & L Account II and III			
Fixed Assets			
1	Fixtures & Fittings	001	001
2	Company Cars	002	003
10	H/P Outstanding	007	007
11	Depreciation	005	005
Current Assets			
1	Trade Debtors	038	038
9	Cash in Hand	143	143
10	Bank Account	089	089
11	VAT Account	069	069
Current Liabilities			
1	Trade Creditors	065	065
2	PAYE & NI Creditor	066	066
10	Bank Account	089	089
11	VAT Account	069	069
Financed By:			
1	Share Capital	091	091
2	Director's Loans	093	093
3	Capital Reserves	092	092

Fig. 8.7 Chart of account. The figures on the left hand side are the nominal codes posted to that heading. Thus Sales (101–104) encompasses nominal ledger codes 101 (System Sales), 102 (Software Sales), 103 (Supply Sales) and 104 (Miscellaneous Sales) (Produced by the SAGE Accounting System, Courtesy of SAGESOFT Ltd)

Inputs
Chart of accounts

Creation and deletion of accounts

Automatic inputs Posted from accounts receivable, accounts payable, payroll and inventory control. These will be posted automatically if an integrated system has been chosen.

Multisoft Systems Company AA	Nominal Ledger Summary Profit & Loss with Budget Comparison				Batch 001/Sample Date 1.07.87			Page 1 Time 09:00
		——Period——				——Y.T.D.——		
Sect Acct Description	Actual	Budget	Variance	%age	Actual	Budget	Variance	%age
M101 Sales – Equipment	110812.42–	115000.00–	4187.58	96.36	680313.15–	690000.00–	9686.85	98.96
M102 Sales – Parts	87443.07–	88750.00–	1306.93	98.52	542434.74–	532500.00–	9934.74–	101.86
M103 Sales – Sundries	22833.79–	22250.00–	583.79–	102.62	132828.90–	133500.00–	671.10	99.49
M104 Sales – Secondhand equipment	21961.04–	19000.00–	2961.04–	115.58	121490.19–	114000.00–	7490.19–	106.57
M105 Sales – Reconditioned Parts	6596.84–	7200.00–	603.16	91.62	45394.19–	43200.00–	2194.00–	105.07
M106 Services	8104.60–	7500.00–	604.60–	108.06	50806.04–	45000.00–	5806.04–	112.90
M107 Discount Given	12039.39	11250.00	789.39	107.01	70732.97	67500.00	3232.97	104.78
M Sales Revenue	248450.00–	245712.37–	2737.63	98.90	1502534.24–	1490700.00–	11834.24–	100.79
P101 Purchases for Resale	200877.40	201000.00	122.60–	99.93	1200997.97	1206000.00	5002.03–	99.58
P102 Direct Wages and Salaries	7139.79	6116.00	1023.79	116.73	37004.20	36696.00	308.20	100.83
P103 Consumable Stores	521.16	460.00	61.16	113.29	3547.25	2760.00	787.25	128.52
P104 Discount Taken	2394.38–	2450.00–	55.62	97.72	13967.76–	14700.00–	732.24	95.01
P Direct Costs	205126.00	206143.97	1017.97	100.50	1227581.66	1230756.00	3174.34	99.74
R101 Staff Salaries	17889.93	17500.00	389.93	102.22	110961.25	105000.00	5961.25	105.67
R102 Rent & Rates	494.90	463.00	31.90	106.88	2940.00	2778.00	162.00	105.83
R103 Insurance	320.00	320.00	0.00	100.00	2386.19	1920.00	466.19	124.28
R104 Heat & Light	471.28	1970.00	1498.72–	23.92	4144.79	3940.00	204.79	105.19
R105 Repairs & Renewals	1466.69	835.00	631.69	175.65	5305.40	5010.00	295.40	105.89
R106 Vehicle Expenses	766.83	850.00	83.17–	90.21	6496.51	5100.00	1396.51	127.38
R107 Stationery & Computer	1438.25	1500.00	61.75–	95.88	10849.41	9000.00	1849.41	120.54
R108 Post & Telephone	936.33	525.00	411.33	178.34	5617.98	6600.00	982.02–	85.12
R109 Accountancy Fees	0.00	0.00	0.00	0.00	0.00	0.00	0.00	100.00
R110 Bad Debts	511.68	500.00	11.68	102.33	3119.74	3000.00	119.74	103.99
R111 Bank Charges & Interest	4910.06	4600.00	310.06	106.74	24912.43	27600.00	2687.57–	90.26
R112 Advertising & Travel	666.88	600.00	66.88	111.14	3866.94	3600.00	266.94	107.41
R113 Depreciation	0.00	1750.00	1750.00–	0.00	0.00	10500.00	10500.00–	0.00
R Overheads	31413.00	29872.83	1540.17–	95.09	180600.64	184048.00	3447.36–	98.13
OVERALL TOTALS	9695.57–	11911.00–	2214.43	81.40	94351.94–	75896.00–	18455.94–	124.32

Fig. 8.8   Trading and profit and loss statement (Courtesy of Multisoft System Ltd)

Multisoft Systems
Company AA

Nominal Ledger
Summary Balance Sheet

Batch 001/Sample
Date 1.07.87

Page 1
Time 09:00

Sect	Acct	Description	Opening Balance	Movements		Account Balance		Comparative Balance	
				Period	Y.T.D.	Debit	Credit	Debit	Credit
	A101	Freehold Property	268530.00	0.00	53436.00	321966.00		268530.00	
	A201	Plant & Machinery	36751.00	2136.20	6060.50	42811.50		36751.00	
	A301	Motor Vehicles	48372.00	0.00	6764.00	55136.00		48372.00	
	A401	Fixtures & Fittings	36009.00	86.38	17510.80	53519.80		36009.00	
A		Fixed Assets	389662.00	2222.58	83771.80	473433.30		389662.00	
	B101	Cash in Hand	200.00	75.00	50.00	250.00		200.00	
	B201	Sundry Debtors	473365.47	9136.36	86767.11	560132.58		473365.47	
	B301	Prepayments	860.00	0.00	860.00—	0.00		860.00	
	B401	Stock in Hand	512836.80	10883.58—	63657.20	449179.60		512836.80	
	B501	Work in Progress	48257.00	1811.76—	16274.00—	31983.00		48257.00	
B		Current Assets	1035519.27	3483.98—	6025.91	1041545.18		1035519.27	
	C101	Bank Account	332328.65—	2891.73—	66032.17—		398360.82		332328.65
	C201	Creditors	298126.53—	13112.58—	66396.90		231729.63		298126.53
	C301	Accruals	2910.00—	0.00	2910.00		0.00		2910.00
	C401	VAT Account	2050.00—	736.12	1280.00		770.00		2050.00
	C501	Bank Loan	250000.00—	0.00	0.00		250000.00		250000.00
C		Current Liabilities	885415.18—	10956.97	4554.73		880860.45		885415.18
	D101	Share Capital	100000.00—	0.00	0.00		100000.00		100000.00
	D201	Retained Profit/Loss	439766.09—	0.00	0.00		439766.09		372112.10
D		Capital Accounts	539766.09—	0.00	0.00		539766.09		472112.10
	E101	Profit & Loss Account	0.00	9695.57—	94351.94—		94351.94		67653.99
		OVERALL TOTALS	0.00	0.00	0.00	1514978.48	1514978.48	1425181.27	1425181.27

Fig. 8.9 Balance sheet (Courtesy of Multisoft Systems Ltd)

Ledger entries   For transferring entries between two or more nominal ledger accounts. This is commonly used for analysing petty cash where a petty cash total is re-distributed amongst a number of other nominal headings, such as travel, entertainment etc.

Sundry transactions   Cash receipts and payments for goods and services not recorded in the sales or purchase ledgers

Files and processes
Files will include the following.

A nominal ledger master file with the facility to create and maintain a chart of accounts.
A transaction file recording all journal entries that are to be posted to the master file at the end of the accounting period.

8.4.2   Other issues
It is desirable to have some flexibility in the creation of the chart of accounts. The software will normally impose some limit in the number of nominal entries permitted, the actual nominal entry headings and in the allocation of nominal account numbers. These will require investigation.

It may be possible to include specific department data and to set up multiple ledgers and multiple bank accounts. This will permit cost-centre reporting and analysis. This is a logical step from the cost and profit centre issues raised in the discussion of the accounts payable and accounts receivable systems. It permits key financial reports to be produced for each cost centre.

It should be clear that there is much to gain from integrating all the financial systems. This greatly simplifies the data entry and reporting requirements. The automatic posting of data should also guarantee the accuracy of the figures.

8.5   Summary

Financial control systems are essential. This chapter has reviewed four major systems and emphasised their inter-connection. It should also be clear that such systems must be subject to checks for honesty, accuracy and consistency. The task of audit will be covered in Part 6 but it is important that packages have internal audit trails recording the nature and value of transactions. An example of such an information trail is given in Fig. 8.10.

Further reading

Anderson R G, *Business Systems*, M&E Handbooks (1977)

Baggott J, *Cost and Management Accounting — Made Simple* (2nd Edition), (1977)

Excellent value for money. Covers many of the fundamental issues that underlie business activity.

Bodnar G H, *Accounting Information Systems*, Allwyn and Bacon (1980)

Useful text with good detailed explanations of the range of accounting tasks. Beware American conventions.

NOMINAL LEDGER LISTING

SAGE SYSTEMS LTD   Nominal Ledger Listing   Date : 31/8/87

Account 101   Colour Brochure Sales

NO.	DATE	INV	DESCRIPTION	DEBIT	CREDIT
			Opening balance	0.00	
60	19/7/82	028	Credit for Carriage	50.00	
44	9/8/82	043	500 brochures		520.00
38	29/7/82	037	1000 brochures		430.10
37	29/7/82	036	2000 brochures		976.30
30	9/7/82	029	1000 4pp brochures		765.87
29	6/7/82	028	1000 4pp brochures		876.24
26	2/7/82	025	500 brochures		278.94
17	23/6/82	016	1000 4pp brochures		410.60
11	14/6/82	01ɔ	3000 4pp colour brochure		1476.30
6	9/6/82	005	1000 4pp brochures		721.60
			Total amount to date:		6405.95

INFOMATION TRAIL

INFORMATION TRAIL

No.	Type	A/C	Date	Inv.	Date	Cheque N/C	Description	Nett amount	VAT amount	Amnt paid	V	A	P-A/C	P-N/C
35	SI	260	22/7/82	034	0/0/70	112	1000 compliment slips	24.26	3.64	0.00	N	N	29	28
36	SI	295	26/7/82	035	0/0/70	100	500 leaflets	180.34	0.00	0.00	N	N	31	33
37	SI	295	29/7/82	036	0/0/70	101	2000 brochures	976.30	0.00	0.00	N	N	36	30
38	SI	310	29/7/82	037	0/0/70	101	1000 brochures	430.10	0.00	0.00	N	N	9	37
39	SI	330	29/7/82	038	0/0/70	112	1000 compliment slips	50.09	7.51	0.00	N	N	19	35
40	SI	201	2/8/82	039	0/0/70	100	1000 letter headings	81.92	12.29	0.00	N	N	20	36
41	SI	230	5/8/82	040	0/0/70	100	500 leaflets	112.47	0.00	0.00	N	N	32	40
42	SI	370	9/8/82	041	0/0/70	100	500 leaflet reprint	196.00	0.00	0.00	N	N	11	41
43	SI	330	9/8/82	042	0/0/70	102	1000 company folders	275.00	0.00	0.00	N	N	39	16
44	SI	220	9/8/82	043	0/0/70	101	500 brochures	520.00	0.00	0.00	N	N	33	38
45	SI	240	11/8/82	044	0/0/70	111	1000 business cards	32.09	4.81	0.00	N	N	34	22
46	SI	260	11/8/82	045	0/0/70	100	500 leaflets	110.00	0.00	0.00	N	N	35	42
47	SR	201		0/0/70	8/6/82	110	Sales receipt	0.00	0.00	63.20	Y	Y	40	0
48	SR	201		0/0/70	15/6/82	112	Sales receipt	0.00	0.00	74.68	Y	Y	47	0
49	SR	201		0/0/70	26/6/82	100	Sales receipt	0.00	0.00	371.35	Y	Y	48	0
50	SR	240		0/0/70	29/6/82	111	Sales receipt	0.00	0.00	28.78	Y	Y	45	0

transaction type
SR = Sales Receipt

nominal code
posted

fields used for
internal software
purposes

Fig. 8.10   Nominal ledger listing (Courtesy of SAGESOFT Ltd)

Best P, *Small Business Computer Systems*, Prentice-Hall (1980)

Haueisen W D and Camp J L, *Business Systems for Microcomputers*, Prentice-Hall (1982)

Computerised business systems are introduced around a case study company. The book is rather expensive but the detail of the case study is very impressive.

9
Generalised software

Chapter 8 looked at specific application areas, using software dedicated to those tasks. In contrast, this chapter examines more general software which in most cases can be adapted for a variety of applications. The customising of this software for a specific task may be relatively difficult and time consuming, but it is feasible. It is possible to use data management software as a basis for a personnel records system, a stock control application, an order entry system etc. In contrast it is not possible to use a dedicated stock control package to manage the personnel records. The price paid for such flexibility is measured in the time needed to understand and construct the system.

The software described in this chapter is readily available on business microcomputers. The size of this market has meant that powerful packages can be sold relatively cheaply. This, combined with the falling cost of hardware, has brought computerisation opportunities to many smaller businesses. It has also given the executives of larger companies a personal tool which frees them from the long development times of the data processing department.

9.1   Word processing

Word processing is concerned with text manipulation, editing and printing. It is worthwhile distinguishing between the following.

- Dedicated word processors. Machines designed to perform only word processing with the programs needed for word processing stored permanently in the memory. These machines usually have special keyboards with individual function keys in addition to the usual typewriter keys.

- Multi – purpose business microcomputers. These are ordinary microcomputers which gain word processing facilities when an appropriate program is loaded into memory. These machines are capable of handling other applications in addition to word processing.

It is probably true to say that dedicated machines perform word processing functions more efficiently than general purpose micros. However, the non-dedicated machine does make up for this relative clumsiness by being able to do other tasks such as financial planning, stock control and data base management. This increased flexibility is often of greater importance in the choice of machine than its ability to handle any particular application.

9.1.1   Word processing facilities
Table 9.1 indicates some of the features that a typical word processing package might possess. The list is not in any particular order — indeed different circumstances will determine different priorities.

Table 9.1

Scrolling	This enables any part of the document to be displayed and is essential for efficient editing.
Deletion	This permits the erasing of unwanted letters, words, lines and paragraphs.
Substitution	Permitting the global replacement of an individual word by another.
Movement	Blocks or columns of text may be moved.
Insertion	Standard paragraphs or other blocks of text can be 'read' from one file to another.
Directory	This enables a check to be kept on files present on a disc and, more importantly, the amount of space left on a disc.
Formatting	This includes such things as right and left hand margin justification the centering of headings alternative line spacing automatic page numbering top and bottom margins headings and footings
Tabulation	Permits columnar alignment of both text and figures. The latter benefits from decimal tabbing.
Glossary	The user may predefine a number of long or complicated words and phrases which can be subsequently entered into the text at the touch of a single key.
Enhancements	Printing features such as boldface, double strike, underlining and strike out.

Word processing eradicates the need for repetitive copy typing of the same article, report or letter. Necessary amendments may be made and the contents re-formatted and printed. Powerful word processing software is currently available even on computers in the inexpensive hobby market.

9.1.2 Merge printing

One of the most useful features of word processing packages is a **merge printing** facility whereby different files may be merged at the time of printing. An obvious example is that of inserting an individual's name and address from one file (a name and address list) into another file (a standard letter). An example using the popular MailMerge package is shown on the following pages. Figure 9.1 represents the template of the letter which is to be sent to all persons listed on a file called DATA1.DAT (Fig. 9.2). An example letter is shown in Fig. 9.3.

9.1.3 Advantages of word processing

Word processing does not solve the problems associated with text and document production but facilitates the implementation of solutions when they are found. A word processor aids efficiency more than creativity.

From the list of facilities given in Section 9.1.2 it might appear that a typical word processor is no more than a sophisticated typewriter. However, while it may be used in that way, to do so is to miss the point of word processing and the benefits it can bring if properly used.

The fundamental advantages of a word processor over even the most efficient typewriter include:

- The ease with which text can be edited and formatted speeds up the production of documents and improves the quality of the final product.

```
.OP
.DF DATA1.DAT
.RV COMPANY-NAME, ADDRESS1, ADDRESS2, ADDRESS3
.RV ADDRESS4, CONTACT-NAME, SAL
&COMPANY-NAME&
&ADDRESS1&
&ADDRESS2&
&ADDRESS3&
&ADDRESS4&

For the attention of &CONTACT-NAME&

Dear&SAL&,

As one of our valued customers we would like to introduce you to our new
product GENESIS designed to reduce maintenance costs in open-plan offices.

We are running a free one day introductory seminar at our offices in High
Holborn and would welcome yourself or any other representatives from
&COMPANY-NAME&.

I will be contacting you in the near future with more details but do not
hesitate to contact me in the meantime if you require further information.

Best wishes.

Roger Jones
Managing Director
```

Fig. 9.1 A letter template created with the WordStar word processing package. The .RV entries are variables to be replaced by the data given in Fig. 9.2. The placement of these entries is guided by the variables enclosed in ampersands in the body of the letter. The entries are available in a file (.DF) called DATA1.DAT also resident on the disk. The .OP command tells WordStar to omit page numbering (Courtesy of MicroPro Ltd)

- Once text has been entered it may be printed out in a variety of formats and at a different times. The updating of documents and lists becomes a simple matter as only the amendments and additions have to be entered, not the whole document. For example, a list of customer names and addresses once entered could be printed out in a number of ways:

  as a straightforward list of names and addresses
  as a record card for sales calls
  as part of a personalised mail-shot
  as a printed address label for the mail-shot.

9.1.4 Implementing word processing
At least four issues require consideration.

Word processing is more than a typewriter
If full benefit is to be gained from the introduction of word processing then the manner in which the organisation generates and uses text has to be re-thought. Text

MRA SERVICES, The Banks, Wellingborough, Northants,, Martin Abram, Martin
CHURCHWARD ENGINEERING, New House, 12 Frinton Road, Weston, Avon,
Contracts Director, Sir
MIDLAND CONSTRUCTION, Tarmac House, Abbey Street, Aston, West
Midlands, Fred Jones, Fred

Fig. 9.2 Contents of the .DF file DATA1.DAT. The entries must be exact if they are to fit the template (Courtesy of MicroPro Ltd)

production is probably one of the most wasteful of all management operations. Documents, memos, reports and quotations are all produced by a variety of personnel in an organisation using words and phrases which differ only marginally from user to user. If a level of agreement and rationalisation on the response to certain recurring circumstances can be reached then much correspondence can be handled quickly and accurately.

Word processing needs a strong filing system
Although word processing embodies a filing system a computer is required to read the files. An efficient manual filing system is required to ensure that time is not wasted trying to trace the file from disk to disk. This means that disks must be properly documented, labelled and stored. This is particularly necessary if documents are to be accessed and updated by several managers and operators.

The training problem
Without proper training of both operators and managers it is unlikely that full benefit will be gained from having a word processing system, even in the long term. Lack of training leads to the under-utilisation of both equipment and staff which can incur substantial hidden costs. The misconception that a word processor is merely a 'super-typewriter' causes particular problems in the planning of training. Management frequently under-estimate the time and guidance needed to pick up these new skills

MRA SERVICES
The Banks
Wellingborough
Northants

For the attention of Martin Abram

Dear Martin

As one of our valued customers we would like to introduce you to our new
product GENESIS designed to reduce maintenance in open-plan offices.

We are running a free one day introductory seminar at our offices in High
Holborn and would welcome yourself or any other representatives from
MRA SERVICES.

I will be contacting you in the near future with more details but do not
hesitate to contact me in the meantime if you require further information.

Best wishes

Roger Jones
Managing Director

Fig. 9.3   Sample output from running MailMerge on Figs 9.1 and 9.2 (Courtesy of MicroPro Ltd)

and consequently do not reap the benefits. They also impose an unfair burden on
typists and secretaries who are often left confused and ill-equipped. Furthermore,
because the word processor is seen to be 'something to do with the typists',
management do not undergo any training themselves and so are left in a position
where they are unsure how to use and exploit the new opportunities.

Pay attention to output
Unlike most other business applications, word processing cannot be effectively
handled with a dot matrix printer. A letter quality device, usually a daisywheel
printer, is required to give an acceptable output quality. This is particularly necessary
if the document is to be photocopied or sent to an important external body, such as a
customer. Letters sent using a dot matrix printer seldom look acceptable.

The type and volume of work also needs careful sizing to ensure that requirements
can be satisfied.

9.2   Spreadsheets

Spreadsheets use the memory of a computer as if it were a large piece of paper divided
up into a matrix of cells. Into these cells may be entered numbers, text and formulae.
The power of these systems is that the data held in any one cell can be made

dependent on that held in other cells and changing a value in one cell can set (if wanted) a chain reaction of changes through other related cells.

In addition the 'paper' can be 'cut' and 'stuck' together in different ways as appropriate. Some or all of the spreadsheet can be printed out directly or saved on disk for insertion into reports using a word processing package.

9.2.1 Spreadsheet facilities

Spreadsheets are available with widely differing facilities often reflected in their relative prices. However, their fundamental power is derived from the 'chain reaction' facility described above. This means that a model can be built in which the effect of changing key parameters may be observed. This leads to the term often used to describe spreadsheets—'what if software'. The example shown in Fig. 9.4 has been built with the package Multiplan. It can be used to evaluate the effect of changing the sales commission rate. Simply entering a new value in the commission rate cell will lead to the automatic re-calculation of all dependent cells.

	A	B	C	D	E	F
1	Quarterly Sales Figures					
2						
3	Salesman	1st Qrtr	2nd Qrtr	3rd Qrtr	4th Qrtr	Total
4						
5	Alan Adams	5600.00	8750.00	10500.00	8500.00	33350.00
6	Brian Brown	5250.00	7500.00	9500.00	8625.00	30875.00
7	Chris Cooke	5625.00	8250.00	8200.00	9500.00	31575.00
8	Don Davis	4585.00	6500.00	7525.00	7200.00	25810.00
9						
10	Total	21060.00	31000.00	35725.00	33825.00	121610.00
11						
12	Commission	1.5%				
13						
14	Salesman	1st Qrtr	2nd Qrtr	3rd Qrtr	4th Qrtr	Total
15						
16	Alan Adams	84.00	131.25	157.50	127.50	500.25
17	Brian Brown	78.75	112.50	142.50	129.38	463.13
18	Chris Cooke	84.38	123.75	123.00	142.50	473.63
19	Don Davis	68.78	97.50	112.88	108.00	387.15
20						
21	Total	315.90	465.00	535.88	507.38	1824.15

Fig. 9.4 A simple spreadsheet. Note the formatting of the 'cells' to display numerical fields to two decimal places; values for commission in the lower half are found by multiplying the sales figures by 1.5%; totals are stored as the SUM (column or row); the borders showing column letters and row numbers may be omitted (Courtesy of MicroSoft Ltd)

A spreadsheet may also offer the features shown in Table 9.2.

Table 9.2

Presentation	Right and left justification. Facility to draw lines.
Formats	A range of formats to display the text and numbers; scientific, fixed decimal etc.
Copying	Powerful copying facilities. This means that the logic of, say a column addition, only has to be entered once and then it is copied to other columns.
Functions	Functional commands such as SUM and NPV (Net Prevent Value) greatly cut down the time needed to develop models. The scope of such commands will vary from product to product. However, the inclusion of such commands as Future Value (FV) does aid the construction of certain financial models.
Programming	The inclusion of programming constructs such as IF. . . THEN. . . ELSE greatly extends the control that may be built into the model. In some respects this may be something of a mixed blessing. On the one hand it provides an effective system development tool, whilst on the other it provides problems of program and system maintenance. Spreadsheet programming constructs are usually terse and unfriendly.
Consolidation	The facility to bring several spreadsheets together into a summary sheet. This is a facility often required by users and which is provided for in a variety of ways by competing products. Indeed a comparison of consolidation methods gives a good insight into the philosophy behind the package construction. Compare, for example, the different approaches of Multiplan and Lotus 1-2-3.
Graphs	Graphs may be available as an integral part of the spreadsheet software (as in Lotus 1-2-3) or as output which has to be used in a specific graph package. The range and scope of graphs will also vary enormously.
Others	Windows to permit the simultaneous viewing of dispersed areas of the spreadsheet. The provision of data tables to permit sensitivity analyses may also be a useful facility. Some spreadsheets also offer statistical regression and matrix manipulation.

9.2.2   Preparing a spreadsheet model

The user of a spreadsheet has two distinct problems.

● Learning the basic commands of the spreadsheet. The 'learning curve' gets longer as spreadsheets become more sophisticated and offer more facilities.

● Preparing and specifying the model. This is often a difficult and time consuming task. The logic of the model has to be carefully specified so that it works properly when entered into the computer. This is not only concerned with the logic of the *application* — i.e. that the standard cost labour unit is calculated correctly — but also with the requirements for 'what if?' experiments. Values cannot be increased by 5%, only formulae. Thus if you wish to see the effect of different inflation rates on a certain set of figures then these figures must be set up so that they reference an inflation multiplier. This may be set to 1.00 to start with, but may then be changed as required. I have met many managers who have established their model in such a way that 'what if?' experiments were completely impossible. The conceptual problems of model building should not be under-emphasised.

It is also important to recognise that most spreadsheets are constructed in RAM. Therefore a memory status check is very helpful so that worksheets can be saved to disk before the memory runs out. Memory size also provides a restriction on the size of the model that can be built. It is likely that this restriction will be met before the theoretical limit of the software. This problem has been recognised by, amongst others, the Lotus Development Corporation who have sponsored and encouraged the development of expanded memory boards giving up to an extra 4 megabytes of extra memory on top of the 640K RAM limit of IBM PC hardware. This permits the construction of models closer to the theoretical limits of Lotus 1-2-3 Release 2 and Symphony, although doubts have been expressed about the performance of such models.

Spreadsheets are powerful personal decision support tools. In addition, the programming facilities of products such as Lotus 1-2-3 and SuperCalc IV also make them important system development products.

9.3   Data management

Data management packages may be thought of as very flexible filing systems. In a manual filing system the records are usually placed in one order, for example, an alphabetical list of employees. This makes the retrieval of such requests as 'give me Benyon's record' relatively straightforward. However, 'give me all records of employees who have not been on a course since 1977' will require a long search.

Data management packages are designed to answer complex queries quickly. Three more examples are given below.

'Which customers have not placed an order for over £1000 for six months?'
'Who worked on the County Council project and left before completion?'
'What stock items exceed their maximum levels?'

The data management software gives the 'facilities' of the system; the content is decided by the user. This places greater stress on prior analysis and understanding and also aids the selection of the package most appropriate to the particular application. Data management packages vary in scope, facilities and friendliness. Some have been developed to meet specific needs such as bibliographic retrieval, whilst others are more general. The large number of competing products presently available means that careful selection may provide particular facilities which are felt to be important for the task in hand. This saves building such features with a less appropriate package.

9.3.1   Facilities of a data management package
The flexible filing system concept introduced above remains the heart of any data management package. The features shown in Table 9.3 may also be present.
Two aspects are worth exploring in a little more detail.

How data is entered and retrieved
The interface between the user and software varies enormously across the range of packages on offer. Some are **menu driven**, others use **masks** or screens, while yet others use **raw syntax**. Understanding the nature and implications of the interface is an important step in package selection. It is made more complicated by the fact that certain packages offer a variety of interfaces. The popular Ashton-Tate package dBASE III will serve as an example. A list of persons aged over 65 and earning more than £20 000 per annum could be obtained by the following syntax.

LIST FOR AGE > 65 .AND. SALARY > 20000

However, it is possible to use the programming facilities of the package to write a series of menus in which the users define their requirements in response to a number of prompts — friendlier to use, but at the cost of programming time and disk space.

Table 9.3

File structure	Easy creation of files and, more importantly, the maintenance of those files. It should be easy to add, delete and amend field structures.
Editing	Change, amend and delete entries. The deletion facility might include a recall option, so permitting the retrieval of wrongly deleted data.
Speed	Facility to sort and index files. Unlike spreadsheets, data management packages are disk-based. Consequently there is a large amount of disk activity in processing a retrieval. Fast retrieval will require indexes.
Reports	Flexible reporting facilities permitting the creation of user defined reports. Control over presentation of screen layouts.
Programming	The provision of programming constructs to extend control over the file structures. This is again a mixed blessing. The inclusion of a programming language gives the package great flexibility but it does so at the cost of difficulty for non-programming users.
External	Facility to transfer data to other software packages. For example the data management software could be used to retrieve names which fulfill a certain criterion. These can then be transferred to a merge-print package for the insertion of details into a standard letter.

A comparison of interface types is a useful exercise. Examine the difference between the raw syntax method of dBASE III and the mask driven interface of Compsoft's product Delta.

Speed of retrieval
In Section 9.2 on spreadsheets it was explained that they are resident in RAM whenever actions are performed on them. This is not true of most data management packages. As a result disk accessing may lengthen the retrieval time to a point where it becomes unacceptable. The relative speeds of packages should be investigated before purchase. The time taken by different packages to undertake a variety of tasks (so-called benchmarks) is regularly published in the computing magazine *Personal Computing World*.

9.4   Integrated software

In the preceding sections of this chapter reference has been made to the passing of files between different software types. This has been taken to its logical conclusion by the marketing of integrated software packages. Lotus 1-2-3 offers spreadsheet, data management and graphics facilities. Its newer relative Symphony extends and enhances these facilities. Open Access offers communications and a diary system in addition to its word processing, data management, spreadsheet and graphics. However, as such packages become more sophisticated three aspects demand further discussion.

● Greater training requirements. The scope and functions of the package demand a longer, and hence more costly, training period.

● Increased debate about the relative performance and facilities of the 'parts' of the system when compared to dedicated stand alone packages. This has led to questions about whether a user really needs the range of facilities on offer.

- The packages tend to be consuming more memory and disk space. This has led to costs associated with hardware expansion. For example, the data management facility of Lotus 1-2-3 is relatively under used. This is partly due to the fairly complicated method of specifying a retrieval, but also because of the problems of memory space. If the selection criteria are poorly specified then most of the records on the spreadsheet may be extracted. These are listed on another part of the spreadsheet so taking up even more memory.

At the time of writing, the market penetration of integrated products has been relatively small. It is quite interesting to note that software vendors are beginning to 'unbundle' their software, offering a number of stand-alone modules, permitting users to decide their own degree of integration.

9.5 Summary

The market success of these generalised software products demonstrates their relevance and importance. However, within each application area, care should be taken in software selection, training and implementation. There is a common misconception '. . . that all spreadsheets (for example) are the same.' This is just not true! They vary considerably in friendliness, price, interface and (most importantly) functionality.

Further reading

Kruglinski D, *Data Base Management Systems*, McGraw-Hill (1983)

A good introduction to the basic concepts of data mangement software. Points are illustrated with examples from four major products. Slightly dated by the progress of new launches but the principles remain instructive.

Crider J, *Word for Word: A Comparative guide to Word Processing Software*, Osborn/McGraw-Hill (1985)

Williams A, *What if?-User's Guide to Spreadsheets on the IBM PC*, Wiley (1984)

10
Software selection

The preceding chapters have considered two important areas of software: specific application packages (such as accounts receivable) and generalised application software (data management and spreadsheets are two examples).

It is important to adopt a formal approach to the selection of appropriate software. This is particularly necessary in the microcomputer market place where the large number of packages available means that they must be given careful consideration. The following 'pecking order' is suggested as an appropriate framework for software selection.

10.1 Software pecking order

10.1.1 Logical system specification

There is little doubt that carefully identifying system requirements is a crucial part of successful computerisation. This is the traditional task of systems analysis and represents the fact identification and documentation discussed in Part 2 of this text. The aim of this approach is to produce a paper based specification that employs a number of models and diagrams representing the system that will eventually be delivered. A number of reservations about this approach to systems development have already been expressed. A further drawback concerns its validity in an environment where the likely solution is the selection of a software package. In such instances much of the detailed specification of files and processes is largely wasted as these factors are not under the control of the system developer. Indeed it can be argued that the four other main areas of design — inputs, outputs, interfaces and controls — should receive priority as it is these which largely distinguish packages from one another. In many instances the main file and process consideration will be file sizing and process definition. In the latter case this should be concerned with defining what *should* be expected in processing, not *how* to achieve it. Thus a mini-specification is suggested that:

- identifies data items required in output documents

- identifies input data items that must be supported

- defines interface levels and types to fit in with user expectations and skill levels

- defines the controls that are required or expected

- suggests a rough file format with data volume

- contains required process definitions.

The content of the mini-specification will vary from system to system and it is inappropriate to discuss it in depth in this text. However, an attempt should be made to maintain a balance between time, detail and cost. The emphasis should be on tasks which aid the identification of *what* the system must achieve, not *how*.

A completed mini-specification can be used as a basis for all further evaluation. It may be given in advance to a salesman with a statement that explains that 'these are the outputs I want, can your package produce them?. Will you show me?'. This is much better than a checklist because the package is now being evaluated in the context of a particular application, appropriate criteria are now being brought to bear. Checklists are unable to give priority and they deal with complexity by just adding more questions. They may, admittedly, suggest issues which may not have been considered and hence can prove useful in establishing the application requirements. However, it is important that they are not slavishly adhered to so as to disturb the priorities of the system under consideration.

The mini-specification now forms the basis of selection.

10.1.2 Specific application package
Question Does a specific application package exist that will fully, or substantially, fulfil the mini-specification?

This step is particularly significant in the selection of microcomputer software where there are many competing packages in a defined market segment. These segments may be fairly esoteric (e.g. golf club systems) or be of general application (e.g. payroll packages). It seems both wasteful and unwise to develop say, a bespoke payroll application, until a number of the marketed products have been examined, evaluated and, if found to be inappropriate, discarded. The very variety of products now means that there are many circumstances where the ability to perform a competent evaluation of packages is more important than specific programming skills. General issues in package selection are covered in Section 10.2.3 but it must be recalled that the most significant criteria for evaluation is *how well the package fits the target mini-specification*. The *latest* product may not be the most appropriate.

If all the specific packages require unacceptable compromises and changes to the target specification, then a second question may be asked.

10.1.3 Generalised application package
Question Can a generalised application package be used to fully, or substantially, meet this mini-specification?

In some circumstances the detail of a particular application may lead to requirements beyond the flexibility of a specific software package. In other instances the application may be in a unique functional area where there has been no well defined market demand. In both these circumstances it is possible that the application shows strong elements of the following.

- Data filing, retrieval and reporting. Hence an appropriate data management package may be purchased and tailored to the application.

- Mathematical manipulation and experimentation. Spreadsheets such as Lotus 1-2-3 are powerful development tools and may be used to build customised applications.

- Manipulation and retrieval. An integrated software package such as Framework or Open Access may be appropriate for system development.

The observation that many systems appear to share the same fundamental structure is supported by the success of these generalised development packages. However, if they are again deemed to be inappropriate a third question may be posed.

10.1.4   Program generators

Question   Can the system be developed using an appropriate program generator?

A **program generator** is a computer program designed to write computer programs. It does so by helping the user through a number of screen definitions which it uses as a basis for program construction. Generators again make particular sense in the microcomputer field and a number of products are available. A useful review was made in 1983 by Chris Naylor (see Further reading).

Only after all these options have been rejected should a conventional high level language, such as COBOL or BASIC, be used for the construction of the system.

10.2   General issues in package selection

It must again be stressed that evaluation against *need* is the most significant issue in package selection. However, there are a number of general points which are worth looking for in all packages. Before examining these in a little more detail it is helpful to summarise the differences between packaged and bespoke or tailor-made system implementation (Table 10.1).

Table 10.1   Package versus tailor made

	Package	Tailormade
Fit	Rough	Exact
Cost	Cheap	Expensive
Changes	Expensive	Cheaper
Applications	Standard	Anything
Delivery	Off the Shelf	Months
Others	Poor?	Good?

A number of points must be stressed.

● There must be an element of compromise in package selection. It is unlikely that a product will be found that will match the implementation exactly. A reluctance to waive any requirements is likely to lead to a bespoke solution.

● Package solutions are much cheaper. One package known to the author consists of about 60 000 lines of COBOL and its authors conservatively estimate the development cost at £300 000. The package sells for about £2 500. The buyer is getting a high quality, tested product for a fraction of its production cost. In a bespoke development virtually *all* of the development costs are borne by the user.

● Packages are supposed to be generalised answers to specific problems. Vendors will make changes with varying degrees of reluctance. There are many examples where software changes made for specific clients have led to operational difficulties with the package, particularly when upgrades, changes and enhancements have been issued.

● The 'off the shelf' nature of packages is something of a mixed blessing. It means that the product is immediately available but time must quickly be found to

Learn the operations of the package.
Enter data into the system so that it is operationally useful.

These tasks must be carefully planned so that they coincide with the delivery of the package. A failure to recognise training needs and data entry overheads will lead to under-use of the package and lose the immediacy that this type of solution offers

In general, a bespoke solution should offer better documentation, training and support. Packages are usually sold with manuals which try to be 'all things to all men', by suppliers who do not really understand them and at prices which have no margin for support or training.

Seven issues repay careful consideration in the evaluation of competing package products.

10.2.1 Facilities
- Calculations performed. Can the VAT amount be calculated from either gross or net input values? Can the VAT rate be varied if legislation alters it from its current 15% rate?

- Reports and analyses. One of the most valuable facilities is the ability to define the contents of customised reports. Some packages only offer standard report formats forcing the combination of several reports with scissors and adhesive tape if none of the offered formats fit the requirements.

- Print options. Are certain reports 'screen only'? Can printer modes (such as condensed print, underscoring etc.) be controlled from within the package? How easy is it to enter these codes?

- Field types. Account codes may only be numeric. This will make it impossible to implement a current faceted alpha-numeric code.

10.2.2 Sizes
- Field sizes. Are these limited? For example, only a six digit product code may be permitted.

- File sizes. There may be a restriction on how many customer records may be created. In other instances the number of records may be unrealistic given the constraints of the rest of the package.

- Number of transactions. In some circumstances the combination of the file structures and sizes affects how many transactions can be held on the system. This is particularly significant in an accounting system and as a result all such software should be accompanied by a sizing algorithm. An example is given in Fig. 10.1

10.2.3 Speed
- Record retrieval. This is an instance where visits to reference sites can be very rewarding. Demonstrations of packages are usually given on a limited number of records and as a result most of the features appear to work very quickly. This speed is unlikely to be maintained as the number of records approaches realistic operational volumes.

- Report production. Purchase of a slow printer can compound the slow production of reports. Can the machine be used for other tasks during the print out or is the operator effectively 'locked out'?.

10.2.4 Security
- Investigation of facilities to permit recovery from catastophic failures.

- Time taken to produce back up copies of data and the implication of this for administrative arrangements.

A.	Total disk space available (drive B)		bytes
B.	No. of sales accounts	◯ × 50 bytes =	◯
C.	No. of purchase accounts	◯ × 50 bytes =	◯
D.	No. of nominal accounts	◯ × 50 bytes =	◯
E.	No. of nominal categories	◯ × 30 bytes =	◯
F.	TOTAL SPACE REQUIRED (B + C + D + E) =		◯
G.	SPACE AVAILABLE FOR TRANSACTIONS =		◯ ÷ 90
H.	Number of transactions possible, per data disk		◯

Example

A.	Total disk space available (drive B)	600 000 bytes	
B.	No. of sales accounts	600 × 50 bytes =	30 000
C.	No. of purchase accounts	350 × 50 bytes =	17 500
D.	No. of nominal accounts	300 × 50 bytes =	15 000
E.	No. of nominal categories	120 × 30 bytes =	3600
F.	TOTAL SPACE REQUIRED (B + C + D + E) =		66 100
G.	SPACE AVAILABLE FOR TRANSACTIONS =		533 900 ÷ 90
H.	Number of transactions possible, per data disk	5932	

Fig. 10.1 Sizing algorithm. The letter H represents the number of transactions (sales invoices, credit payments etc.) that can be supported on one disk). This can then be compared with the transactions passing through the present system (Courtesy of SAGESOFT Ltd)

10.2.5 Privacy and control
- Passwords. Existence and levels of passwords.
- Audit. The package should satisfy both internal and external auditors (see Part 6).
- Privacy. The package should allow the purchaser to comply with the requirements of the Data Protection Act (see Part 6).

10.2.6 Accuracy
- Calculations. How does the package deal with rounding errors?
- Errors and warning messages. Does the package trap all user errors or does it permit arithmetical operations which are logically correct but are likely to be administratively meaningless? — for example, the calculation of negative stock levels. What error messages are given and how easy is it to recover from various types of error?.

10.2.7 Interface

- Type and consistency of the software interface

- Flexibility of the interface. Can the package produce a variety of interfaces to suit different user types and skill levels?

- Clarity of the documentation

- Arrangements for installation, training and software upgrades.

10.3 Summary

The selection of software has been presented in a definite 'pecking order'. This order reflects the changing nature of the market place and is particularly relevant to microcomputer applications. General guidelines for package selection have been given but the principle of evaluating against requirements has been stressed.

It will be necessary to assess the software vendor on the same grounds as selecting suppliers of other goods and services. This will include financial viability, experience, geographical location and terms of payment. All suppliers will also supply **reference sites**. These must be visited and the operations of the package and the support of the supplier discussed in detail. Such visits give the potential purchaser an oportunity to see the package working under operational conditions and volumes. He can discuss the type of support given by the supplier and learn about problems and difficulties, as well as opportunities, that he had not foreseen.

Further reading

Isshiki K R, *Small Business Computers* Prentice-Hall (1982)

Good coverage of application software with emphasis on checklists. Misses very little out!

Naylor C, *Programs that Write Programs* Sigma Technical Press (1983)

Useful comparison of program generators. You will either enjoy or dislike the rather jokey writing style.

Part 5
Systems Management

Computer systems bring change and that change has to be carefully managed if the project is to be successful. This part examines a number of elements of management that concern the computer system professional. The first chapter concentrates on the role of the computer as a shared corporate resource and examines how competing claims upon it may be fairly evaluated and compared. In doing so it reflects upon communication difficulties that often arise between system users and developers and introduces the ideas of participative system design in this context.

Chapter 12 concerns the organisational structures of computing. Both external (where should information systems sit in the corporate hierarchy?) and internal issues are examined, and a project based approach is recommended for the latter. A brief review is also made of typical information system jobs and how these might change in the foreseeable future.

One of the major tasks of an information systems section is the selection of the hardware and software necessary to fulfill the organisation's information needs. The management aspects of this are the subject of Chapter 13. Issues covered include tender invitation and evaluation, contractual arrangements and financing options.

Finally, Chapter 14 looks at project division and management and the popular control technique of critical path analysis is demonstrated in detail. This detail may be greater than in most corresponding texts, but it may be justified on the grounds that if system development is primarily project based, then project management is an essential skill for its practitioners and students.

11
Managing the shared resource

11.1 General issues

The tasks of systems analysis, design and development, described in Part 2, are usually undertaken by staff in a **data processing** (DP) department. This function may be organised in different ways (see Section 12.1) and have different titles, but essentially it remains the part of the corporate structure charged with providing computer systems and services for the rest of the organisation. In general, the term **information systems** (IS) function will be used to describe such activities. This name reflects the wider contemporary scope of computing. However, more conventional terms, such as data processing and **computer unit**, will be used as synonyms.

The head of this function has similar managerial responsibilities to other senior colleagues. These tasks include staff selection, career planning, maintenance of morale and motivation, setting and meeting objectives, agreeing and monitoring budgets and establishing and adhering to corporate standards and procedures. Many of these general requirements of management are especially acute in the administration of the information systems department. Some examples are given below.

- Staff motivation and morale. IS staff are often young, energetic and ambitious. They are aware that demand for their skills comfortably outstrips supply. Most installations have a high staff turnover with the result that many staff who begin projects have left the firm before they are completed. This creates a problem of continuity and such difficulties are often tackled by demanding copious documentation so that all aspects of the project are described in written detail. In some circumstances the stifling bureaucracy of this documentation actually fuels the dissatisfaction of the computer staff. More effort should be given to tackling the root problems of staff turnover. This may involve better career planning and more flexible staffing structures and remuneration.

- Problem of control and assessment of staff. It is very difficult to measure the *productivity* of a computer department. Efforts have been made to measure programming proficiency but these are not widely used and the problem of effectiveness is even more acute in the tasks of systems analysis. Reference has already been made (see Part 2) to Daniels and Yeates' statement that documentation is often the only tangible result of months of analysis. It should be clear that the number of pages of documentation produced by each analyst is not a useful measure of their relative worth.

- Managerial proficiency. It is traditionally difficult to find people with an appropriate combination of technical and managerial abilities. Many technically competent employees appear to lack the necessary political and personnel skills required of an effective manager.

Finally, it must be recalled (see Chapter 3) that information systems is a *shared resource* of the company. It can rarely produce income directly. It is a service department to support the organisation's *doers and makers*. The costs of the data processing overhead must be shared out amongst the rest of the company. A formal charging system is one of the ways of distributing computing costs.

11.2　Information systems as a shared resource

11.2.1　Formal cost sharing — a charge out service

Some organisations choose to re-distribute overhead costs equally across other departments of the company. Others make the adjustment by relative size so that a department with twice as many people will pay twice the cost. These methods are relatively easy to *administer* but they are often demonstrably unfair in practice because they do not take the actual *use* of computing resources into consideration. A charge out system works on the principle that users 'pay' for what they use. This means that the cost of services and systems will come out of the user department's budget which forces proper budget management and project assessment. The use of the system has a financial cost which must be weighed against the benefits that should accrue when the system becomes operational. The costs also provide an 'income' for the IS department permitting a measure of its 'profitability'.

　Costs may be levied for the following.

● Transactions. The number of payslips produced is an example. This is slightly unrepresentative because most jobs have a given set up cost and economies of scale accrue as the number of transactions increases. It does not cost twice as much money to produce 2000 payslips as it does 1000. A set up charge and volume discounts should be included in the costing system.

● Resources. An example is the use of CPU time. Some tasks effectively tie up the computer for long periods of time. This must be taken into consideration. Printer time and consumables — disks, paper, ribbons — are amongst the other resources that must be considered.

● People. Charge out rates for analysts, programmers, training courses, maintenance. It must not be forgotten that salary costs make up a large part of the computer unit's costs. These have to be passed on to users.

　For a charge out policy to work effectively it must be understood by the users. If other departments do not comprehend the basis on which charges are made then they are unable to plan requirements sensibly or control their use of current facilities.

　Effective cost monitoring is also necessary. It must be possible to log the use of CPU time and count and record transactions and transaction types. The time spent by analysts and programmers on different projects must be meticulously recorded. Most importantly, the user department's account must be kept up to date so that users know where they stand. Account balances can be compared with projected budgets and corrective action taken where appropriate. Most dissatisfaction occurs where accounts are presented infrequently and without supporting documentation. In such circumstances the user's first reaction is usually disbelief!

　The importance of charge out systems is growing as more organisations choose to establish their information systems departments as profit centres or as separate companies. Many such sections are then required to bid for work within the company *against external agencies and consultants*. Clearly, a strong internal recording system is required if they are to produce sensible, profitable bids.

11.2.2   Priority setting and the invisible backlog

One of the difficulties of being a shared resource is that the facilities and services provided are always subject to competing bids from the rest of the organisation. In these circumstances it is essential to develop an agreed method of establishing the priority of a project. This may require users to submit a formal, standard request for resources and competing bids are evaluated against agreed criteria. The criteria are available to the users so that requests may be presented within the required framework. It is important that every effort is made to establish a *fair and equitable* way of allocating priorities to projects and that *users understand the criteria used in the allocation*. One of the greatest complaints of user departments whose projects are given little importance is that the method of priority allocation was never explained to them. This leads to dark whispers of 'politics' and contributes to a general dissatisfaction with the information systems department.

The development of an agreed publicised approach also has important benefits for the computing section. If the selection method has been decided on a corporate basis then it can be reasonably certain that the projects selected are likely to fit in with the corporate objectives of the organisation. This is a better method than simply giving priority to projects which have enthusiastic, important or assertive sponsors. Projects must be seen from the corporate level, not from the partial view of individual users.

Most organisations have a development 'backlog' in that more projects are requested than can be delivered. Projects awaiting development are placed on a waiting list. Evidence concerning the average length of this waiting list varies, but all research seems to agree that it is substantial. Lobell (see Further reading) quotes figures from a Xephon survey on IBM UK sites.

- Average size of backlog — 166 person-years.
- Estimated elapsed time to deal with this backlog given current tools and resources — approximately five years.

Martin (see Further reading)

- One typical corporation had a backlog of 70 applications. In the last twelve months only 19 applications were created.
- One New York bank estimated a backlog of seven years.

Martin also makes the valid point that when the documentated backlog is several years then users do not even consider making requests for the applications they need. He terms this the **invisible backlog**.

There are many factors contributing to these sizeable backlogs and there are as many recipes and suggestions for reducing it. These include

- more powerful software tools (see Chapter 6)
- improved system development methodologies
- computer aided design and development.

There is evidence of success in all these fields but there is also a strong possibility that as the perceived backlog falls then more of the invisible backlog will appear. Ironically, the use of some of the techniques listed above may actually *generate* demand for IS services and so the total backlog remains the same or actually increases.

Whatever the size of the backlog, or the remedies adopted, there must be a method for allocating priority to projects and resources. Furthermore, the principle and detail of the method must be understood by all users and potential users. It is also beneficial if users denied reasonable priority are given alternative opportunities (training, packages, external software support).

Finally, doubts must be expressed about any eventual disappearance of the application backlog. Mumford (see Further reading) once made the point that innovating groups such as systems analysts and programmers can only gain from change and that their future career prospects *depend* to a large extent on its continued implementation. Thus information systems departments are constantly seeking opportunities to extend computerisation. This ensures the existence and growth of the department. In many respects the computing profession has a vested interest in the maintenance of a healthy (but not too healthy!) application backlog.

11.2.3   Communication difficulties

Data processing is essentially a service to the rest of the organisation and so many of the tasks of the section require communication with users, clients and operators. There are often difficulties in harnessing the technical skills of the computing staff with the business knowledge and information needs of the users. While acknowledging the dangers of generalisation two arguments can be put.

- Many users lack an understanding of the detailed tasks of system development. Some questions posed by the analyst appear trivial or irrelevant. The *time – scale* of development often looks unreasonable and apparently simple changes take months to implement. Delivered systems sometimes appear visually disappointing — 'I can produce better colour on my son's home computer.' Users quickly become frustrated by the analyst's lack of basic business knowledge.

- Analysts rely too heavily on technical expertise and do not understand the business framework in which their systems operate. This leads to them posing inappropriate questions which undermine the users' confidence in their ability. Detailed operational information is requested but the reasons for requesting such detail are seldom explained. Analysts become frustrated by the user's lack of basic computer knowledge and their inability to perceive potential applications and benefits.

It is quite easy to develop a split between analyst and user where the mutual trust required for successful development has irretrievably broken down. This split has been recognised by Land and Mumford (see Further reading) and is summarised in Fig. 11.1. Indeed Land and Mumford have seen this basic division as one of the main factors at the root of unsuccessful computer systems development. They have pioneered an approach to system development which is based around the disappearance of this split with the design work undertaken by a group of users of all grades. This design group is advised by an analyst but his or her role is to *transfer* skills not to *impose* them. The design group reports to a steering group of senior user management, senior system management and senior trade union officials who sanction and assist when required. A summary of the approach is given in Fig. 11.2.

Participative systems design is underpinned by certain value judgements and supported by specific recommended techniques (see Further reading). It has raised fierce controversy because of its perceived threat to the data processing establishment and because of its rather (some claim) manipulative attitude towards users. However, as Mumford once wrote

'The argument. . . is related to both ethics and to expediency. We believe that people have a moral right to influence the organisation of their own work situation and also that if this right is conceded then there are likely to be gains both in job satisfaction and in efficiency.' *Computer Weekly* 09/11/78

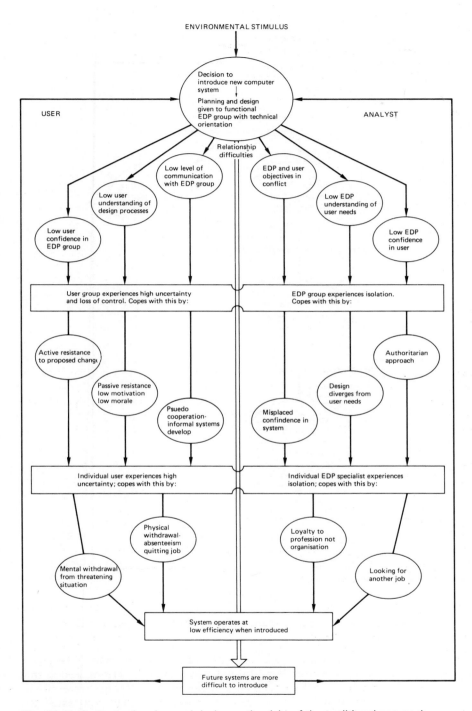

Fig. 11.1   Systems planning and design — the risks of the traditional approach

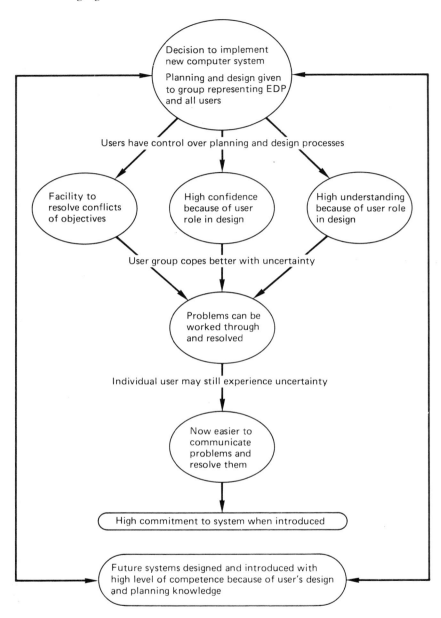

Fig. 11.2   Systems planning and design — the advantages of the participative approach

The central role of communication was also identified by Freeman (1981) (see Further reading) in an article entitled 'Why Johnny can't analyse'. He suggested that the core of 'the systems analysis activity is communication' and 'the first reason why Johnny can't analyse. . . is that he or she can't communicate.' He contrasted the informal, vague nature of user requirements with the formal precise methods with which analysts tried to capture them.

11.3   Summary

This chapter has reflected upon general issues caused by information systems being a shared source of the enterprise. Management and allocation difficulties have been considered and the existence of an application backlog has been demonstrated.

The problems of communication do not have simple solutions. Land and Mumford's approach is worth investigating because if offers a different angle on systems development. Prototyping (Chapter 6) also represents a change in opportunity and perspective. However, above all, the communication skills of analysts need to be nurtured, not hindered, by the framework chosen for system development.

Further reading

Freeman P, 'Why Johnny can't Analyse', in Cotterman W etal (Ed.), *Design — A Foundation for the 1980s,* North Holland (1981)

A useful collection of papers reflecting upon the role of the analyst in the 1980s.

Lobell R F, *Application Program Generators — A State of the Art Survey*, NCC (1981)

Also includes a survey of application generators.

Mumford E, Land F and Hawgood J, 'A Participative Approach to the Design of   Computer Systems, in *Impact on Society*, *vol.***25**, No. 3, 1978.
Mumford E and Henshall D, *A Participative Approach to Computer Systems Design*,   Associated Business Press (1979)
Mumford E and Ward T, *Computers: Planning for People,* Batsford (1968)

The three references given above provide a reasonable flavour of the 'Participative School'. I personally still prefer Mumford's older work (as in *Computers: Planning for People*).

Martin J, *Application Development without Programmes*, Prentice-Hall (1982)

12
Information systems in the corporate structure

12.1 Organisation structures

In many organisations the present location of the IS department was decided by historical chance. The first implementation in the firm became its reporting ground and, despite changes in scope and size, it still remains in that part of the administrative structure. Some data processing departments show their accounting tutelage by continuing to report to the Financial Director, others show their stock control roots by remaining in the operations department. The reporting structures and arrangements created by this first implementation may remain applicable. However, it is more likely that they will cause difficulties and constraints as the section tries to expand to cope with computerisation in other departments. There are many examples where the growth of computing has been retarded by its inappropriate place in the organisation structure.

Some organisations have relocated the data processing department into a wider management services section. This will also encompass operational research, statistical support and organisation and methods. In certain instances this section has been established as a separate trading company and required to make 'bids' for projects in the rest of the group (see Chapter 11). Such autonomy is also likely to extend to permitting the section to market and sell its products and services to a wider market. It is not unusual to find software developed as a bespoke system for the main group subsequently marketed as a software package aimed at other companies in the industry. In this way the section becomes an important revenue earner and hence joins the doers and makers of the group.

Establishing the management services section as a separate trading company may have positive effects on staff motivation and morale. However, its very success may affect the services offered to the other companies in the group. It is also likely to create a very centralised approach to data processing which may not fit in with user preferences. One major company initially established a large management services section and then took 'the logical step' to establish it as a separate company within the group. The company was free to offer computer time, products and resources to other companies but at a dearer rate than charged to member firms within the group. The company traded with relative financial success, but such was the demand for its services that most of the work was undertaken for non-group companies where the returns were higher. As a result an increasing amount of group work was contracted to external firms who underbid the quotes given by the group company. Eventually, senior management decided that this was not an acceptable state of affairs and so disbanded the separate trading company and re-distributed information systems staff around the user departments of the group companies. Their role was defined as the 'catalysts and experts' required to bring computerisation into all departments of the group. This in itself was only partially successful as it did not readily encourage the development of company-wide integrated systems. Thus a new systems section was created to deal specifically with such issues. The wheel had almost come full circle!

Thus the position of the information systems department in the corporate hierarchy is subject to fashion, experiment and technological trends. It is difficult to be prescriptive. As Keen (see Further reading) points out, every computing department is different and its functions and purpose will vary with:

- the size of the organisation
- whether a decentralised or centralised philosophy is prevailing
- the size and type of hardware configuration
- commercial or scientific installation
- the geographical distribution of the company
- management personalities
- experience of individual managers
- types of computer applications
- length of time that the company has been involved in computing.

However, it must be stressed that a structure built around the 'first application' may create difficulties and slow down the growth of computerisation. The computer section needs to be placed in an organisational structure which encourages rather than inhibits its activities. The most appropriate arrangements will vary from firm to firm dependent upon such factors as organisational size, marketplace, geographical distribution, and management expertise.

These issues will also affect the *internal* arrangements of the data processing department. Keen identifies three ways of organising a department.

- A simple hierarchy where junior programmers report to senior programmers who report to a programming manager. He/she reports to a DP Manager who is responsible to a Director of the company. Similar hierarchies exist for systems and operations staff. This is a **rigid people-centred structure**.

- Pools of skills and expertise are created and teams are selected from those pools; teams are headed by a team leader. This is a flexible arrangement and is **work orientated**.

- A permanent multi-skill team arrangement where team leaders report directly to the DP Manager. These teams may specialise in certain specific functional areas (finance systems) or have specific technical skills (telecommunications).

Keen suggests that the selected method should demonstrate an (elusive) combination of the following:

caring for people
a strong emphasis on work
ensures that this work is relevant
encourages the development of expertise
breaks down inter-departmental barriers
improves the effectiveness of corporate jobs.

He proposes an arrangement based around projects. Such a structure should provide

- the wide spectrum of skills needed as the project progresses.

- A more applicable structure. The project orientation of most departments does not fit well into a simple hierarchy.

● A separate management structure for production and maintenance. It should not be assumed that reporting arrangements for staff on development projects should be imposed on other aspects of the department's work.

Keen illustrates his preferred structure with an example for a management services division (reproduced as Fig. 12.1). Three groups are identified.

DP operations   Concerned with the day-to-day running of the computer systems. Two aspects should be noted.

● Each project team should include a representative from this section. This is needed to plan and control testing, operating requirements, data entry instructions, hardware and software use etc.

● Maintenance is placed outside projects. Keen argues that the easiest way to slow up project development is to distract staff with time consuming and demoralising maintenance. Maintenance occurs once a project is over. Therefore it should be given to those staff who are in daily contact with users and who are responsible for the *operational* phase.

Systems development projects   Projects represent the most important part of the management services task. They are supported by operational staff and technical experts. Projects are headed by full-time team leaders reporting to the project manager. The team members are selected, *as required*, from the pools of specialists and the operational staff. Thus the team controls all activities. No other departments are involved.

Specialist pools   These are the source of staff for the projects. Each group is headed by a technical manager who is responsible for maintaining staff expertise. This is important. Such managers are concerned with the development of skills and knowledge *not* with the conduct of projects.

Keen's suggestions are primarily aimed at companies with large management services functions. Smaller departments will require fewer management layers and projects will be less formal. However, the principles of **project-orientated** activity still apply.

12.2   Information systems functions

12.2.1   Systems analysts
The tasks of the systems analyst have been described in detail in Part 2. They are usually responsible for all stages of the system cycle except program development. Thus the analyst defines the system required in a system specification document and then receives the working version back from the programming section. Final testing and implementation are usually the analyst's responsibility.

12.2.2   Programmers
Programmers prepare, test and document computer programs from the specifications provided by the analyst. Programs will be written in an agreed programming language to a defined discipline — such as structured programming. Programmers are usually responsible for program testing but not system testing. Elements of the programming task were discussed in Part 1.

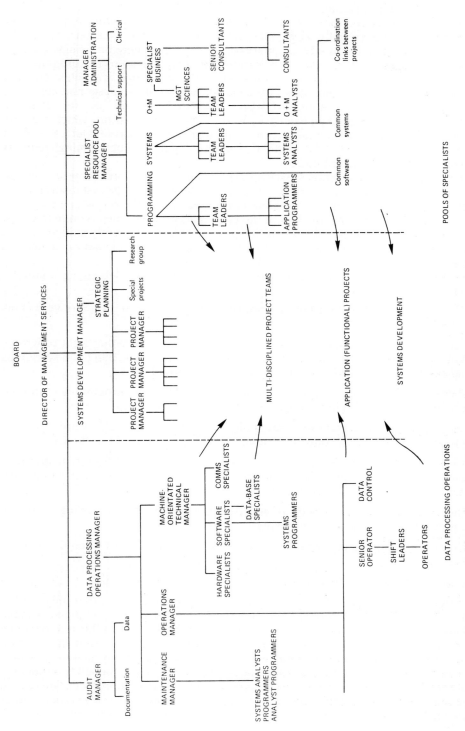

Fig. 12.1 A structure for a management services division (adopted from J Keen, *Managing System Development*, Courtesy of John Wiley Ltd — note that staff numbers have been omitted)

12.2.3   Analysis and programming

The relationship between the tasks of the analyst and the programmer requires some discussion. In some (usually larger) organisations the two areas are rigorously separated along the lines briefly summarised above. There may be formal arrangements for the signing over of the specification from the analysis to the programming department and reciprocal documentation when the programs are delivered. The detail of the specification may also vary considerably. Some analysts may leave the programmer with a fair amount of scope, allowing opportunities for flair and initiative. However, such scope can easily lead to maverick programs which are hard to understand, debug and maintain. As a result many analysts closely define the logic of their systems and essentially deskill the programming task. Programming creativity is reduced to straightforward coding.

In contrast some organisations, particularly smaller ones, prefer to employ analyst programmers who have responsibilities throughout the whole of the system cycle. This has the attraction of making the complete development task the responsibility of one person or team, so reducing one link in the user-analyst-programmer communication chain. However, it may be difficult to find staff who are sufficiently skilled in both analysis and programming. The two tasks are essentially different in *nature*, a fact well summed up by Tom de Marco (see Further reading).

He identifies the following features in programming and debugging computer systems.

- The interpersonal relationships are not very complicated nor are there very many of them.

- The work is very definite. A piece of code, for instance, is either right or wrong. When its wrong, it lets you know in no uncertain terms by kicking and screaming and holding its breath — acting in obviously abnormal ways.

- The work is satisfying. A positive glow emanates from the programmer who has just found and routed out a bug.

He concludes that implementation disciplines are largely 'straightforward, friendly, definite and satisfying.' In contrast systems analysis is none of these things.

- It certainly isn't easy. Negotiating a complex target document (system specification) with a whole community of heterogeneous and conflicting users and getting them to agree is a gargantuan task.

- The interpersonal relationships of analysis, particularly those involving users, are complicated, sometimes even hostile.

- There is nothing definite about analysis. It is not even obvious when the analysis phase is done.

- Largely because it is so indefinite, analysis is not very satisfying.

The difference in nature between analysis and programming means that they tend to require different types of people. This helps fuel the 'Do good programmers make good analysts debate?'. The answer is, of course, that some do. But this is likely to be less to do with their programming expertise than with the possession of a certain temperament and an empathy with people. The problem of the analyst and programmer divide is focussed even more sharply where promotion depends on moving out of programmer grades into the analysis section. Internal staff problems are caused by the tendency of some organisations to regard programming as a subordinate rather than complementary skill. The policy of regarding them both as specialist skills (see Fig. 12.1) seems to be most sensible.

12.2.4 Operations staff

The computer operations staff are responsible for the day-to-day running of the computer department. This will include data control, data preparation and the loading of the machines. The latter task embraces disk loading, printer control and paper changing, output despatch and the logging of hardware and software use. A traditional operations section would roughly coincide with the arrangement under the Operations Manager in Fig.12.1. Although Keen argues for maintenance to be undertaken by the operations section it is usually seen as a programming task. Operations staff perform a much needed but under-valued service. However, the lack of prestige and promotion opportunities often leads to low morale and high staff turnover.

12.2.5 Data analysts

The development of formal data analysis methods to support data base design (see Chapter 5 — Further reading) has led to a new group of specialists versed in these techniques. Staff in this area are still relatively scarce and so salaries are usually quite high.

12.3 The information centre

In this part the terms data processing and information systems have been used interchangeably. However, in reality, they may be distinguished as relative stages of computing maturity. Data processing is usually associated with *operational systems*, typically similar to those described in the Chapters 7 and 8. In contrast, information systems are perceived as applications supporting management decision making. These systems are usually characterised by uncertainty (managers rarely understand their decision making well enough to specify definite requirements) and flexibility. This change in computing emphasis has already been considered in Part 3 where it was seen as one of the major forces behind the growth of prototyping and fourth generation software.

The different levels of management decision making are illustrated in Fig. 12.2. Decisions at the top of the hierarchy are often one-off, unstructured policy decisions which may require access to a large amount of external data. Thus operational data becomes both *summarised* and *less important* as judgements become increasingly strategic. Furthermore, a need for systems based on external data arises for the first time. Information systems based solely on internally generated operational data are demonstrably bogus.

The extension of computer systems into tactical and strategic decision making has been accompanied by three important trends.

- Growth of packaged software. Many operational systems may be implemented by using a package.

- The emergence of powerful, flexible microcomputers accompanied by versatile development software (see Chapter 8).

- Increased computer familiarity in both middle and senior management.

A recent organisational reflection of these trends is the concept of the **information centre**. Proposed originally by IBM, it is conceived as a centre where users have access to both development tools and information systems advice. This gives users the opportunity to explore their requirements and problems using application development aids. The culmination of these experiments may lie anywhere along the

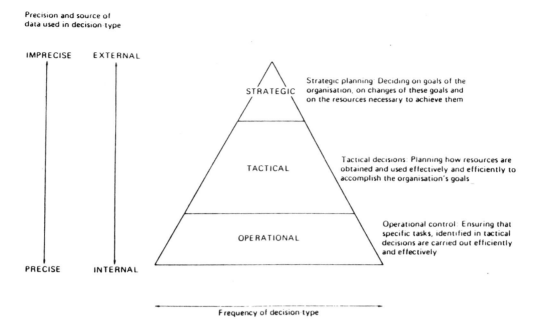

Precision and source of
data used in decision type

IMPRECISE   EXTERNAL

STRATEGIC — Strategic planning. Deciding on goals of the organisation, on changes of these goals and on the resources necessary to achieve them

TACTICAL — Tactical decisions. Planning how resources are obtained and used effectively and efficiently to accomplish the organisation's goals

OPERATIONAL — Operational control. Ensuring that specific tasks, identified in tactical decisions are carried out efficiently and effectively

PRECISE   INTERNAL

Frequency of decision type

Fig. 12.2   Management decision types

development spectrum, from a completely user-written system to an application developed by the IS section from a conventional specification. The information centre concept should be based around experiment and choice. The latter is particularly important as it should provide an opportunity to select from a number of different strategies, all of which have been experienced in some (albeit limited) way. The information centre should be a source of advice, experience, training, standards and good practice. It should seek to foster intelligent and efficient end-user computing, not to inhibit it. Used properly, it could become standard practice in the next stage of computing maturity.

12.4   The changing role of information systems staff

It should be clear from many of the issues discussed in this text that computing is in a stage of transition. Several factors, all discussed in detail elsewhere, contribute to this.

- Technological factors. Falling hardware costs, communication opportunities, powerful application development software, cheap versatile microcomputers.

- Methodological issues. New analysis and design techniques, data analysis, prototyping.

- Market forces. Large new markets, Increased computer familiarity. Exploiting opportunities provided by technical advances.

How will these changes, and others, affect the tasks of analysis and programming, the two core tasks of information systems development?

Martin (see Further reading) has addressed these issues in *The Information Systems Manifesto*. Briefly, he sees much of programming becoming automated, but that more skilled programmers will be required for the production of software tools and program generators. Thus the number of 'coding' programmers will fall but there will be a need for a highly skilled elite. The role of systems analysts will also change. They will become *developers*, skilled in fourth generation languages, who can help users build their systems with these powerful new tools. The days of the hands-off analyst who seldom touched a computer are numbered!

12.5   Summary

The position of the information systems section in the corporate hierarchy can critically affect its morale and influence. The internal structure of the section benefits from a project-orientated approach which provides flexibility, motivation and is appropriate to the project nature of most systems activity. The chapter concluded with a brief review of the tasks of analysis and programming and how these may change in the future.

Further reading

de Marco T, *Structured Systems Analysis and System Specification*, Prentice-Hall (1979)

Keen J, *Managing System Development,* John Wiley (1981)

Many textbooks on management issues are too theoretical for the average reader. Keen's book is full of good sense and covers a wide spectrum of systems tasks. His suggested organisational structures are 'project based' and this seems to fit in well with the project approach to system development.

Martin J, *The Information System Manifesto*, Prentice Hall (1983)

James Martin's books are usually entertaining and controversial and this is no exception. He sets out his vision of the future of information systems development and discusses the implications of predicted changes on current practitioners and professionals.

13
Hardware and software selection

The tasks described in Part 2 and 3 lead to the definition of a paper based system specification. This will be made operational by purchasing and developing appropriate hardware and software to support it. Chapter 9 looked at some of the software possibilities and concluded with a suggested 'pecking order' for software selection. This was based on developing a match between requirements (as described in the specification) and the facilities and features of the software. This chapter now examines some of the management issues that will be faced in choosing appropriate hardware and software.

13.1 Tenders

The system specification may be used as a basis for an invitation to tender. It is unlikely that all the detail will be needed and indeed it may be preferable to use the concept of the mini-specification (see Chapter 9) which concentrates upon key operational and technical requirements. The detail of the invitation to tender will clearly vary with what stage the tender is issued at and what is being requested. A tender distributed at the end of a feasibility study requesting bids for system specification will obviously be different from one sent out at the end of detailed design asking for hardware bids.

The invitation to tender may also include details about the organisation's business, tasks, priorities, turnover and structure. This gives the potential supplier a structure in which to place a response. Work undertaken in firms of a similar size or function can be highlighted and appropriate references given. The proposed project cost and time-scale may also be provided so that suppliers can gauge the level and timing of the commitment required.

The tender document must also request specific details about the potential supplier. These might include:

description of the organisation
size of the organisation
turnover
years trading
number of systems implemented
two reference sites
specific expertise in this application area
installation proposals
training and maintenance policies.

Once the invitation to tender has been constructed it may be sent out to potential suppliers. Advice on how many suppliers should be contacted varies considerably. Edwards (see Further reading) suggests that only four or five names should be selected and that an independent consultant is employed to aid in the selection of those names. He feels that 'too wide a range of choices may hamper decision-making.' Dilloway (again see Further reading) is more concerned with the selection of packaged software in the microcomputer market place. He suggests that the invitation to tender is sent to as many as 100 possible suppliers of which 20 will make a reasonable response and three to five will eventually be short-listed. He makes the following point;

'Those readers who feel that it is not fair or good business to approach 100 possible vendors may make a preliminary enquiry if they wish. However, I feel that most suppliers would prefer to see the whole ITT (Invitation to Tender) rather than a pre-qualification questionnaire.'

In general it may be wise to approach all suppliers that do either of the following.

- Provide software for that *vertical market*. These suppliers have a good understanding of the application area and have specific products and expertise in that industry. Such knowledge may more than compensate for the geographical distance from the client's premises.

- Are established in the client's immediate geographical area. Some companies prefer to deal with local firms who should be able to respond quickly to problems and queries. This feeling of 'being able to get at them' may outweigh their inexperience in the particular sector of industry.

It helps subsequent evaluation if the proposals are requested in a fairly standard format. The claimed features may then be placed within a columnar schedule with weights assigned to different features if this is deemed to be appropriate. There are likely to be four main considerations.

- Technical. How well does the proposed hardware and software fulfill the requirements of the specification?

- Contractual. What are the formal terms of agreement between supplier and client?

- Financial. What are the relative costs and how can these be financed?

- Support. The features, experience and flexibility of the supplier.

These are now considered in turn.

13.2   Technical evaluation

The evaluation of technical factors is confused by the inter-relationship of hardware and software. There are dangers if one is given too much priority over the other — the following example illustrates this.

One firm evaluated software first and selected an appropriate multi-user software package. However, none of the machines which supported this package could produce the speed of response required with the planned operational volumes. Too much emphasis had been placed on software *features* rather than on practical speed. Furthermore, the software had been evaluated in single-user mode only. All the demonstrations referred to its multi-user function but this had *not actually been seen*. When a multi-user demonstration was given the software gave very slow response times due mainly to the hardware configuration. When the salesman was asked why the system was advertised as supporting 16 users when it appeared to keel over with only four he replied 'It does support 16 users *as long as they are not all using it at the same time!*'

Key technical factors may greatly constrain the software choice. For example, the need for **multi-user** microcomputer data management software will drastically reduce the software choice.

However, there are also problems caused by allocating too much priority to hardware. One organisation spent most of its time evaluating different hardware choices and assumed that the software was bound to be available — 'after all, it's only a straightforward accounting application.' But, when they completed their selection and purchased the equipment, they found that their application was not catered for by the restricted number of accounting packages available on that machine. They compromised and used a package that did not closely fit their needs. The amount of extra clerical work created by this solution eventually persuaded the company to abandon the project and commission a customised bespoke system. The exercise had been expensive in both time and money and had led to a dramatic fall in staff morale.

Thus software and hardware selection has to go hand-in-hand, with priority probably given to software, if only because the natural tendency is to attach most importance to hardware due to its relative cost and tangibility. It is important to request both *demonstrations* and *reference sites* and to evaluate the configuration in the light of requirements and operational volumes. This point has already been made with reference to software selection (see Chapter 10), but it is worth re-emphasising — the buyer must beware!

Evaluating paper proposals and interpreting other companies' business and volumes is a difficult intellectual exercise. It is hard to feel very confident about any judgement! Dilloway has suggested a way of reducing uncertainty by employing a 'trial period' where it is decided if the product is satisfactory. The trial is established on the assumption that it will be satisfactory and so as much effort is put into it as a full implementation. It almost takes the form of a 'money back if not fully satisfied' guarantee. The (welcome) trend of software suppliers providing limited record evaluation copies of their software also encourages the trial idea. These are usually available at a nominal cost which is allowed against any subsequent purchase of the full system.

13.3 Contractual issues

Items are usually supplied with specified terms of contract. These are provided by the supplier and are almost bound to favour him. The terms of the contract are often taken as given and are not seen to be subject to negotiation. This is not the case; it may be both practical and desirable to negotiate the terms of supply. Edwards gives the following instances where the terms may be particularly negotiable.

- Smaller suppliers may be much more willing to accept amendments. Their desire for business may outweigh favourable terms of supply.

- Software development is difficult to predict and categorise. Agreements to provide such services should be more flexible and negotiable than contracts for more tangible and well-understood goods, such as hardware.

- Suppliers offering relatively new hardware and software which is unproven may vary their normal terms of supply.

- Large customers may be able to impose their own conditions of supply.

It may be preferable at the outset to insist upon standard terms of supply such as those developed by the Institute of Purchasing and Supply. These are described in detail in Dilloway's book. Three issues are worth further reflection.

- Copyright. Software packages are not 'bought'. The copyright remains with the originator who licences the product to be used in a particular way. This licence covers the extent and terms of copying. The purchaser is, in effect, a licencee who can use the software under the terms of the contract. The licence is a legally binding contract. The licence is usually 'non-transferable', so that it cannot be sold to other users. The licence agreement for dBASE III is shown in Fig. 13.1.

- Performance. It is impossible to be sure if software is completely free from errors. Most suppliers will fix program errors for a long period of time after acceptance and they will do this free of charge. This refers, however, to errors of execution and not to errors of content. Dilloway comments that 'it is well nigh impossible for an intending licensee to sufficiently understand a computer software product from its "published specification and Documentation" to be able to sufficiently appreciate how the product will work in practice.' It is also unlikely that suppliers will agree to the inclusion of certain speeds and response times. Such factors are so difficult to determine that it is the brave (or foolhardy) supplier who commits them to contract. Finally, there is a growing (but disturbing) trend towards disguising the fixing of product bugs as 'upgrades', and requesting money for the privilege of receiving the newer version.

---

dBASE III version 1.00 14 June 1984 IBM/MSDOS ***

COPYRIGHT © ASHTON-TATE 1984
AS AN UNPUBLISHED LICENSED PROPRIETARY WORK.
ALL RIGHTS RESERVED.

Use of this software and the other materials contained in the software package (the "Materials") has been provided under a software License Agreement (please read in full). In summary, Ashton-Tate grants you a paid-up, non-transferrable, personal license to use the Materials only on a single or subsequent (but not additional) computer terminal for fifty years from the time the sealed diskette has been opened. You receive the right to use the Materials, but you do not become the owner of them. You may not alter, decompile, or reverse-assemble the software, and YOU MAY NOT COPY the Materials. The Materials are protected by copyright, trade secrets, and trademark law, the violation of which can result in civil damages and criminal prosecution.

dBASE, dBASE III and ASHTON-TATE are trademarks of Ashton-Tate.

Press the F1 key for help
Type a command (or ASSIST) and press the return key (*DY*).

Fig. 13.1

- Delivery schedule. Agreed milestones for delivery must be set and the terms of payment associated with those milestones established. The financial consequences of 'project slippage' must be negotiated as well as the formal means of product acceptance. This latter aspect may include the specification and duration of defined acceptance tests.

Finally, it must be accepted that business must take place in an atmosphere of mutual trust and understanding. If this breaks down, or does not exist in the first place, then it seems unreasonable to progress with the supply. Legal contract forms are not a substitute for commercial respect and tolerance. This is particularly true in the supply of computer systems and software. If negotiation becomes a 'battle of forms' then it does not augur well for the delivery and implementation of the system.

13.4   Financing the system

Payment is usually associated with the delivery of products at an agreed sequence of milestones (see above). The client firm may fund these payments in a variety of ways.

- Cash payment from resources. This may be the preferred way of purchasing microcomputer hardware and software. This method should be avoided if it is likely to cause cash-flow problems. Cash is usually used to finance day-to-day activities (so-called working capital) and not to buy longer term assets such as a computer. A medium to long term asset like a computer is normally funded by a medium to long term debt.

- Leasing. This is a popular way of buying a larger computer. The client selects a machine which is then purchased by a finance company. The computer is then leased to the client at a charge which repays the capital plus a fixed interest rate over an agreed number of years. The 'term' of the lease is usually three or five years. Thus leasing gives the client a machine right away which can be funded out of future earnings. Furthermore, the future payments are predictable and their real costs will fall due to the effect of inflation. If the lease is of a 'full-payout' type where the amount repaid equals or exceeds the total cost of the equipment then the lessee will normally be able to 're-hire' the equipment at a nominal rate. However, it is likely that this option will not be taken up as the equipment will almost certainly be substantially out of date. The operational life of a computer is the basis of a different type of lease which runs for less than the expected usefulness of the machine. In this instance the finance company may be looking to lease the machine to two or three clients during its operational life. This may typically occur where equipment phased out of a company that wishes, or needs, to be at the leading edge of technology, is used as a workhorse in another organisation concerned mainly with transaction processing.

- Rental. This is most useful for short-term hire but it is usually an expensive way of procuring equipment. While I am writing this I have in front of me a brochure advertising a £75/week hire charge for a computer which only costs £1200 to purchase outright. Rental may be more attractive with larger computers and gives the opportunity to trade-in regularly to remain at the forefront of technology. It has the advantage that rentals of this type are usually with the actual supplier rather than with a third party, such as the finance company in the leasing arrangement.

The method selected for computer procurement will vary with:

- the cost of the purchase

- the cash position of the company

- the current taxation arrangements. The allowances against taxation may tip the balance in a certain direction. The position tends to change from budget to budget.

13.5   Supplier/client relationship

In general the arrangement between client and supplier is not a short one-off relationship. The transaction is not the same as the purchase of a simple consumer good where the only subsequent contact with the supplier is likely to be if there are grounds for complaint. Computer system purchase often requires a long term commitment from both sides involving many interactions between supplier and customer staff. Thus the supplier has to be someone the client has confidence in, feels they can work with and, furthermore, is someone who also seems to be committed to a long-term trading relationship. I have seen projects begin in a climate of antagonism and these have usually deteriorated into mutual contempt. The supplier complains of 'a customer who is always bothering me' and the client of 'unhelpful staff who never return phone calls'. This is not an appropriate climate for the implementation of change.

13.6   Summary

Thus hardware and software selection is affected by financial issues, technical performance, supplier relationships and contractual arrangements. The eventual selection will be a compromise between these four categories, although they should not be given equal weighting. There is little to be gained by buying a cheap under-performing system from the nicest man in the world!

Further reading

This chapter is based around three books.

Dilloway C, *Purchasing Computer Software Products*, Gower Press (1985)

Dilloway's book provides entertaining reading, as well as a detailed annotated guide to the Institute of Purchasing and Supply's model forms for licence agreements.

Edwards M, *Understanding Computer Contracts*, Waterflow (1983)

This book has a wider remit than Dilloways and adopts a more legalistic approach. There are many interesting examples of case law, used to illustrate the problems of computer system acquisition.

NCC, *Software Contracts*, NCC (1980)

A useful guide on all aspects of software contracts.

14
Information systems
— a project-based
function

14.1 The concept of the project

Information systems development is largely project based because it is usually concerned with the delivery of one-off products by teams which have no permanent place in the administrative structure. The fact that most development will be a joint effort between line management and IS staff means that some temporary organisational structure must be established to permit the development to take place. This temporary structure is 'the project'. The central importance of the project was recognised in Keen's suggested organisational structure (Chapter 12).

Non-trivial projects require formal management so that they are both controlled and effective. Keen suggests that project success is directly related to formal project management and that greater formality is required where

a large number of departments and people are involved
the system is technically complex
the business application is complex
new technology is being used
the risk of financial loss is high.

This is particularly so if several, or all, of these elements are present.

A formalised approach to project management provides a mechanism for dealing with the technical and political complications that are bound to arise. There is, of course, an overhead in terms of meetings, minutes and reports, but these should be outweighed by the discipline imposed by the management framework.

14.2   The tasks of the project

14.2.1   Project manager

Projects are undertaken by teams which must be headed and directed by a suitable Project Manager. It is wise to establish such a post very early on in the project discussions so that the appointed person can influence the project direction and the membership of the team. It is often difficult to find people with suitable business, technical and project management experience to fulfill the role of Project Manager.

The Project Manager must be given suitable terms of reference so that he or she knows *what to try to achieve*. These terms will usually cover

- what should be delivered

- when it should be delivered

- what resources will be given to deliver it by the defined date.

Formal terms of reference should prevent misunderstandings and misconceptions. They will permit the Project Manager to visualise the scope of the project and so better identify the constituent tasks.

14.2.2 Identifying manageable tasks

The project will require the delivery of a product. This might range from a written report to a fully tested application system. Whatever the required outcome, the job of producing it will have to be reduced to manageable, complementary, inter-related tasks. The detail of these tasks will naturally vary from system to system but Keen believes that eight general **project work streams** can be distinguished. Not all these streams will be evident in every project.

- The user department, which is usually the project's client.
- Other computer projects which are related to the one under development.
- Systems development work.
- Data capture and clerical procedures.
- Application software.
- DP operations implications.
- System software.
- Hardware acquisition, configuration and use.

In planning such activities the Project Manager will have to identify the following.

- Specific tasks that must be completed.
- How each specific task affects other tasks in the project. Two issues are important here.

    What tasks are required before this activity can commence?
    What other activities in the project cannot commence before this task is completed?

- The duration of each task so that sufficient staff may be allocated.

  Information about activities may be illustrated and controlled by **network analysis (critical path analysis)**. This technique permits the overall project to be sized, costed and displayed. More importantly, it helps identify tasks which are critical to the project's planned duration as well as illustrating the effect of delays on both project tasks and times. Network analysis is both straightforward and powerful. It is treated in detail in Section 14.3.

14.3 Network analysis — a project management tool.

14.3.1 Notation and rules

A network shows the inter relationship of **activities** which have to be undertaken in a project. An activity is a task which takes time and resources — e.g. lay drains, plastering, painting, are all activities in the construction of a house. An activity is represented in a network by an *arrowed line*. The head of the arrow indicates where the task ends and the tail where the task begins. Thus before network analysis can be undertaken the planner must determine what activities are involved in the project. This may pose problems of identification which can only be solved by close involvement with those responsible for undertaking the project. This involvement should also permit the planner to uncover the logical relationships of the project's activities. These relationships must be correct otherwise the network and any subsequent conclusions will be inaccurate. An estimate of the time of an activity is also required. An activity and its associated time span is shown below:

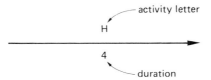

Activities link **events**. An event is a point in time which represents the start or finish of an activity. It is represented by a *circle*.

It may be necessary to show an activity which preserves the logic of a network and ensures that the rules of drawing networks are not violated (these rules are given later in this section). Such an activity does not consume time or resources. It is termed a **dummy activity** and is shown on a network by a *dotted arrow*. A network is a

combination of activities, dummy activities and events. A simple network may look like Fig. 14.1.

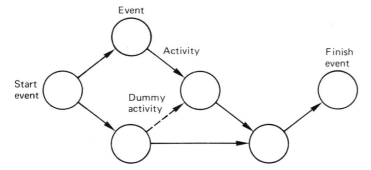

Fig. 14.1   The structure of a simple network

A network should have only one **start** event and one **finish** event.

Every activity must have one **tail** event and one **head** event. Many activities may use the same tail event and many use the same head event. The following are permissible except at the finish or start of a network.

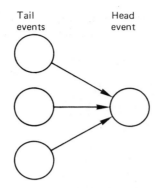

Tail event | Head events | Tail events | Head event

In this instance many head events share the same tail. This would not be permissible at the finish of a network

In this instance many tail events share the same head. This would not be permissible as the start of a network.

However an activity must not share the same tail event and the same head event. This is not permitted.

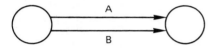

In such an instance the logic of the network may be preserved by using a dummy activity.

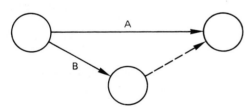

No activity can start until its tail event is reached and no event is complete until all activities leading to it are complete. The importance of the rule will be demonstrated later.

Loops are not permitted because networks essentially show the progress of a project in time. This progress is generally represented by the network proceeding from left to right.

All activities must be tied into the network. Activities which do not link into the overall project should be discarded. The following is not permissible.

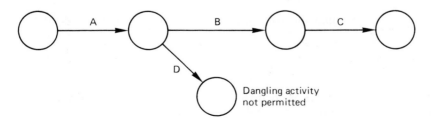

Dangling activity not permitted

Networks are not drawn to scale. The length of the arrow is not proportional to the time of the activity.

Identifying events   Events should be numbered from left to right.

Identifying activities   Activities may be identified by:

- a shortened description of the job — e.g. testing

- an alphabetical code, A, B, C etc.

- giving the tail and head event numbers — e.g. 2–7, 8–11 etc.

14.3.2   Network analysis — an example

A computer system project leader has identified eleven activities in a project. These are shown in Table 14.1.

Table 14.1

Activity		Preceding activity	Duration (weeks)
A	Pilot survey	–	6
B	Investigation of computer requirements	–	4
C	Preliminary data analysis	A	5
D	Write initial report	B, C	2
E	Program design	B	7
F	Program testing and debugging	E	6
G	Main data collection	B, C	5
H	Data collection	G	3
I	Run program on collected data	F, D, H	2
J	Discussion and analyse results	I	2
K	Final report	J	3

The following are hints for drawing the network.

- Start on a sheet of paper at least four times as big as you think you will need.

- Draw a network in pencil — have an eraser available.

- Begin by drawing an arrow.

- Do not be afraid of untidiness at first.

- Try to avoid drawing arrows which cross each other.

- Try to keep arrows as straight lines.

- Try to avoid too great a variation in the length of arrows.

- Try not to let estimates of duration affect the length of your arrows.

- Be willing to rearrange and redraw!

Let's work through this example illustrating possible errors. First draw an arrow representing activity A.

$$\xrightarrow{\qquad\qquad A \qquad\qquad}$$

This activity links two events. If we wished to name these events we might use the terms 'commencement of the project' and 'pilot study completed'.

The second activity, B, does not have any preceding activity and so may share the same tail event as A. This also obeys the rule that the network may have only one start point.

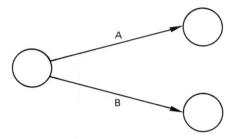

The following representation is wrong.

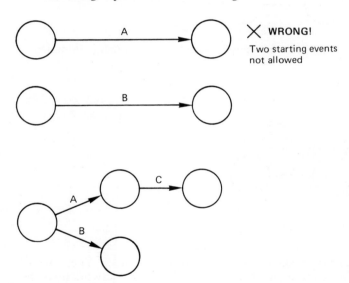

✗ WRONG!

Two starting events
not allowed

Activity C may be inserted quite easily (see above) but D represents something of a problem because it is preceded by both B and C. This may be surmounted by inserting D after C and linking the event which marks the completion of B with the event that represents the commencement of D. This does not represent a real activity and thus a dummy is used to preserve the logic of the network. In the first run through it is useful to insert plenty of dummies which can subsequently be rationalised in the final network.

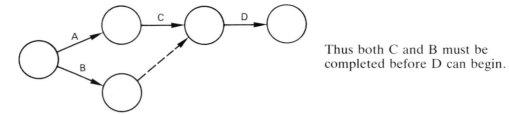

Thus both C and B must be completed before D can begin.

E, F, G, and H present little problem.

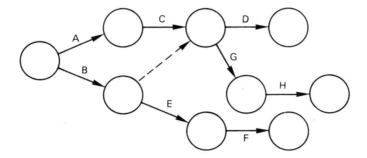

However, I is preceded by F, D and H. This may be represented by using dummies as below.

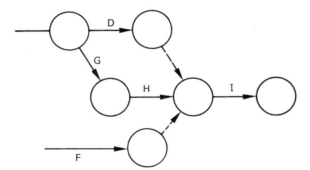

Closer inspection of these dummies shows that they are unnecessary. The rules of network analysis permits the sharing of head events. Thus the network may be redrawn with J and K added for completeness.

This network may be checked against the rules.

- Does it have only one start and one finish event?   Yes
- Do any activities share the same tail event and the same head event?   No
- Are there any loops in the network?   No
- Does the network proceed from left to right?   Yes
- Are all activities tied into the network?   Yes
- Are the minimum number of dummies used?   Yes

Having established the logic of the network we now wish to ascertain the duration of the project and the critical activities in achieving that project time.

14.3.3   Time analysis in networks

The critical path of the network gives the shortest time in which the whole project may be completed. There may be more than one critical path in a network and it is possible for the critical path to pass through a dummy. The critical path is established as follows. The earliest start time (EST) is determined for each event: this is the *earliest possible time* at which a succeeding activity can start. The ESTs are inserted by working through the network annotating the events as follows:

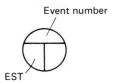

The EST of a head event is obtained by adding the EST of the tail event to the activity duration. The network begins at time 0 (zero).

When two or more routes arrive at an event the *longest route* time must be taken. The logic of this should be obvious. If activity Z depends on the completion of X and Y and X is completed by day 7 but Y is not finished until day 9, then Z cannot start until day 9.

The network for our example is given in Fig. 14.2.

Note that at event 3 routes AC (taking 11 weeks) and AB (4 weeks) converge. Activities D and G cannot start until both B and C are finished. Thus the earliest start time is at the end of the eleventh week.

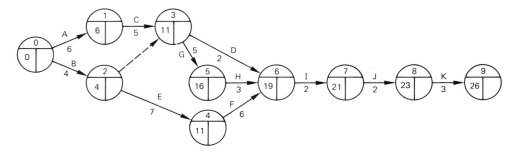

Fig. 14.2   The network: ESTs completed

The blank sector on the circle is for the insertion of **latest start times** (LSTs). This is the latest possible time at which a preceding activity can finish without increasing the project duration. These are determined by working backwards from the final event subtracting each activity duration from the previous LST. Where the tails of activities both arrive at an event the lowest number is taken. This is illustrated in the example given in Fig. 14.3.

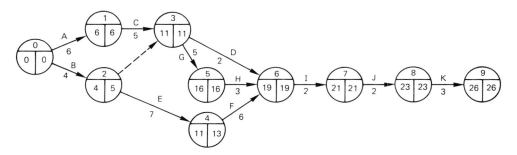

Fig. 14.3   The network: LSTs completed

Note that at event 3 activities D and G converge. The LST cannot be 17 because G and 11 take 8 days and so this would lengthen the project duration. Thus the lowest number is taken.

The critical path may be determined by examining the network for the following conditions.

● The EST and LST of the two events it connects are identical.

● If so the **total float** of the activity must be zero, where

total float = latest head __ earliest tail __ activity
              time   time   duration

By inspecting the network given above it is clear that A, C, I, J and K are all critical activities. However, does the critical path pass through D or G and H? If the second test is applied Table 14.2 shows that G and H are the critical activities.

The critical path may be indicated on the network by two small transverse lines on the activity arrow.

Table 14.2

Activity	Latest head time	Earliest tail time	Activity duration	Total float
D	19	11	2	6
G	16	11	5	0
H	19	16	3	0

The critical path identifies the activies that must be completed on time if the project duration is not to be extended. All activities that are not critical have an associated float representing spare time. The duration of the project is given in the final event circle. In our example the project time is 26 weeks (see Fig. 14.4).

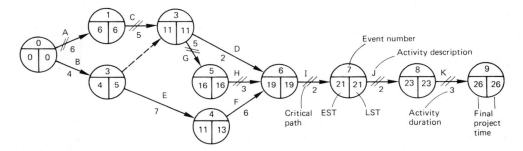

Fig. 14.4 The network: critical path identified

A number of developments of the basic initial path idea may be identified.

14.3.4 Cost scheduling
In this instance the *costs* of the activities are given and used to calculate the cost of various project durations. The project may be completed at a given cost but project duration may be *decreased* by putting in more resources — overtime, plant etc. Some ways of reducing the project duration will be cheaper than others and network cost analysis seeks to select the cheapest way of reducing the overall duration. Four sets of data are needed to perform this so-called 'crashing' of the network.

- Normal costs. Costs associated with a normal time estimate for an activity.

- Crash cost. Cost associated with the minimum possible time for an activity. These will take into acccount many factors and are usually higher than normal costs.

- Crash time. The minimum possible time that an activity is planned to take.

- Cost slope. This is the average cost of shortening an activity by one time unit. The slope is usually assumed to be linear and is calculated by

$$\text{cost slope} = \frac{\text{crash cost} - \text{normal cost}}{\text{normal time} - \text{crash time}}$$

14.3.5 Resource scheduling
Networks may provide assistance in planning and controlling resources. The resources used on a project (men, materials, money etc.) are subject to varying demands and loadings as the project proceeds. Management may wish to know if resource

limitations may delay the project and may also wish to ensure, as far as possible, a fairly constant workload throughout its duration. This would eliminate unnecessarily high costs at peak periods and idle resources in slack times. The understanding of the project gained from network analysis facilitates such project control. The resource implications of a project can be shown on a **Gantt chart**. On a Gantt chart the activities are shown by lines with lengths proportional to the activity time. The Gantt chart for the computer system project is shown in Fig. 14.5.

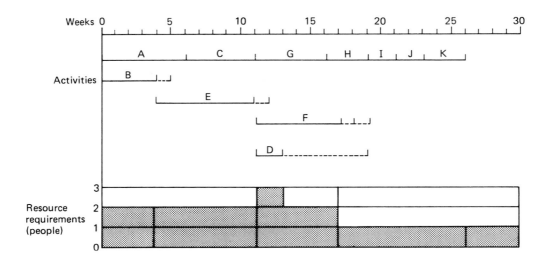

Fig. 14.5 Histogram and Gantt chart – original estimates

Note that it assumes that each activity starts at its earliest time and the dotted continuation line shows the float for each activity. If we assume that we require one person for each activity then the staffing needs can be shown in a histogram at the foot of the Gantt chart. This is compiled by counting the number of solid horizontal lines in each column. The histogram demonstrates the weekly labour requirement.

If labour requirements are unevenly distributed then the histogram may be smoothed by delaying activities which have float. For example, the histogram for the computer project suggests that three people will be required in weeks 11–13 to undertake tasks D, G and F. However, this can be reduced to two people by simply rescheduling D to be done after F. By using the float in this way the staffing needs of the project are evened out. There is no need to second an extra member of staff, or take on a contract worker, for the one 'peak' week. The Gantt chart and histogram now look like Fig. 14.6.

14.3.6 Pert and probability
In the example of the computer project leader the time estimates were presented as a single definite figure — e.g. six weeks to do the pilot survey. Such estimates may be difficult to ascertain. It may be easier to attach estimates of *probability* to a number of different durations. An example is given in Table 14.3.

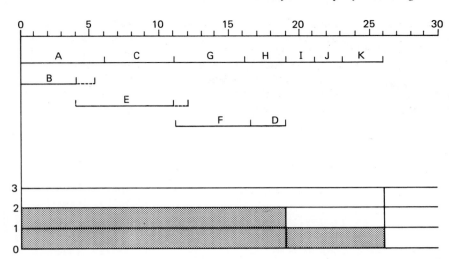

Fig. 14.6   Histogram and Gantt chart – tasks re-scheduled

Table 14.3

Length of pilot study

Duration	Comment	subject probability
4 weeks	We might get it done if Smith gets a move on.	0.2
6 weeks	Seems what we are likely to achieve.	0.5
7 weeks	If they start playing up in the computer department.	0.3

In this instance the project leader has given three different probabilities based on different circumstances. These may be combined into one duration by the notion of **expectation**. Thus

$$(4 \times 0.2) + (6 \times 0.5) + (7 \times 0.3) = 0.8 + 3.0 + 2.1 = 5.9 \text{ weeks}$$

In subsequent analysis the composite time of 5.9 weeks is used.

This example depends on the leader giving subjective probabilities. Most people find this quite difficult. In **PERT** (project evaluation and review technique) this is avoided by asking for the pessimistic, optimistic and most likely activity durations. The **optimistic** time is the time in which the estimator considers that the activity can be completed if all goes well. The **most likely time** is the time which would most often be needed if the activity was carried out many times under normal conditions. The **pessimistic** time is when everything (within reason) that can go wrong goes wrong. This is extremely difficult to estimate particularly as the estimator has to decide on the degree of pessimism warranted. The three estimates are then combined by using the following formula:

$$\text{estimated time} = \frac{\text{(optimistic time + pessimistic time + 4x most likely time)}}{6}$$

For example

Length of pilot study	comment
4 weeks	optimistic
6 weeks	most likely
7 weeks	pessimistic

$$\text{PERT duration for this activity} = \frac{4 + 7 + (4 \times 6)}{6}$$

$$= \frac{35}{6}$$

$$= 5\tfrac{5}{6} \text{ weeks}$$

$$\simeq 5.8 \text{ weeks}$$

14.3.7   Final comments

Network analysis is a very useful technique to aid the planning and control of projects. Lack of control may produce high costs, missed deadlines and missed opportunities. Many problems exist in establishing the original data and much care must go into identifying activities, their interrelationships, the likely time of completion and the resources they require. However, if these can be reliably determined, the processing of the data has been eased considerably by the ready availability of computer packages. Two example packages available on microcomputers are Hornet and Superproject. Network analysis is an underused technique. It offers many benefits in the all too often uncoordinated and unplanned field of project estimation and control.

14.4   Sharing the project load

The last example has illustrated how there may be varying calls on resources throughout a project. These may sometimes be re-distributed, as in Section 14.3, but in many instances there will be a need to bring in short term **contractors** to help the full-time staff through a heavy period of work. Contracting is a feature of the computing industry. It is a useful way of employing relatively scarce skills for a defined period of time without having the overhead costs of full-time employment. However, contractors must be closely supervised to ensure that their time is used effectively. Contract rates are high and so a good rate of return is required. Furthermore, the morale of the full-time staff must be considered. It is rather demoralising to manage a team where the contract team members are earning more money than their notional manager!

It may also be sensible to employ people on short term contracts to fill areas where the firm lacks specific expertise. This may, for instance, be on telecommunications, methodology, hardware trends etc. These may be short term one-off requirements or long term advisory needs. In most instances the firm is looking for advice, guidance and assessment. This is the role of the **consultant.**

A **computer bureau** may also be chosen to support both short and long term needs. Indeed the organisation may decide not to establish any internal data processing at all and to sub-contract all of it to a bureau. Bureau's are essentially organisations with substantial computing facilities that sell part of these facilities to client organisations. Thus it is possible for a relatively small company to have access to a large amount of processing power without the overheads that this would normally incur. A number of processing alternatives are available.

- Simple batch. Raw or pre-coded data is delivered to the bureau with regular and ad hoc printouts provided in return.

- Remote batch. Data is keyed into a terminal at the client's offices and transmitted to the bureau's computer via the telephone lines. Printouts are returned by courier or results returned down the line for outputting on a printer in the client's office. The use of an in-house terminal may be logically extended to interactive processing where the client can access the machine as required, producing reports and analyses on demand.

- Time sharing. The bureau operates the computer but sells or leases rights to a certain proportion of the facility to its clients. This provides a fixed cost which may be budgeted for by the client organisation. This is conceptually different to the other two arrangements where there is a large element of variable costs associated with the actual use of the bureau's machine. These variable costs are usually on top of a fixed annual standing charge.

14.5 Summary

Chapter 12 argued that information systems development is a project-orientated activity. This chapter has examined the implications of this in some depth. It has considered the tasks and management of the project, together with some strategies for spreading or sub-contracting the workload.

Further reading

Cohen S S, *Operational Research*, Edward Arnold (1985)

Introduces many mathematical models within business examples.

Keen J, *Managing System Development*, Wiley (1981)

Moore P G, *Basic Operational Reasearch*, Pitman (1976)

A valuable introduction to O R techniques with a realistic network analysis example.

Owen F and Jones R, *Modern Analytical Techniques*, Polytech (1973)

A comprehensive and relatively cheap book with an easy to follow network analysis example.

Part 6
System Controls

Controls are insufficiently stressed in most texts, and indeed in many practical implementations. They are often viewed as something 'bolted on' at the end and not as an integral part of system development. This Part attempts to re-dress this by dwelling in some detail on three aspects of control.

Chapter 15 deals with privacy. The elusive nature of privacy is contemplated and the effect of computers on this debate is briefly reviewed. An illustrative example is included from the National Health Service. This is followed by an examination of the development and contents of the 1984 Data Protection Act.

Chapter 16 suggests a framework for examining computer-related risks (from Wong) and then examines each level of risk in this framework. Each examination includes at least one example, together with possible counter-measures.

Finally, Chapter 17 looks at the role and tasks of the computer auditor. A number of types of control are suggested and examples, problems and opportunities are identified for each control type. The operational implications of audit are reviewed and special problems identified in microcomputer and on-line systems.

15
Privacy and data protection

15.1 The nature of privacy

One of the major difficulties of discussing the problem of 'privacy' is that there can be little agreement on the nature of this elusive concept. What one person considers private and confidential may be felt, by another, to be suitable for public broadcast. Warner and Stone (see Further reading) commented that 'Privacy is an exceedingly slippery virtue — intangible, hard to define and harder still to measure.' The elusive nature of privacy makes it difficult to legislate for it, a problem that has been acknowledged by most government commissions set up to examine the subject.

Furthermore, the changing nature of society and the values and norms of individuals within that society make privacy a central issue, subject to regular changes in perception and importance. John Stuart Mill in his classic essay 'On Liberty' accorded it a vital place in the organisation of human activities.

'There is a limit to the legitimate interference of collective opinion with individual independence: and to find that limit, and maintain it against encroachment, is as indispensable to a good condition of human affairs as protection against political despotism.'

Thus privacy may be viewed as a balance between the individual's desire for secrecy and anonymity and the collective societys' need to know for the good of all.

This balance has been affected by two distinct trends since Mills' time.

- An individual desire for increased privacy and isolation. This has been aided by the opportunity of individuals to secure *physical isolation* in private dwelling houses. Such 'rights' have also been encouraged by democratic forms of government which stress the importance of the individual.

- The increasing complexity of modern society, and the inter-dependency of so many of its parts, demands more information about individuals if that complexity is to be managed successfully. The delivery of welfare, policing and other regulatory controls, necessarily requires individual information if they are to operate successfully.

Thus there have been (and continue to be) important pressures on both sides of the privacy see-saw. A number of textbooks explore the political and social issues in great depth (see Further reading) and you are encouraged to dip into these. However, the main concern of this book is computers — how have these affected and shaped the notion of privacy?

15.2 Computers and privacy

Sieghart (see Further reading) contends that computers have changed information systems in seven fundamental ways. Compared with their manual predecessors, computerised information systems tend to lead to the following.

- More transactions being recorded.

- Records being kept for longer. The use of a computer means that there is no premium on space. Thus it is possible to record more information 'just in case it is needed' and there is no pressure to discard old records to 'free some filing cabinets'. This means that colossal data bases may be built up:

  'By December 1977 details of 17.7 million vehicles and owners were recorded on the Police National Computer (PNC), and by the time of writing (summer 1979) the total had reached almost 19 million.' D. Campbell *Computing* 20/03/80

  It also means that yesterday's mistake may be recorded for much longer, even when that 'mistake' is purely a matter of interpretation. Jones (see Further reading) quotes the case of a young Austrain boy who came to Britain as a refugee and was living in Coventry. He organised a number of regular social evenings with fellow Austrians, collecting a small sum from each person to pay for a room at the local YMCA.

  'Years later, having become a research engineer and a British subject, he found himself refused visas to the USA and Canada. Inquiries made by cousins in America disclosed that the black mark on his record was having been treasurer for the "Young Austrians of Coventry".'

  Thus the candidate was not only being punished for a past activity, but also for the connotation placed upon this by recruiting personnel. They obviously associated this club with subversive rather than social activities.

- Information is given to more people.

- Data is transmitted over public communication channels. Norman (see Further reading) noted three reasons for concern about the vulnerability of telecommunications. Firstly, a variety of unclassified (US) government information should be kept private in the national interest. He cited plans to support the US dollar in international financial markets as a typical example. Secondly, private and public networks were vulnerable to undetected interception. Protection against unauthorised monitoring was not a major design criteria for these or other nation's telephone networks. Finally, the government is a major user of common-carrier telecommunication systems.

  'The General Services Administration's Federal Telecommunications System makes extensive use of the facility logging over 200 million voice, data and facsimile calls each year. Some undetermined number of these calls undoubtedly warrant better safeguards against interception than are currently in place.'

- Fewer people know what is happening to the data.

- Data tends to be easier to access.

- Data may be manipulated, combined, correlated, associated and analysed to provide information which could not have been obtained without computers.

It is really the last facility that distinguishes the computer system from its manual predecessors. There are many examples where the cross-correlation of files has identified some person, trait or anomaly. The following example illustrates this and shows the potential, and dangers, of linking previously independent clerical systems.

15.3   National Health Service (NHS) — child health system

The NHS Child Health system consists of four separate, but linked, modules designed to monitor the health of a child from birth to school leaving age. These are shown diagrammatically below.

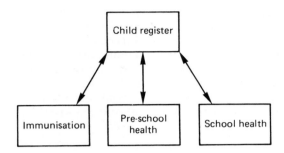

A flavour of the system may be obtained by listing the key parts of two of its sections.

Child register   (a)   Birth notification form filled in. Details of birth entered onto the system and lists of births produced automatically for the Registrar of Births.

(b)   On defined date, immunisation consent cards are sent to the child's Health Visitor.

(c)   After discussing immunisation issues with the parents, the Health Visitor returns the completed consent card and the record is updated with this information.

(d)   Facilities are provided to record children moving in and out of the area so that the file remains complete.

Immunisation   (a)   Immunisation invitations are raised at the appropriate time. These detail the time and place of the session together with the type of vaccinations that will be given. These appointment cards are sent directly to the child's parents or guardians.

(b)   At the same time a list of these appointments is sent to the General Practitioner (family doctor) or health clinic responsible for administering these vaccinations.

(c)   At the end of the scheduled vaccination session the appointment list is returned to the computer section annotated to show attendance.

(d)   Children who have not attended are immediately re-scheduled. If they fail to attend again their Health Visitor is informed and is expected to make a visit.

(e)   The annotated list is used a basis for automatic payment of the General Practitioner.

The system is designed to help the individual as well as society as a whole. For the latter it offers the 'basis for health, education and social services planning in the future.' It is designed to help increase the penetration of child health services and to improve the uptake of vaccination programmes. The data stored should provide a comprehensive profile of the young population aiding administrators to plan services and facilities accordingly. Thus birth rate trends may be identified and extrapolated permitting the planning of education provision and teacher training programmes that take into consideration the bulges and dips that regularly pass through the demographic structure of a nation. This seems to offer an attractive alternative to the panic recruitment and cuts that mark so much contemporary education policy.

On the other hand, the individual is also helped by the system's ability to identify certain persons or groups that are not using the child health services correctly or adequately. Thus parents who have not taken their children for immunisation may be quickly identified and Health Visitors sent to offer advice. Furthermore, certain sections of the community are notoriously reluctant to take up the services on offer. These may be listed out (say, all those in a certain ethnic group) and sent a special mailing in a given dialect or language. Identifying certain groups to offer positive help is not uncommon. Another example — taken from *Computer Weekly* — is reproduced below.

'Council system picks poor tenants' 26/11/81
by Philip Hunter

'The question of computers invading privacy arose when unclaimed benefits were paid to council house tenants in Harlow, Essex. An ICL 2904 was used to identify 315 poor families who had failed to claim their welfare benefits out of a total of 3740 tenants.

The exercise was part of a pilot study conducted by Harlow Council aimed at reducing a mountain of unclaimed benefits. Many people entitled to benefits are not on record.

The idea of computers conducting means tests from files of poor people is anathema to many but according to Harlow Council's head of information services, Martin Kaye, there was no question of invading privacy.

'This was purely aimed at people whose records we already have and who, because of stigma, shame or embarrassment fail to claim social security or family income supplements,' he said.

This facility of identifying distinct population targets is also a feature of the Child Health system. In the summer of 1978 the medical press was particularly concerned with the merits and disadvantages of the system. Many letters contained anxieties about the privacy of information and the usurption of the 'special relationship' between patient and doctor. This culminated in a letter sent from Dr John Dawson, an assistant secretary of the British Medical Association (BMA), to David Ennals, the then Secretary of State, criticising the system on the grounds that it would threaten fundamental principles of confidentiality. . . (letter to David Ennals and all other MPs 31/08/1978).

Two specific issues are worth further discussion.

15.3.1 Concern about the actual data gathered
For example, suggested data items on the birth notification form included:

Previous abortions
One-parent family (Y or N)
Ethnic group

while the example immunisation consent card asked for

Does the child's surname differ from the mother's?
Father's occupation

The latter was used for social class coding.

The forms also included a number of medical data items which many doctors felt transcended the limits of privacy. Whether such data items are *actually* a threat to individual privacy is a question which does not have a general answer, it depends solely upon the perception of the individuals concerned.

15.3.2   The coordination of files

The majority of the data collected had previously been available in separate files, offices and locations. The Child Health system depended on the coordination of such information for its very success. This may be acceptable whilst a benevolent government is in power. However, if the political environment changes, then files which were once used for identifying groups with certain health risks may now be accessed for providing a hit list for state exterminators. The system cannot preserve the anonymity of the individual and 'who knows who will be the next operators of this or other data banks. Russian experience suggests that doctors may be subject to political pressure.' (Dr Forrester, letter to the *British Medical Journal*, 09/08/1971).

This latter point is difficult to contest. Such systems may seem acceptable (or not) in the current political climate, but if this were to change radically then they would become a powerful tool of repression. No amount of security and legislation can overcome this. Sensitive systems will not self destruct if the Blue Meanies come to power!

15.3.3   Summary

The correlation of data files is always likely to cause controversy. Public opinion has been mobilised in cases where such association has been both criticised and advocated. The latter cases are distinguished by errors made by social care authorities where information unwittingly relevant to the case was held by another public body. This has led to unnecessary suffering and death, and pleas for 'more co-ordination' to reduce such incidents. This is also true of police investigations, where outdated manual records have not permitted the flexibility of retrieval and correlation permitted by computer systems. Thus computerisation creates both problems and opportunities.

15.4   Data Protection legislation

A number of attempts were made to introduce Data Protection legislation in the 1960s. These were mainly private member's bills and stood little chance of reaching the statute book. In 1970 an official committee, under the chairmanship of Kenneth Younger, was established to consider privacy intrusions. However, they were restricted to examining the private sector, a limit that caused some concern.

The Young Committee took evidence as well as undertaking a limited amount of field research. Lindop (in Benyon and Bourne — see Further reading) describes how people were asked

'If there was freely available in your public library a list in which all the properties in the various streets in your town were listed in numerical order, and against each number there was the full name of those people who lived there, would you regard that as in invasion of personal privacy?'

35% of the respondents said 'yes' and moreover, 'there ought to be a law against it.' This was, in fact, a description of the electoral register which is available in public libraries in the United Kingdom. Not only was it not recognised as such in the Younger fieldwork, but 35% of the people questioned saw it as a significant privacy threat.

The Younger Committee made a series of recommendations and the Government reacted to these by producing a White Paper on the subject in 1975 — three and a half years after the Younger Commission had reported! This paper also established a Data Protection Committee to advise the government on legislative requirements. The Chairman of this later committee was Sir Norman Lindop and his team reported in December 1978. However, much of his work was lost in the change of government in 1979 (form Labour to Conservative) and the subsequent White Paper of 1982 did not borrow many of its principles. The Data Protection Authority proposed by the Lindop Committee was replaced by a Registrar appointed by the Crown. Similarly, statutory codes for practice favoured by Lindop were rejected as impractical as they would impose 'an unacceptable burden on resources'. It was the 1982 paper that formed the basis of the subsequent Data Protection Bill considered in Section 15.5.

Pressure for Data Protection legislation came from three sources.

15.4.1   Council of Europe Convention

The Council of Europe (which has no connection with the EEC) drew up a voluntary charter which individual countries could agree to if they so wished. This agreement is established by signing the Convention and then passing national legislation that enshrines the principles of the charter. When five countries have ratified the Convention by passing appropriate laws, then its terms become mandatory on all ratifying countries. The United Kingdom signed the Convention in 1981 but its failure to develop national legislation meant that it ran the risk of economic discrimination. Ratifying countries might oppose the export of data to a country that did not have Data Protection legislation. This point is recognised by the UK Data Protection Registrar who explained that one of the concerns of the 1984 Data Protection Act was to counter problems:

'arising from the possibility of damage to our international trade which might occur if the United Kingdom were not to ratify the "Council of Europe Convention for the Protection of Individuals with regard to Automatic Processing of Personal Data". Countries ratifying this Convention might place restrictions on the transfer of personal data to countries which have not ratified it.'
The Data Protection Act — 1984   Guideline No. 1.

15.4.2   UK industry

There was great concern that trading losses might result from the lack of legislation. Non-European countries were also beginning to enact laws that specifically disallowed the export of data to countries that did not have adequate Data Protection legislation. This was of particular significance to multi-national companies and one large corporation cited it as their main reason for considering the re-location of their headquarters to a European country that had already implemented the requirements of the Council of Europe Convention. Certainly *The Times* saw industry pressure as a significant issue:

'Commerce — not liberty is the motive power behind the Government's legislation in the field of data protection. Fear of losing markets, not the desire to defend individual Privacy against computer driven intrusions colours the clauses of the Data Protection Bill. . .' *The Times* 12/02/83

15.4.3   Human rights and professional groups

Civil liberty pressure groups, especially the National Campaign for Civil Liberties (NCCL), were active in the fight for adequate legislation. However, there has been little apparent concern from the public at large, despite a number of well researched TV documentaries that recounted a series of harrowing tales. Indeed, Norman Lindop once commented that 'what we needed at the time was a jolly good scandal to give us some political leverage.'

Despite this indifference the Data Protection Registrar feels that individual privacy is an important concern of the Data Protection Act. He sees it as dealing with the problems

'arising from the threat which the mis-use of the power of computing equipment might pose to individuals. This concern derives from the ability of computing systems to store vast amounts of data, to manipulate data at high speed and, with associated communications systems, to give access to data from locations far from the site where the data are stored': Data Protection Act   Guideline No. 1

15.5   Data Protection Act — 1984

The first bill was presented in 1982 but it was lost as a result of the General Election. The bill was re-presented in 1983 and received the Royal Assent on the 12th July 1984. There are a number of excellent books and pamphlets on the subject (see **Further reading**).

15.5.1   Data Protection Act — brief details

Definitions

Data   means information recorded in a form in which it can be processed by equipment operating automatically in response to instructions given for that purpose.

Note   the word 'automatic' is important. The Act excludes manual records.

Personal data   means data consisting of information which relates to a living individual who can be identified from that information, including any expression of opinion about the individual but not any indication of the intentions of the data user in respect of that individual.

Note   identification may be direct (through names) or through codes.

Data subject   means an individual who is the subject of personal data.

Note   A company is not an individual unless that company is a sole trader.

Data user   means a person who holds data and/or controls the contents and use of the data

Note   A data user will apply to the Data Protection Registrar for details of his data to be placed on the Data Protection Register.

Principles

The information to be contained in personal data shall be obtained, and personal data shall be processed, fairly and lawfully.

Personal data shall be held only for one or more specified and lawful purposes.

Note   these purposes will be specified on the Register.

Personal data held for any purpose or purposes shall not be used or disclosed in any manner incompatible with that purpose or those purposes.

Personal data held for any purpose or purposes shall be adequate, relevant and not excessive in relation to that purpose or those purposes.

Personal data shall be accurate and, where necessary, kept up to date.

Note   where accurate means correct and not misleading as to any matter of fact.

Personal data held for any purpose or purposes shall not be kept for longer than is necessary for that purpose or purposes.

An individual shall be entitled:

A)   At reasonable intervals and without undue delay or expense to

- be informed by any data user whether he holds personal data of which that individual is the subject, and
- to access any such data held by a data user; and

B)   where appropriate, to have such data corrected or erased.

Appropriate security measures shall be taken against unauthorised access to, or alteration, disclosure or destruction of, personal data and against accidental loss or destruction of personal data.

Rights of individuals

The data subject has right of access to data held about him or herself. This is in accordance with one of the principles of data protection and is laid down in detail in the Act itself. An individual shall be entitled to

- be informed by any data user whether the data held by him includes personal data of which that individual is a data subject; and
- to be supplied by any data user with a copy of the information constituting any such personal data held by him.

The request from the data subject for such information must be made in writing and be accompanied by the required fee.

The courts may order data users to pay compensation for damage or distress suffered by data subjects as a result of:

loss of data
destruction of data without the authority of the data user
disclosure of, or access to, data without the authority of the data user
inaccurate data

Exceptions

The data user does not have rights of access to the data if it is held for certain circumstances or for certain purposes or reasons. Briefly, these are as follows.

- Data held for

  'the prevention or detection of crime'
  'the apprehension or prosecution of offenders'
  'the assessment or collection of any tax or duty'.

- Data held by a government department, supplied by a third party, in connection with the making of judicial appointments. This covers the appointment of judges but not of jurors.

- Data to which legal professional privilege (as between lawyer and client) could be claimed.

- Data held solely for statistical or research purposes.

- Data whose disclosure is prohibited by law where the Secretary of State decides that this prohibition should override the subject access provisions in the interests of the data subject or any other individual and makes an order conferring exemption.

- Data covered by the Consumer Credit Act 1974.

- Data held solely for recovery or 'back up'.

- Data held by regulatory bodies discharging statutory functions in connection with the protection of the public against dishonesty, incompetence or malpractice in financial matters.

The Secretary of State may also make Orders exempting from the subject access provisions or modifying these provisions in relation to:

- data concerning physical or mental health or social work.

The exemptions above apply to **subject access**. Certain systems are excluded from the act *as a whole*. These include the following.

- Personal data which are required to be exempt for the purpose of safeguarding national security.

- Personal data held for the purposes of payroll, pensions or accounts.

- Data held by an individual 'concerned only with the management of his personal, family or household affairs or held by him only for recreational purposes.'

- Data held by an unincorporated members' club and relating only to members.

- Data consisting only of names and addresses and used only for the distribution of articles or information.

15.5.2 Reaction to the Act

The Data Protection legislation has, to date, largely been greeted with dismay or indifference. There was an undeniable feeling that the bill exempted most of the systems that people really cared about and which caused most reported privacy incursions. On the other hand a large amount of trivial information would have to be registered at a significant cost to the data user. Applications for registration have run considerably below expectations.

However, it must be recognised that the Data Protection Registrar acknowledged the partial nature of the Bill in his first Guideline.

'The Act lays down a framework of law within which its purpose can be achieved. This approach has two consequences.

- There will inevitably be uncertainty about the application of the Act in particular circumstances.

- Some uncertainties may only be definitely resolved following decisions by the Data Protection Registrar, the Data Protection Tribunal or the Courts.'

Furthermore, it now appears that blanket exceptions will not be granted. Elbra (see Further reading) makes the point that the exception of data held for the 'prevention or detection of crime' should not give the police the right to refuse access to any data that they hold. In the case of the police 'they might be entitled to refuse access to their modus operandi files or their files of suspected persons, but not the criminal records, which refer to crimes which have already resulted in prosecution.'

Thus the Data Protection Act has to settle down and its scope must be determined through case law. Attention will also have to be increasingly focused on the *software implications* of the Act. At the time of writing most firms are concerned with the administrative burden of the Act: filling in forms, appointing responsible staff, circulating information etc. However, complaints are already being made about the cost of implementing system changes so that software complies with the requirements of the Act. Jeff Pipe, assistant city treasurer of Birmingham City Council, described the provisional figure of £13m in costs overall to local authorities to implement the legal requirements of the Act as 'laughable' (*Computing* 13/09/84). The same article describes just one of the software requirements of the legislation.

'to resist a charge of holding incorrect data on your file you have to indicate whether the data was supplied by the data subject or by a third party. Computer files will have to be amended to include that indicator.'

15.6   Summary

Thus privacy is not only a difficult concept to define, but is also subject to changes in definition and importance. Cases of abuse are well documented (see Jones for example) but it has never been a significant public issue. Legislation has been slow in coming and the presented bill has faced severe criticisms. However, it is fair to say that the law is only in its early stages and the real test of its enforcement and relevance will be when the first cases come to the courts. This is something that should be carefully observed as the implications of court decisions are likely to have a significant effect on software developers and users.

Further reading

Bourn C and Benyon J, *Data Protection: Perspectives on Information Privacy*, Leicester University (1983)

An account of contributions made to a conference on 11th May 1983 at the University of Leicester. The contribution of Paul Sieghart is particularly relevant, coherent and incisive.

Elbra R, *Guide to the Data Protection Act*, NCC (1984)

A useful, short (32 pages) guide to the Act.

The Data Protection Registrar, *The Data Protection Act – 1984   Guidelines*, 1985 onwards

The Data Protection Registrar publishes a series of guidelines on the Act. Guideline No. 1 appeared in February 1985 and provided an introduction and guide to the Act. It promised a 'living series which will be used to illustrate new or changed circumstances as the operation of the Act developes.' The first examples of these guidelines were well presented and written. More information should be available through contacting the

Office of the Data Protection Registrar
Springfield House
Water Lane
Wilmslow
Cheshire
SK9 5AX

Younger K (Chairman), *Report of the Committee on Privacy*, Cmnd 5012, HMSO,   July 1972
Lindop (Chairman), N *Report of the Committee on Data Protection*, Cmnd 6353,   HMSO, December 1975
Data Protection: the Government's Proposals for Legislation, Cmnd 8539, April 1982
Data Protection Act 1984

These reports and bills give a valuable insight into how privacy issues have been viewed by legislators and investigators. The scope of the study has narrowed over time and the final Data Protection Act is a pale shadow of the measures suggested in the Younger and Lindop reports.

Sizer R and Newman P, The Data Protection Act, Gower Press (1984)

An in-depth look at the Act, with each paragraph diagnosed in detail. The implications of the Act for managers and professionals are also examined.

Three more general books on privacy are given below.

Jones, M *Privacy*, David and Charles (1974)

This book is essentially a collection of articles, papers, quotes and examples collected under a number of appropriate headings. It is one of a series of 'Sources for Contemporary Issues' published by David and Charles. Extensive sections from the Younger Report, together with earlier debate by MPs on the issue.

Warner M, and Stone, M *The Data Bank Society*, Allen and Unwin (1970)

An excellent book which examines privacy from a number of angles. Useful discussion on the nature of privacy and very well researched. Do not be put of by its age. You may also find it in second hand book shops. My copy cost 25p!

Sieghart, P *Privacy and Computers*, Latimer (1976)

Another excellent book, written by one of the acknowledged experts on the subject.

16
Security

16.1 Security and controls

Controls have to be implemented at all levels. Too many texts stress operational controls at the cost of considering those in system development and the corporate structure. This chapter uses Wong's (see Further reading) 'onion-skin' approach which provides a framework for systematically identifying computer-related risks. The basic areas of risk are shown in Fig. 16.1. Each of these will be considered separately, with examples and counter-measures suggested where appropriate.

16.2 Areas of risk

16.2.1 Corporate objectives

These risks occur where the computer installation is affiliated to a company whose objectives do not command general approval. This may be due to a number of factors such as pollution, warfare contracts, personal injustice or political animosity. Wong states that

'extremists, urban guerillas or radical pressure groups who may be prepared to resort to indiscriminate violence to achieve their objectives, may well regard the computer installation as an attractive target.'

The computer centre is an appealing target as it represents a very valuable asset in a small geographical area. Computer systems have already been singled out for terrorist activity. Norman (see Further reading) identifies five cases where the motive for destruction was primarily political. Two will be covered here.

Case 1
New Society (17/04/80) reported two attacks on central installations at Philips Data Systems and CII-Honeywell Bull in Toulouse, France. Unidentified intruders sabotaged both hardware and software. At Philips cassette tapes, floppy discs and punched cards holding vital programs and data were all burnt. At CII-Honeywell Bull a petrol bomb was used to destroy a small computer used for demonstrations. The most likely perpetrator of the attacks was CLODO — The Committee for the Liquidation and Misappropriation of Computers — an organisation which has carried out subsequent attacks on computer installations in France. CLODO (a slang word for tramp) stated that

'we are workers in the computer sector, and therefore well placed to understand the current and future dangers of data processing and telematics. The computer is the favourite tool of the dominant. It is used to exploit, put on file, control and repress.'

The claim that the saboteurs were computer professionals was supported by a director of Philips who felt that 'they were not vandals, least of all amateurs.' The damage had not been indiscriminate.

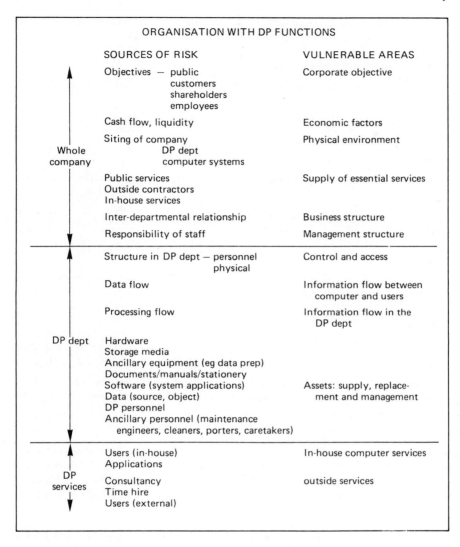

ORGANISATION WITH DP FUNCTIONS

SOURCES OF RISK	VULNERABLE AREAS
Objectives — public customers shareholders employees	Corporate objective
Cash flow, liquidity	Economic factors
Siting of company DP dept computer systems	Physical environment
Public services Outside contractors In-house services	Supply of essential services
Inter-departmental relationship	Business structure
Responsibility of staff	Management structure
Structure in DP dept — personnel physical	Control and access
Data flow	Information flow between computer and users
Processing flow	Information flow in the DP dept
Hardware Storage media Ancillary equipment (eg data prep) Documents/manuals/stationery Software (system applications) Data (source, object) DP personnel Ancillary personnel (maintenance engineers, cleaners, porters, caretakers)	Assets: supply, replace- ment and management
Users (in-house) Applications	In-house computer services
Consultancy Time hire Users (external)	outside services

Left-margin labels (top to bottom): Whole company · DP dept · DP services

Fig. 16.1 The 'onion skin' approach to the systematic identification of computer related risks (adopted from K K Wong, *Computer Security: Risk Analysis and Control*, Courtesy of the National Computing Centre Ltd)

Case 2
Norman states that in a two year period (1976–8), the Italian 'Communist Combat Unit' carried out bombing attacks against at least ten computer centres. The cost of these operations was estimated at ten million dollars. Two examples must suffice.

- 10/06/77 Univac 1110 — Rome University
  CPU covered with petrol and ignited.

- 03/12/78 Honeywell 66 — Italian Ministry of Transport computer covered with petrol and set on fire. Files destroyed included those holding data on stolen vehicles and false number plates.

Honeywell was identified as a particular target because of its 'imperialist aims to infiltrate and direct the information services of the bourgeois state.'

Wong suggests the following counter measures.

- Frequent inspection of information sources to observe changes and review security strategy.
- Education of the public. (By this I think he means propaganda!)
- Observation of safety regulations.

16.2.2   Economic factors
Trade problems and recession may create a number of circumstances which affect the security of the computer department. Economic issues will be important both to the individual (who may be suffering personal money problems) and to the group involved in organised collective bargaining. Precautions will also have to be taken to secure continuity of supply and maintenance.

Case 1
Computer Weekly (24/07/80) ran an article on a dispute involving operators and programmers at the West Midland Regional Health Authority which showed 'once again, the importance and power of computer staff.' Staff at the computer centre were unhappy with a pay offer which, if accepted, would break the traditional link between the NHS and Civil Service annual pay awards. Their action was to refuse to process the pay awards made to Midlands doctors and dentists. The back pay owed stood at about £3.5 million at the time of the article, which concluded with the news that

'the doctors and dentists are understandably rather annoyed about waiting for their 31% pay rise and have issued a writ against the WMRHA, claiming breach of contract.'

Case 2
The Times (24/030/1973) reported on a cashier who embezzled $1 500 000 from a savings bank in New York. The cashier was a compulsive gambler and every cent was spent on this obsession. Fraud was undertaken by altering input data and juggling accounts to produce the correct information when required. Undetected mistakes were explained away as teller errors.

Wong suggests a number of counter-measures including contingency plans for industrial action, perhaps using back-up personnel. The cashier in Case 2 also gave ideas for precautions.

'Banks place an almost unshakeable trust in their employees. I was not polygraphed when I was first employed. And the bank did not have a policy for periodic polygraphing. If they had, it would have stopped me cold.'

'. . . this could have happened at any bank where too much supervisory authority was placed in one individual's hands. . . . Any bank with only one supervisor is asking for trouble. If there were another supervisor with the same responsibilities as myself, I do not think I could have stolen from the bank.'

16.2.3   Physical environment
Typical problems are fire, floods, pollution and explosions. Other risks may include air crashes (if the computer centre is built near an airport), road accidents and vandalism. Wong feels that

'of the many problems which threaten the computer operation, those affecting the physical environment are perhaps the easiest to comprehend and for which to organise safeguards.'

Case 1
Norman describes the fire at the Lyon-Sevigne national network station on 09/11/81. The exchange is a major switching point for telecommunications networks and contains telephone, telex and data switches. In less than half an hour two floors of equipment had been burnt and water and smoke damage extended to the telex equipment on the ground floor. Norman (whose source was a private communication) described the cost as incalculable.

Case 2
An indication of the ever-present hazard of fire is provided by the case of the Pentagon fire of 1959 where three complete computer systems were destroyed, valued at $6.3 million.

Case 3
A gas leak caused the $290 000 explosion at Fort Wayne which destroyed a Honeywell 200 of the Phelps-Dodge company.

Counter measures against natural hazards include:

* secondary, emergency sources of supply
* back-up generators
* recovery procedures and disaster plans
* off-site storage of back-up data and programs
* fire-proof safes and other precautions.

In the latter two cases described above, the fireproof cabinets survived and tapes and disks were undamaged.

16.2.4 Supply of essential services
Essential services include water, heat, gas, and most crucially, power. Loss of these facilities may either be deliberate (due to an industrial dispute) or accidental (a dog chewing through a power cable). Whatever the reason a back-up generator is essential if computer operations must continue. Security problems may also result from breakdown of communication lines or wire tapping.

Case 1
Computer Weekly (21/07/77) reported the effects of a power failure in New York on 13/07/77. Most systems continued on their back-up generators, but the buildings they were housed in often had no lights, lifts or air conditioning. Power was not restored for 24 hours. Most computer problems were due to incomplete file transactions.

Case 2
Norman reports the case of a stray dog chewing through a cable, necessitating the cancellation of a trial session while cable repairs were made.

Suggested counter measures include back-up supply services and disaster planning. Wong also suggests the taking out of insurance with special coverage.

16.2.5   Business structure

This will encompass fraud, industrial action and boycotts by user departments. It will also include circumstances where the management structure too easily permits fraudulent activity which can be blamed on 'computer errors'. Norman lists 20 cases where fraud was perpetrated by non-computer staff, and an example of over-delegation has already been identified in an earlier example. Two further cases must suffice.

Case 1

Three employees of a New York securities firm embezzled at least $500 000 over several years by taking money from customer's accounts. Clients who noticed these mistakes were told that they were due to 'computer errors' and that the true amount was known to the company and so the statements produced by the computer system could safely be ignored. Some customers became very suspicious when subsequent statements were also incorrect.

Case 2

Norman gives another example which illustrates that even the well paid employee is not above fraud. A Vice President of a bank was given authorisation to balance differences between accounts during the conversion of a manual ledger system to a computerised one. In collusion with an outsider, the Vice President embezzled about $6 000 000 by omitting transactions from the manual system. The balances were maintained by adjustments that he had been empowered to make.

Controls will also be required over the management structure *within* the data processing department. Senior DP management are in powerful positions because they realise that few of their colleagues are technically able to question or assess the performance or activity of the computing department. It is difficult to see *what is actually going on* in the section. Poor controls and over-delegation can quickly lead to opportunities for fraud. Norman lists 27 cases where the perpetrator belonged to the computing staff.

Case 1

An Operations Manager at a branch of the Wells Fargo National Bank in Los Angeles pleaded guilty in August 1981 to embezzling $21 000 000 from his employees. The fraud was undertaken by creating a network of fictitious bank accounts with an increasing number of transactions used to overcome automatic error detection. The operation became increasingly complex and the manager was able to have fewer vacations. In the event, a clerical error led to the discovery of a fraud which had been going on for two years. The money was largely spent by his conspirators on high living and unsuccessful boxing promotions.

Case 2

Another case involving the Operations Manager was reported in *Computerworld* (15/08/73 and 22/08/73). This concerned the issue of one part of an in-house four part cheque to a conspirator, while the other three parts showed a legitimate contractor. The fraud had been going on for four and a half years (netting some $300 000) before it was eventually discovered during the Operations Manager's vacation. One of the false cheques was spotted by an employee and a subsequent investigation exposed the fraud.

The large number of fraud cases which were permitted, perhaps encouraged, by lack of attention to management reporting structures illustrates the need for effective counter measures in these areas. Careful consideration of the organisational structure is essential. Adequate reporting and auditing controls must be established in a structure that recognises a proper segregation of duties.

The risks identified so far are relevant to the whole company. However, there are also significant security problems within the data processing section itself. These may arise from staff relations, information flow, supply, replacement and management of computer resources, supplying or receiving computer services.

16.2.6 Staff relations
Wong states that 'demotivated staff are unlikely to obtain satisfaction from their jobs, and may well believe that they are inadequately rewarded or receive insufficient praise for their efforts. . .'. This may lead them in to temptation, attempting to by-pass the security system either as a challenge, or for financial gain. The incidence of crime by computer staff has already been commented upon and management examples given. Two further cases illustrate how personal problems led the protagonists into criminal activity.

Case 1
Norman recounts the case of a debt-ridden programmer who managed to transfer $100 from 41 different accounts into an account his wife had opened under an assumed name. The money was designed to fund a planned holiday.

Case 2
A 21 year old programmer developed a cheque handling system that ignored overdrafts in his own account. This was only discovered when the computer system broke down and the account processing had to be done by hand. By this time the overdraft stood at $1357.

Wong suggests some counter-measures that can be taken to prevent problems arising from staff relations. These include:

- job enrichment
- improved appraisal techniques
- staff motivation programmes
- profit sharing schemes
- worker participation.

16.2.7 Information flow
This encompasses flow of data from the DP department to the user and also within the computer section itself. This will include the disclosure or misuse of confidential information, perhaps for blackmail, by users and DP staff acting in collusion. Risks within the DP department include negligence, accidents and a lack of discipline in the development of systems. An example of the latter is provided by the computerisation of the Driver and Vehicle Licencing records at Swansea, Wales (the DVLC).

Case 1
The DVLC has been bedevilled by problems. Norman quotes examples of cost over-runs, implementation delays, errors in data handling and poor service to users. These were compounded by poor planning.

'It was originally intended that the system should be fully operational by the beginning of 1975, cost just over £9 million per annum and employ 4000 people. However, in the late seventies, the DVLC in fact cost around £45 million a year, employed nearly 8000 people and did not handle licence renewals, which were delegated to 81 local offices.'

Case 2
The entry of undetected erroneous data is a problem that can affect any software. One of the developer's key tasks is to define validation checks so that such data is not produced on output documents. These 'computer errors' usually make national headlines and give the media an opportunity to ridicule technology. Sometimes these errors are humourous, sometimes tragic and, occasionally, involve financial loss. Norman gives an interesting example of a 17 year old student who was expecting a tax refund of $14.39. Instead he discovered that he had been sent a cheque for $800 014.39. This was caused by part of the post-code being entered in the amount field by mistake. The tax authorities conceded that it was unlikely that this error would have ever come to light without the student's honesty. The books had been automatically balanced and all software checks had been made.

Audit controls are required to safeguard installations from these risks. These would include:

- auditing software
- data control techniques
- data validation procedures
- good documentation
- auditing of data and programs
- access control into computer systems
- good operations management.

Details of many of these controls are given in Chapter 17.

16.2.8   Risks arising from the supply, replacement and management of computer resources
Wong includes the following risks in this category:

- faulty equipment, stationery and software
- breakdown of hardware, software and systems
- arson, theft and sabotage
- business interruption
- misplacement or destruction of data, programs etc.
- out-of-date program and system documentation
- sickness and injury to senior staff
- industrial action and blackmail
- misappropriation of computer resources
- data corruption and decay of storage media.

Case 1
Computing (16/06/76) reported the theft of computer time by two programmers at Sperry-Univac. They used this time to run a music arranging business, developing a program to turn out sophisticated musical arrangements as well as recording their business transactions.

Case 2
Computer Weekly (06/08/81 and 07/01/82) reported the case of an analyst who ran his own business on his employer's (an insurance company) computer. He had written an accounting suite for his girlfriend's catering company, of which he was a Director and a company secretary. The programs were discovered while he was away on vacation when a programmer undertook some routine maintenance checks. His subsequent appeal was also reported in *Computer Weekly* (07/05/81) where an industrial tribunal was told how

'an insurance firm's IBM 3031 system was used to make pictures of Raquel Welch, Mickey Mouse and the Mona Lisa. . . (the computer was also used) to work out football permutations and (running) unauthorised programs which could have helped his girlfriend run her catering business.'

The employee's case claim of unfair dismissal was unsuccessful.

Adequate audit controls are required to counter these risks. These will include

- access controls
- reporting structures and responsibilities to handle irregularities, accidents and breakdowns
- good housekeeping and operating procedures
- establishing and maintaining rigorous standards.

16.2.9 Risks from supplying or receiving computer services
These arise from the moral and legal liabilities associated with offering services to both internal and external users. Such risks are particularly significant in offering services to external customers. Thus organisations selling DP services might have the following problems.

- Mis-routing of output.
- Poor delivery of services.
- Liabilities associated with late delivery and/or poor performance.
- Contractual risks.
- Staff misconduct.
- Professional errors and omissions on consultancy assignments.

Case 1
Norman reports the case of a service bureau specialising in payroll processing offering it for about half the normal cost. This low cost, and the completeness of the service, attracted some 425 clients. All aspects of the payroll were handled, including all withholding taxes. The bureau ran successfully for a while, although some payroll cheques did bounce — a mistake that was blamed on a 'home-town bank'. However, the bubble soon burst and

'when last seen, the service bureau owner, who had used his brother's name in conducting the operation, was heading East with his wife in a rented car. . . The total taken was probably in excess of $5 000 000.'

Case 2
The *New Scientist* (19/12/74) reported how a 15 year old Westminster schoolboy cracked the security system of a major London computer timesharing service. This was done without 'special technical gadgets and (he) started with no special knowledge of the computer's inner workings — instead he relied only on ingenuity and a teletype terminal in his school.'

Norman gives a series of examples where mischief was the main reason for fraudulent activity. These were committed by persons who he terms as the new generation of 'computer freaks' who explore computer systems and make mischievous changes. The term 'hacker' is now in general use.

Wong suggests a number of audit and contractual counter-measures designed to define the legal framework in which services and products are offered.

16.3　Summary

Thus security risks occur at a number of levels and the extent of computer fraud is debatable. Some commentators feel that it is under-estimated whilst others believe that the whole problem is inflated out of its true proportion. Norman comments that

'the vast majority of all computer insecurity incidents can be traced back to application programs. Most computer goofs are application program errors, either in program specification or writing. Most reported "computer fraud" has been achieved either by writing (rarely) fraudulent programs or by exploiting (commonly) loopholes deliberately or accidently left in programs'

Developing software controls that identify errors and unauthorised access is an important task and such controls are examined in detail in Chapter 17. However, having acknowledged this, it must also be stated that many lapses of physical security have also been recorded. Norman lists a catalogue of incidents identified by Lewis Security Systems. Three examples are listed below and they serve to demonstrate that computer security is perhaps not taken as seriously as it should be.

Case 1
The report of an open side door to a secure computer centre. This was used to pop outside for fresh air, although 'we are air-conditioned.'

Case 2
The case of an alert guard who noticed a visitor wearing the wrongly coloured badge, stopped the man, and immediately issued him with the correctly coloured badge for that area, without any interrogation.

Case 3
The computer complex with three computer halls protected by 11 locked doors each with a card lock. All 11 locks were jammed or distorted but 'we have not had them repaired because the large number of temporary staff on shifts would necessitate our issueing them all with cards.'

Further reading

This chapter is based around two books.

Norman A R D, *Computer Insecurity*, Chapman and Hall (1983)

A well-written catalogue of computer fraud cases. Extensively referenced and cross-referenced. Cases are organised by date, geographical area, target, victim type, loss, perpetrator, motive, legal action and source order.

Wong K K, *Computer Security: Risk Analysis and Control* NCC (1977)

This book provides the framework used in this chapter. Rather tersely presented and some of the counter-measures seem too general to be truly informative.

Other references include:

Martin, J, *Security, Accuracy and Privacy in Computer Systems*, Prentice-Hall (1973)

Farr, R *The Electronic Criminals*, McGraw-Hill (1975)

Parker, D *Crime by Computer*, Scribners (1976)

An interesting novel on the subject is
The Consultant, Ballatine Books (1978)

This was the basis of a short TV series of the same name, starring Hywell Bennett. Watch out for a repeat showing!

17
Auditing

Chapter 16 illustrated how security risks existed at many different levels and how a security policy is required that recognises this. This chapter examines some of these controls in greater detail. The term 'auditing' is used to cover all such controls, although some of the checks discussed here might be implemented by personnel who would not consider themselves to be auditors in the conventional sense.

Financial Auditors have existed for many years. Kelman states that 'their duties are settled by law and have been so since 1898 when Lord Justice Lopez gave judgement in the Kingston Cotton Mill Case.'

'An auditor is not bound to be a detective or. . . to approach his work with suspicion or with a foregone conclusion that something is wrong. He is a watchdog and not a bloodhound. . . If there is anything to excite suspicion he should probe it to the bottom; but in the absence of anything of that kind he is only bound to be reasonably cautious and careful. . .'

The 'watchdog' role of the auditor also applies to the more recent development of computer auditing.

17.1   The role of the computer auditor

Thomas and Douglas (see Further reading) suggest that it is not possible to give a definitive role for the computer auditor. However, they believe that the overall work should encompass:

- ascertaining the systems and reviewing the organisational and operational controls of the computer department
- ascertaining and reviewing application systems which are under development or being run
- carrying out audits of live data and results for systems in use
- carrying out an efficiency and effectiveness audit

They suggest three levels of control.

17.1.1   Organisational
This covers an overall review of general principles, management and organisation. Tasks might include the following.

- An investigation into how system developments are established, controlled and resourced.
- A review of whether there are adequate controls and division of duties in the specification, development, testing and incorporation of program amendments.

- An inspection of operating logs to see if they are properly maintained, scrutinised and filed.

17.1.2   Application review
This will consist of a general review of each separate application or procedure. Tasks which might be included are given below.

- A consideration of the feasibility study report to see whether it meets the defined terms of reference. An inspection of the development timetable to see whether it is realistic and fits in with corporate plans.

- An evaluation of the planned training strategy to see whether it is both reasonable and realistic.

- An inspection of system costings and the method adopted to 'charge' these out to users. An assessment of the principle and fairness of such charging arrangements.

17.1.3   Detailed review
This examines each part, routine and program in the system. It should consider such questions as the following.

- What checks are carried out on individual documents, and are these checks laid down in the manuals. Are such checks properly made and are they adequate?

- Is there any validation carried out during data preparation, and if so, is the correction of errors properly controlled?

- How is the confidentiality of information preserved, and how is the correct circulation of output ensured? What controls exist to stop unauthorised copies of data from being produced?

- Are there adequate on-line recovery and back-up procedures, so that the requirements of the system can always be met?

Thus auditing has a wide scope and is not purely concerned with compliance to established accounting and financial procedures. This range of activity may not be recognised by the organisation, or indeed by the auditors themselves. Chambers (see Further reading) believes that

'. . . auditing has been linked with the accounting function, and on the whole has not extended its scope to become interested in compliance or security within the data processing area.'

17.2   Types of control — specification and development

The auditor should be able both to participate in and critically evaluate the system specification document produced for development projects. It is essential that audit is considered at every stage of the system development cycle and not just tagged on at the end as a series of operational controls. Such participation will ensure that checks are both relevant and timely. It should also mean that the auditor has a detailed and complete picture of the system which has been built up over a long period of time. The task of auditing a system 'cold' is really quite daunting. The following stages can be identified in system audit.

17.2.1   Initial system proposal
The auditor will be concerned with such issues as:

- A review of the terms of reference to see if they are unambiguous and adequate for the task at hand. Sloppily defined terms of reference can lead to project difficulties and disagreements between the parties involved.

- The inspection of the time-table for the project, itemising the different stages and the resources needed. Project plans may be put together too hastily and without sufficient attention paid to the staff and computer resources required. Furthermore there may be a tendency to under-estimate requirements either because of genuine optimism or in the belief that 'this will get the project approved'. The auditor should scrutinise plans carefully and may also be responsible for the establishment of standards for project proposal documentation.

17.2.2   Audit of the outline proposal
At this stage the auditor will be able to make more specific recommendations. These will involve the review and assessment given below.

- A review of adequacy of the internal controls and checks through the system. At this stage these will not be specified in detail but the auditor will be looking for evidence that controls have been considered and that these appear to be both relevant and valuable.

- An assessment of the likelihood of the stated objectives of the system being achieved within the agreed time-scales and resource constraints. It is accepted that many computer projects over-run both in time and money. These factors have to be reviewed, so that changes in plans are justified, understood and sanctioned.

17.2.3   Audit of the detailed proposal (system specification)
It is at this stage that the auditor will be able to look at the system in greater detail. He or she will be able to assess more accurately the chance of project success and the resources that will be involved. Furthermore, the auditor will be able to consider the detailed audit checks that are planned and evaluate their relevance and completeness. Detailed tasks might include the following.

- An assessment of the clerical activities scheduled for the new system and the quality of staff to be used for those tasks. It is sadly true that many system developers do not give sufficient consideration to the clerical activities that surround their computer system. Norman made the point that many of the difficulties faced at the DVLC (see Chapter 16) were due to clerical rather than computer problems. These were sometimes caused by poor staff performance, but on other occasions by the designers under-estimating the time taken to perform certain clerical tasks.

- Adequate control procedures and checks are written into the system at each stage, so that some sort of checking can be performed independently of the computer system. These controls need to be scrutinised and evaluated. All parts of the system need to be examined to see if there are circumstances where the auditor feels that there should be checks but none appear to be planned.

17.2.4   Audit of programming and program testing
The auditor will have checked the system specification and will also evaluate the final delivered system. Therefore, he might consider that no audit is required in the program development stages. Some auditors might like to check program code, but it

is probably more sensible to restrict controls to program development standards and documentation. In general, standards are a good way of imposing controls and the auditor should be actively involved in their definition.

17.2.5 Auditing system implementation
This will involve the planning of the system delivery, including documentation and training. Suggested tasks include

- An examination of the manuals provided, ensuring that they are complete, up-to-date, and relevant to the users or operators that they are intended for. Back-up and emergency procedures should also be detailed. The manuals should be written in an appropriate language and, most importantly, be *correct for the current state of the system*. Manuals which do not reflect the present system configuration are both confusing and potentially damaging. Users expect to see the screens and report formats produced by the system to be the same as those that appear in their manual. When they do not do so, they become both confused and doubtful, and their confidence in the delivered system is reduced.

17.2.6 Audit of system testing
The auditor must be convinced that systems have been tested properly and in accordance with defined standards. He or she may request active participation in the system tests and help check out printed reports and forms. The auditor may also use this opportunity to test out the checks that he or she has suggested or authorised by entering invalid data. Once the system has been delivered the auditor should be an important member of any post-implementation review. At this stage the auditor will be reviewing the controls of the system to ensure both that they are adequate *and* that they are being adhered to. This will include the maintenance of back-up copies, files and documentation, which must be open to his or her inspection.

17.3   Audit — the control of data

It has been stressed that audit and security has much wider scope than purely operational controls. They are as much concerned with corporate responsibilities and management structures as with the correct input, output and processing of data. This wide ranging nature of control should be recognised in the definition and scope of the auditor's tasks.

However, it must still be said that most documented errors are caused by accident; the wrong input of data, incorrectly defined processing, misinterpreted output. These are due to genuine mistakes, mis-keying and misunderstandings. It is the task of the system developer to design systems that minimise the chance of such errors reaching processing or system outputs. Controls will be required on data at all stages of its collection, processing, storage and retrieval. Data should be accurate and complete at all times, and its manipulation both authorised and legitimate. It is important to recognise that the necessary controls will be implemented in the clerical procedures of the system as well as in the software itself.

17.3.1   Clerical controls
It may be possible to implement **control totals** that are summed both manually and automatically. These totals are compared and if they agree then the data is assumed to have been entered correctly and the batch can be posted for processing. Such totals are particularly common in accounting systems where the accuracy of data is paramount. For example, the SAGE accounts program maintains four totals which

should be checked against a manually compiled equivalent. Only if these four totals are correct may the batch of transactions be accepted and the appropriate ledgers and accounts be updated. Two of the control totals are net amount and VAT amount; the other two are the sum of the account numbers and the addition of all the nominal codes entered on the batch. These are useful accuracy checks but clearly they have no particular significance. These meaningless sums are often termed **hash totals**.

Clerical controls are also of importance where source documents are posted around sections of buildings. It is very easy for forms or returns to be 'lost in transit' with the result that certain transactions, such as employee payments, do not take place. Movement control is usually enforced by the completion of **batch control documents** that give sufficient information for the recipient to check for the completeness of contents. Typical of data on a control sheet would be the following.

- Serial number of the batch. To check whether this follows the last received batch of documents. Has a whole batch gone missing in the post?

- Count of batch contents. The number of forms that should be in the batch.

- Serial numbers of forms. The serial numbers or number range(s) of the enclosed forms.

Such checks will be a part of a data capture system that is designed around the guidelines offered in Part 2. You may recall that reducing entry errors was a major concern of input design. Similarly, a large data processing centre will have a section dedicated to data control, responsible for checking input data, enforcing input schedules, locating errors, organising and validating output etc. They will also wish to impose standards of good house-keeping so that disks are properly and clearly labelled, unused files deleted, proper control documentation established and maintained. This is often sadly missing in microcomputer installations where disks go unlabelled (or labels are never changed), hard disks become cluttered with obliquely named files which no-one can recall creating, let alone naming, and backup procedures are ignored because 'we haven't got enough spare disks.'

17.3.2   Software controls
The source for most of these checks will be a data element data dictionary definition. These will permit the formulation of a whole range of controls performed by the *software* itself. Thus the machine is now being used to trap input errors using the skill and knowledge of the system's developer. Some typical checks are given below.

Range checks
   The data has to lie within certain values. These may be set globally (e.g. Property Reference Code must be between 100 and 200) or may be more selective to identify uncommon occurences. Thus, if 90% of all Property Reference Codes are between 100 and 110, then legitimate, but infrequent codes may trigger a request for operator checking.

'You have entered code 121. This is a Warehouse. Please confirm that this code is correct. . .'

Sequence checks
   Used to test that transactions that are supposed to be in a certain order are actually arranged this way. Thomas and Douglas comment that

'although well-known, this check is not applied in systems as widely as it could be. Coupled with the issue of sequentially prenumbered stationery, where stationery control is exercised, this check can provide control over a number of aspects of the non-computer part of the system'.

Format checks

That data always conforms to the specified format. Thus a product code designated as two letters followed by four numbers is always entered this way. Invalid entries such as A2341 or AS231 are rejected.

Consistency checks

Two data items may be related in some way. Thus maternity leave is always associated with sex = 'female'. Many such relationships exist and should be exploited to the full. It should stop some of the more ludicrous errors like those quoted in Warner and Stone of one air*man* discharged on the grounds of pregnancy, and the award of a flying badge to a carpenter.

Record and item counts

Counting the items (how many invoices have been entered) represents a simpler but less reliable alternative to control and hash totals.

Flag fields

The inclusion of flag fields that record whether a certain state or process has taken place. These are essentially included in the file definition for *control purposes only*. Thus if a salary field has been up-dated the flag is set to a value which traps all subsequent attempts to access the salary information. It can be viewed as a switch that is set once and prevents any subsequent activity until it is re-set.

Code design

It may be feasible to implement a code design which has elements of self-checking. Thus the first facet of the code (say the first three numbers) may be split off and certain checks performed. Included, amongst these might be consistency checks against other parts of the code:

'If the first three numbers of the code are less than 100 check that the fourth number is not greater than 7.'

This code was part of one used for supply requisitioning. The first three numbers were employee codes. Those with a code beginning with less than 100 could not order more than £7(000) worth of goods.

A code is helped by the addition of a **check digit**. This represents a number added to the end of the code which permits the rest of the code to be checked for transcription, transposition and random errors. One of the most common methods of allocating a check digit is the modulus 11 algorithm. This is best illustrated by an example.

A company uses product numbers of six digits. 345213 is a typical example. It wishes to incorporate a check digit into the code in an attempt to reduce the number of clerical input errors. This will make a new seven digit code.

The method of calculation is as follows:

Number	3	4	5	2	1	3
Multiplier	6	5	4	3	2	1
Product	18	20	20	6	2	3
Sum of products	69					
Divide by modulus 11	6 remainder 3					

The remainder is added to the code to make the new one:

3452133

Everytime this code is entered by the operator the software undertakes a modulus 11 check to validate the check digit. If the last entered figure is 3 *and* the rest of the code is correct then the input is permitted. The value of this can be demonstrated by the effect of a simpler transposition error.

Number	3	5	4	2	1	3	3
Multiplier	6	5	4	3	2	1	
Product	18	25	16	6	2	3	
Sum of products	70						
Divide by modulus 11 remainder 4							

The check digit is incorrect and so an error has been made in the entry.

It should be recognised that all these checks should be applied together. The erroneous input 3542133 may have survived format and range checks only to be tripped up by the check digit. However, the latter is not a coding panacea. Thomas and Douglas point out that it will not prevent the mistake of a user who has a list of valid and verifiable numbers and applies the wrong one by mistake. They suggest 'a check digit system always has some value, but the auditor should assess how much reliance should be placed on it.'

17.4   Auditing techniques

17.4.1   Test data method

In this method, the auditor prepares some dummy data and passes it through the system. The effect of this data is predicted in advance: how it will be presented in reports, the effect of processes on it, which data items should be rejected or questioned etc. These predictions are then compared with the results from the system run and any discrepancies are investigated. In many respects it is like the system testing covered in Part 3, but in this instance it is undertaken by an external observer — an auditor — and not the system developer.

Test data may be constructed to examine the processing of normal, unusual and ridiculous figures. These figures must be carefully controlled within the system, so that legitimate transactions are not sparked off by them. There are many, perhaps apocryphal, stories of vanloads of goods touring the European mainland looking for fictitious addresses entered by auditors as part of the test data. In such instances the dummy nature of the data had not been recognised and as a result the usual administrative arrangements had been set in motion.

This latter problem can be overcome by establishing areas of the system which are specifically for audit testing purposes. Thus a firm may set up a customer, a department or an account specifically allocated to audit. This section of the system works like all the rest but the usual physical consequences of the processing are withheld. This so-called integrated test facility is usually feasible where the system has been designed with audit as one of its main design objectives. The weakness of this approach is ensuring that the dummy audit sections are actually working the same as the rest of the system and have not been singled out for special, legitimate processing! Chambers (see Further reading) states that the test data method may be used to good effect in the following circumstances.

- Test input data controls, including data validation.

- Test processing logic and controls.

- Test computation of such values as discounts, payslips, VAT and commission.

- Test related manual controls.

He feels that it is a useful audit tool but that it is very time consuming and only gives a snapshot of the system's activities. It only deals with dummy data and so 'it cannot be said to directly contribute to the verification of balance sheet and operating statement items, or any other items.' The external auditor will be more concerned with verification and so is more interested in an auditing technique which permits him or her to interrogate real data. This will not only give the verification required but also provide an insight into the system's controls. Direct access is provided by audit enquiry programs.

17.4.2 Audit enquiry programs

These packages vary widely in sophistication but they are primarily used to examine files, retrieve data and produce requested reports. They permit the auditor to access the system files and data directly and to make the required tests and enquiries on the actual operational figures. Chambers feels that such packages help the auditor in five ways.

- They compensate for the loss of visual evidence. The records may be read almost as if they were their physical equivalents.

- Data may be extracted for futher audit investigation. Thus problems and inconsistencies may be pursued through subsequent enquiries. In this way the audit enquiry program is a much more sensitive tool than the test data approach.

- They provide independent verification of the values, details and analysis of the presented data. The test data method cannot do this because it cannot use the real figures.

- Complex calculations may be conducted faster, more accurately and more completely than with clerical audit procedures.

- 'They allow identification of items which do not comply with the laid down system rules or which, while complying, seem unreasonable.'

An example of the use of an audit enquiry package and guidelines for their selection is given in Chambers.

17.4.3 Audit: the operating system

The operating system may be a useful source of audit information. Most operating systems maintain **operational logs** that record what use has been made of the system. In many practical instances it has been the operating system which has provided important clues about fraudulent activity. Evidence has included statistics about use, aborted attempts to log into certain files, high activity on files at unusual times and overuse of certain terminals.

A very useful review of the audit facilities of a selection of mainframe operating systems is given in Douglas (see Further reading) where Burroughs, Honeywell, IBM, ICL and Sperry operating systems are assessed and contrasted. Sandra Bennett describes the Burroughs System Log and lists the utilities which are available to interrogate it. These include an 'analyser' which can print all or part of either the current or previous logs.

'The utility provides facilities for printing information relating to periods of time, particular jobs or particular types of messages. One of these options will print a list of security violations. Another option will provide information on hardware faults . . .'

17.5 Audit — some further considerations

Special difficulties may be encountered in auditing certain types of configuration. This will be illustrated by considering two particular problem areas — on-line processing and microcomputers.

17.5.1 Audit of on-line systems

Many of the controls outlined earlier can only be sensibly applied to **batch** systems. In most instances they depend upon the existence of a physical document which can be used to verify the transaction. However, this is unlikely to be true of on-line systems where data is entered straight onto the system without any intervening form or paper document. The problems this can cause led to Hooper (quoted in Chambers) claiming that

'where on-line systems are concerned the matter of audit trails becomes more important than ever because the use of visual display input terminals is like writing in invisible ink.'

This creates the major problem of ensuring that the user can only gain access to authorised data and that he or she can only make the changes that are permitted. This requires a systematic approach to allocating security passwords and levels, and supporting these with appropriate application and system software. This is easier said than done! Even operating systems, which are generally the result of considerable software effort, may be breached by knowledgeable users.

Case 1
Computing (23/03/78) described how students at Thames Polytechnic were asked to break the security routines on a DEC System 10. Three students succeeded, breaking into a file that contained examination marks and amending their results.

Case 2
Norman (see Further reading) quotes the case of a programmer who breached a rival software company's security to locate and display the code of a proprietary software package.
   Many operating system developers have tried to offer flexibility in their software by giving more optional security facilities. These are useful when the computer section *know they exist, know how to use them and,* as importantly, *know when to use them.* However, such flexibility can lead to more opportunity for fraudulent activity. Bennett, in her review of the Burroughs Master Control Program (MCP), reveals that

'it is possible to compile and run the MCP with both the system log and the job log required options set off. Burroughs do not recommend this, but it is possible.'

Thus operating systems may not possess, either through omission or choice, adequate audit features. This is even more true of application software, particularly where audit and security has been given relatively low priority in the system design.

Thomas and Douglas list 21 checks that the auditor should make on the access controls of on-line systems. Four representative examples are given below.

- There is a limit to the number of false attempts permitted when trying to gain access from a terminal. After this limit has been passed, the terminal is locked out from the centre until the activity has been investigated.

- There is a logging system which records the use and work of the terminals, and summarises the nature of the valid use of each terminal and itemises its misuse.

- Passwords are used at different levels and for different operations such as access to the system, enquiry, input and update. A user may be issued with more than one password.

- There is a limit set on the amount of time during which a terminal can be actively continuous, and after that time it is required to repeat the 'sign-on' procedure. This limit should be monitored, reviewed and enforced.

Thus, the complexity of developing and operating an on-line system poses additional audit problems which have to be considered and overcome.

17.5.2 Audit of microcomputers
Many microcomputer implementations use packaged software. The auditor must evaluate the audit features of competing packages and so contribute to the eventual selection of an appropriate product. Features of importance include the following.

- The provision of a complete and adequate audit trail.

- Data validation facilities, particularly in input control.

- An assessment of the product's documentation.

- Password levels and flexibility. Password maintenance and security. How easy is it to find out the allocated passwords and change them?

The operating system is one of the most fundamental sources of audit information. Mainframe computers maintain detailed logs as a matter of course (unless they are turned off!) and have often provided the information required to trap unauthorised activity. Microcomputers usually have very rudimentary logging facilities, if any at all! The log might detail only the name of the file, its size and the date and time that it was last accessed. Thomas and Douglas recognise this and suggest that 'a manual log be maintained in an agreed form. The auditor should review the type of logging system in operation, and should carry out random checks on the log to ensure that programs were run as scheduled, and they only accessed permitted files.' This may appear to be good sense but it does seem rather optimistic. It is unusual for many users to know what files are on a disk, let alone details of the last amendments and updates. The security and audit shortcomings of microcomputer operating systems are likely to continue reducing the chance of performing an effective microcomputer system audit.

17.6   Summary

An interesting insight into the extent of system audit is provided in a paper by Chambers (see Further reading). He quotes US research showing that 73% of internal audit departments audit computer systems whilst they are under development. 58%

are involved in system testing, 35% are required to sign-off new systems before they can be implemented and 19% are subsequently asked to sign-off program modifications. 64% claim to review program code, but only 10% do this regularly. In contrast a 1977 UK report (Chambers further reading) showed that 'whereas 96% of public sector organisations use computers for financial systems, only 16% employs specialist audience and 28% make no audit checks at all of computer based systems.' Certainly, auditors profession has been slow to come to terms with computer systems and has rarely controlled them with the thoroughness that they deserve. Furthermore, there has been a tendency for computer specialists to give too little weight to audit and not to plan for it properly in the system design. Audit and security features often appear as 'optional bolt-on extras' and may be the first things to be sacrificed when software has to be cut down in size to improve its speed or portability.

There are signs that the two professions are coming closer together and realising their complementary roles in software development. It is slightly ironic that this is taking place at a time when the proliferation of uncontrolled microcomputers with their rudimentary operating systems is making many applications virtually unauditable.

Further reading

This chapter is based around four excellent books

Chambers A *Computing Auditing*, Pitman (1981)

Chambers A and Court, J *Computing Auditing (Second Edition)*, Pitman (1986)

A very readable and comprehensive book covering most aspects of computer auditing. It also includes a useful guide to audit enquiry packages and their selection. Less complete on the technical aspects of software control.

Thomas A and Douglas I *Audit of Computer Systems*, NCC (1981)

Wide coverage of auditing tasks. Its more comprehensive treatment of computer issues makes it an excellent complement to the Chambers book discussed above.

Douglas I (ed), *Audit and Control of Systems Software*, NCC (183)

This text covers the security aspects of system software in detail and is well worth dipping into. The book is a collection of individual articles and I feel that there is some unevenness in both content and presentation. Authors have not always adhered to the same format and this makes comparisons very difficult. Furthermore, some of the contributors appear to be over-complimentary in their review of products. Sandra Barnett's article on the Burroughs system is both well written and even handed and is recommended reading.

Other references include:

Chambers A, *'Computer Fraud' The Computer Journal*, **21** No. 3, 1978

Pritchard J, *Computer Security: Security Software* NCC (1980)

Millichamp A, *Auditing*, DP Publications (1984)

Index

DRAGON STORM

Skye and Soulsinger

ALASTAIR CHISHOLM

Illustrated by Eric Deschamps

nosy
crow

First published in the UK in 2023 by Nosy Crow Ltd
Wheat Wharf, 27a Shad Thames,
London, SE1 2XZ, UK

Nosy Crow Eireann Ltd
44 Orchard Grove, Kenmare,
Co Kerry, V93 FY22, Ireland

Nosy Crow and associated logos are trademarks
and/or registered trademarks of Nosy Crow Ltd

Text © Alastair Chisholm, 2023
Cover illustration © Ben Mantle, 2023
Inside illustrations © Eric Deschamps, 2023

The right of Alastair Chisholm and Eric Deschamps to be
identified as the author and illustrator of this work has been asserted.

ISBN: 978 1 83994 706 3

A CIP catalogue record for this book is available from the British Library

Printed and bound in Great Britain by Clays Ltd, Elcograf S.p.A.

Papers used by Nosy Crow are made from wood grown in sustainable forests.

1 3 5 7 9 10 8 6 4 2

DRAGON STORM

Skye and Soulsinger

Also in the series:

TOMAS AND IRONSKIN

CARA AND SILVERTHIEF

ELLIS AND PATHSEEKER

MIRA AND FLAMETELLER

KAI AND BONESHADOW

ERIN AND ROCKHAMMER

CONNOR AND LIGHTSPIRIT

ROYAL PROCLAMATION:

There are dragons in the land of Draconis.
The evil lands of Venn and Borolo are
sending dragons against us. His Royal
Highness Prince Harald has seized an
enemy dragon. He is the Dragon Prince
and the one true Dragonseer.
All hail Prince Harald!

Report all dragon sightings. Failure to do
so is treason. Protecting other dragons is
treason. Refusing an order from
Prince Harald is treason.

Obey your King. Obey Prince Harald.
Draconis forever.

SKYE

In Skye's dream she was flying a dragon.

She was in the cool air high above Rivven, looking down at the houses, market stalls, smithies and farms that made up the city. She could see the Royal Palace below, with its white walls and towers, and tiny fluttering flags.

She was sitting on the back of a large dragon. He had a long neck, and his back was pale blue from nose to tail. His wings

were spread wide, riding the air currents like a bird. His back was warm, his skin smooth and dry.

A dragon! thought Skye. But strangely she wasn't scared. It was like something she remembered, like hearing a tune from long ago…

The dragon turned his head and looked at her. He had soft ears like an owl, pale brown eyes and a long snout, and when Skye saw him she felt an odd happiness. "Hello," she said.

The dragon nodded. "Help me," he said.

Skye frowned. "What?"

"*Help me!*"

He lurched and suddenly tumbled through the air, and Skye yelped. She wrapped her arms round his neck as he fell down towards the city, towards the palace!

"Stop!" she shouted. "What are you doing? Stop!"

"HELP ME!" he roared, his voice fierce and wild. The palace roof hurtled towards them, and Skye screamed—

DRAGON STORM

"Ma'am?"

Skye blinked and woke up. In front of her was Moira, her maid, looking worried.

"Ma'am, are you all right?"

Skye rubbed her face. "I was dreaming," she said, yawning. She looked around. "Are we there yet?"

Moira smiled. "Nearly." She leaned back so Skye could see out of the window.

They were in a carriage heading along the South Road. The road was smooth and the carriage swayed gently as they moved. Skye's guards rode ahead and behind, and the air was full of the clip-clop of horses and the jingle of their harnesses. Ahead lay the city of Rivven, glinting and beautiful in the bright autumn sunshine. Rising from the centre was the Palace Rock, and above it the Royal Palace.

"I always forget how good Rivven looks," said Skye.

Moira nodded. "It was lovely staying at Lady Crimson's lodge," she said, "but I miss the old streets here." She smiled at Skye. "Have you had a nice holiday, ma'am?"

It wasn't a question a maid would normally ask, but Moira was only a year or two older than Skye, and as close as Skye had to a proper friend. Moira could get away with saying things to Skye that others wouldn't dare to, and Skye felt she could tell Moira things that she couldn't say to anyone else.

Skye shrugged. "It was fine," she said. "Lady Crimson's nice. But we both know I was only there because Father didn't know what to do with me over the summer."

"We missed all the summer festivals," said Moira sadly. "Except the Maze Festival, remember?"

Skye nodded but didn't answer.

Moira gazed up at the palace. "I wonder what else we've missed?"

The carriage rolled through the gates of Rivven, past the city guards in their polished armour, and the crowds started cheering. Skye smiled awkwardly at them from the window, and waved now and then. She always found this embarrassing, and it didn't help that Moira, hidden in the shadows, was laughing and pulling faces.

They made their way up the curving road that led to the palace, leaving the crowds behind. As they reached the main gate, Skye realised the guards were different. They wore black uniforms with silver flames embroidered on their sleeves, and they didn't salute as the carriage arrived, but stared ahead, scowling with grim faces. Skye frowned. Had something happened?

They reached the palace steps, and Skye frowned again. Her brother, Prince Harald, was waiting for them. But where was Father?

DRAGON STORM

Harald smiled as Skye stepped down from the carriage. "Hello, sister," he said, bowing.

"Hello," said Skye.

Harald had a friendly smile. He looked as if everything he saw made him happy. Sometimes Skye thought she must look very grumpy next to him. Everyone agreed he was handsome, with blond hair swept

back from a strong face and clear blue eyes. He wore a red tunic decorated with silver thread, and pale calfskin gloves. "How was your holiday?"

"Fine," said Skye.

There was a slightly awkward pause. When Skye was younger, she used to adore her big brother. He would joke with her,

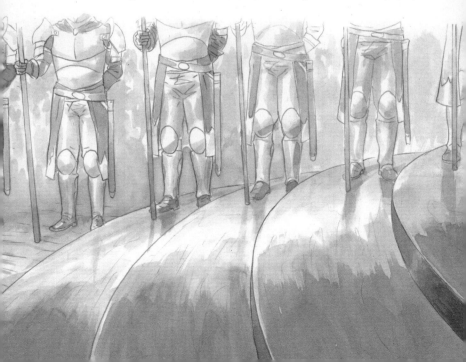

tease her and play hide-and-seek, cheer her up and protect her. But recently things had changed. He still smiled all the time, and still teased her – but his jokes had become a little cruel, she thought. Everyone else still loved him, though…

"Where's Father?"

Harald raised his hands as if to say sorry. "Unable to join us just now," he said. "There have been some changes here. Once you're settled in, I'll tell you all about them."

"Is anything the matter?" asked Skye, suddenly worried. "Is he all right?"

"Everything is fine," said Harald, grinning. "Our enemies have shown themselves, but we are more powerful than they thought."

This sounded alarming, but Harald rubbed his hands together as if looking forward to a feast. "Everything is going wonderfully!"

His gloves slipped a little, and Skye noticed the skin underneath.

"What happened to your arms?" she asked. "They're very red. Did you burn yourself?"

Harald shook his head and straightened his gloves. "Nothing you need worry about, little sister," he said. His voice was light, but there was something about the way he said "little sister" that set Skye's teeth on edge.

"Well … whatever," she snapped. "I'm tired. I'm going to my rooms." She turned to see Moira organising the servants and sorting out her things. When she turned back to Harald, he was already walking away.

Skye's chambers had been prepared for her return. A fire burned in the hearth, the dust had been swept away, and the curtains were open, revealing a view over Rivven. Skye could see the streets stretching out, and beyond them the southern hills and the great River Seek that ran through the city and out to sea.

This was the land of Draconis, and Skye, daughter of King Godfic, was its princess.

Skye loved Rivven, and Draconis. It was an ancient land with a proud history, and she was proud to be part of it. She wanted to be *more* part of it – but King Godfic didn't think that was right for a princess. Instead, he sent her to finishing schools, or to people like Lady Crimson, to practise being a pretty princess. Once upon a time, Harald would have stood up for her, and persuaded Father to let her join him in sword practice and horse riding. But these days…

Moira bustled in suddenly behind her. "Ma'am, you'll never guess what's happened!"

Skye turned in surprise. "What's wrong?"

"There's been an attack!" Moira said. "Last week, the king was attacked! And Lord Smale has been arrested!"

Skye gaped at Moira in astonishment. "What?"

Moira panted. She looked like she'd been running. "And there's more! Right here, in the palace, there's—"

There was a knock at the door, and Prince Harald entered. He glanced at Moira, then smiled at Skye.

"Father will see you now," he said.

FIRE-
DREAMER

Skye and Moira followed Harald through the palace corridors, down to the Assembly Hall.

"It's wonderful to have you back," said Harald, striding ahead. "These are very exciting times for Draconis!"

Skye glanced at Moira, who was clearly desperate to tell her something, but couldn't while Harald was here. Skye said, "Harald, was father attacked? I heard—"

"Yes," said Harald. He stopped for a moment and gazed at her, looking serious. "Yes, I'm afraid so. There are forces trying to destroy us, little sister. The kingdoms of Borolo and Venn are working against Draconis."

Borolo and Venn…? Skye shook her head in astonishment. Borolo and Venn were countries south of Draconis. They'd been friendly for centuries. "And you have Lord Smale imprisoned?" she asked.

"For plotting to kill the king, yes," said Harald.

Skye shook her head again. Lord Smale was the ambassador for Borolo. He was a tall, rather awkward man, and didn't seem much like an evil mastermind. The last time Skye had met him, he'd accidentally spilled wine on her dress and had become so flustered he'd had to go and have a sit-down. How could this be?

They passed guards and servants. Some were the usual King's Guards in their purple sashes, but many were dressed like the guards on the gate, in black uniforms with silver embroidered flames. The palace guards bowed as they passed, and the servants kept their heads well down and scuttled past as if frightened. The Silver Guards saluted to Prince Harald but ignored Skye altogether.

When they reached the great doors of the Assembly Hall, two more of the Silver Guards stood there, fierce and hostile. Harald ignored them and looked back at Skye.

"These are dark times," he said. "Skye ... our father was attacked by *dragons*."

Skye stared at him. She wondered if he was joking, but his face was hard and serious. "Dragons? *Real* dragons?"

Harald nodded. "There are dragons right here in Rivven. They've been hiding all this time – summoned by a cult of deadly wizards. They're working with Borolo and Venn, and they want to seize control of Draconis." He grinned suddenly. "But we have our own surprises. Come!" He entered the hall. Behind him, Skye and Moira looked at each other, and then followed.

Skye and Soulsinger

The Assembly Hall was long, with high ceilings, but the morning sun didn't reach this part of the palace and it was dimly lit by only a few flickering torches. It was usually busy with courtiers and servants, but today there were only more guards. At one end was a throne, and sitting on the throne was Skye's father King Godfic.

DRAGON STORM

"Good morning, Father!" called Harald cheerfully. "Look who's back!"

King Godfic's head jerked up, and he gave a snort. The king was short, and his golden crown and thick robes seemed to push him down into his seat. He looked as if he'd just woken up. He peered at Harald, and then Skye. His eyes widened slightly.

"Hello, Father," said Skye, and bowed to him.

King Godfic nodded. "Good … good to see you, m'dear," he said. His voice sounded thick, and he still seemed half asleep. "Did you have a nice time?"

"Yes, Father. Lady Crimson sends her regards." Skye hesitated. She never knew what to say to her father. He spent so much of his time being the king, regal and haughty. Skye was sure he loved her, but every conversation was like this.

"I was telling Skye about the terrible situation with Venn and Borolo," said Harald. The king grunted. He seemed confused and not himself. "And I told her how you were attacked by dragons!" continued Harald. The king gave a little jump. Harald smiled. "But she doesn't need to be afraid, does she?"

Skye glanced at Moira. What was going on?

Harald turned to Skye. "You're just in time," he said. "We've arranged a Royal

Address for this afternoon. We've summoned every important noble in the kingdom to come and swear loyalty. That's right, isn't it, Father? It was your order, wasn't it?"

King Godfic looked at Harald. He blinked once or twice. He seemed about to say something, and then…

And then, from the shadows at the back of the hall, there came a growl.

Skye stiffened. Her father did too. His eyes darted from side to side, but he didn't turn his head. Instead, he said, "I … yes." His voice sounded scratched, and he coughed. "Ahem. Yes, it was my order. You are to attend the … the…" He looked at Harald.

"The Royal Address," said Harald again.

Something moved in the shadows.

"Yes," said King Godfic.

Skye turned to Harald. "What's happening?" she demanded. "What's that sound? Harald, what's going on?"

Harald smiled. "They underestimated us, sister," he said. "They sent a dragon, but we were ready." Slowly he pulled off his long gloves. Underneath them his hands were bright red, from his fingertips to his wrists. He looked at them. "You asked about my hands," he said. "It's nothing, really, just a side effect of something marvellous. I've learned a trick, you see.

DRAGON STORM

Watch what I can do."

He held up one hand in a fist … and something stepped out of the shadows behind King Godfic.

It was huge-shouldered, as red as blood, with green ridges along its snout and furious golden eyes. Its muscles rippled as it walked, and its mouth hung slightly open, revealing large yellow teeth. With each step the floor shuddered.

King Godfic gave a little squeak. He didn't look behind him, but his hands gripped his throne as the creature approached.

It was a dragon.

"Skye," said Harald, grinning, "meet *Firedreamer*."

24

The creature gave another long, wet growl. Moira whimpered and tucked herself behind Skye, who stood in terror. She wanted to run, but somehow kept herself still.

"This is a great time for Draconis," said Harald. "Things are going to change, little sister." He smiled again. "I hope we'll see you this afternoon for the Royal Address?"

Skye managed to look away from the dragon to Harald. She swallowed. "Yes," she said. "I'll, ah, I'll go get ready."

Harald nodded. "Good idea!"

Skye and Moira bowed to King Godfic, who was still in his chair. They walked, carefully and slowly, out of the hall, and back to Skye's chambers without speaking.

Skye and Soulsinger

Then they stared at each other in horror.

"My lady," said Moira, in a weak voice. *"What is going on?"*

 # THE ROYAL ADDRESS

"A *dragon*, ma'am!" squeaked Moira. "It was a dragon!"

Skye rubbed her forehead. "I don't understand it," she said. Dragons attacking Father? A dragon *here*, in the palace! And Harald's strange behaviour, and his red hands, and the way he'd clenched his fist and controlled the horrible, terrifying creature...

"Did you ever see such a thing?" asked Moira.

Skye and Soulsinger

Skye didn't answer. She stared out of her window to the city below. Why would Borolo and Venn attack? How could Harald control this dragon? And why was Father so *scared*? She shook her head. "We … we should prepare for the Royal Address," she said. "Perhaps things will make sense after that…"

The Royal Address was an ancient tradition, when the most powerful lords and ladies of Draconis came to swear loyalty to the king. Usually it was just for show, but this year seemed different. Harald had arranged for it to take place in the Assembly Hall, and three thrones were set out – one for King

Godfic, one for Harald, one for Skye. Skye sat nervously, aware of the shadows behind her. She was sure she could hear breathing.

Firedreamer, the dragon.

The Oath of Loyalty was laid out on a table. Skye, from her throne, could just make out the words ...*pledge allegiance to King Godfic and Prince Harald...* When had Harald's name been added? Beside the table stood Malik, the king's clerk. He had curly black hair and a faded scar down one side of his face. Normally he was friendly, but today he looked concerned. Skye's father seemed to be half asleep. She worried about him.

Harald strode through the hall, chatting with the nobles, remembering their names,

their families, their estates. Everyone loved
him. Now more than ever, it seemed, as they
nodded and laughed at even his simplest
jokes. It wasn't very warm, but some of the
nobles were sweating. Now and then, they
glanced nervously into the shadows at the
back of the hall.

DRAGON STORM

Harald gave a speech about the noble, ancient kingdom of Draconis. He talked about evil forces from the lands of Venn and Borolo that had plotted to kill the king. He talked about dragons – not seen for over a thousand years but now returning – and their dangers. But also about how this was a chance for Draconis to rise and take its rightful place in the world. Skye wasn't sure what he meant, but some of the lords and ladies seemed to approve.

Then, one by one, they came forward and signed the Oath of Loyalty. Clerks dripped hot wax on to the document, and nobles pressed their signet rings to the wax to make a seal, and that was it. Some looked worried,

some excited.
And some of
them watched
Harald carefully
and kept their faces blank.

"Well, that went well, don't you think, Father?" asked Harald after they had left.

King Godfic nodded. "Yes…" He didn't seem sure.

Harald turned to Malik. "Lady Berin wasn't here. My father ordered *all* the lords and ladies to attend, did he not?"

Malik bowed. "Lady Berin apologises, but she is unwell, sire. She hopes to visit when she recovers. She is keen to swear her loyalty to Draconis."

Harald smiled. "To Father and me, you mean."

"Indeed, sire," said Malik.

"Well, no matter," said Harald, shrugging. "We hope she feels better soon."

The hall doors opened, and a woman entered. She was tall, with long red hair and a strong, jutting chin, and she wore the same black outfit and silver flame as the new guards. She marched forward to the thrones, ignored King Godfic and Skye, and knelt before Harald. "Your Highness," she said.

Harald nodded. "Marshall Flint! Good to see you. How was your mission?"

"Good, sire," she said. "We found it just where you said." She handed Harald a small leather bag, and he pulled out a diamond brooch on a gold base. It shimmered in the light of the hall, and Harald's eyes glinted.

"Oh, well done, Marshall," he breathed. "Well done!" He saw Skye staring and chuckled. "Something special, little sister. It's called a Dragon's Eye. Extremely powerful, so the old books say. It could be useful…" He dropped the diamond back into its leather bag.

"Well, I believe we're done here. Father and I must talk." He turned to Skye and smiled coolly. "Politics. Nothing for you to bother your pretty little head about."

Skye scowled, and was about to snap an angry reply, but then she saw Moira at the back of the hall. Moira was nodding to her. "Fine," she said, and left.

They didn't speak until they were back in Skye's chambers. Then Skye said, "What's going on, Moira?"

"I've been talking to the staff," said Moira. "It's true – there *were* dragons in the palace! *Three* dragons! And Prince Harald was able to control them, or one of them…" She frowned. "It's all a bit confusing. Maybe the other two escaped, or Firedreamer ate them, or, well, I don't know. But Lord Smale is under arrest! And there's something called the Dragonseer Guild, full of evil wizards who can summon dragons!" She shook her head. "Remember Alino? In the kitchens?"

Skye and Soulsinger

Skye nodded. Alino was the royal chef, and had been creating feasts for the palace for years. He was a cheerful, red-cheeked man from Borolo, and he'd often let Skye come into the kitchen and taste the food when she was younger.

"Alino says it's not good for Borolans just now. People have been saying horrible things. Calling him a traitor, can you believe?"

Skye didn't know *what* to believe. And this Dragonseer Guild...

She took a deep breath. "Moira," she said slowly, "I need to tell you something, but you have to keep it completely secret. Can you do that?"

Moira looked surprised but gave Skye a firm look. "You know I can, ma'am."

Skye nodded. "That Dragon's Eye thing, that Harald had there. I've seen one before. It's not really an eye, it's a jewel. But it *is* magical. You can use it to find things. And one time…" She stopped. "Do you remember the Maze Festival?"

"Of course, ma'am."

"Father wouldn't let me take part," said Skye. "He just wants me to be a pretty princess. But I entered secretly. I met a boy there called Ellis. And he had…" She hesitated. "He had a dragon."

Moira put her hand over her mouth in shock. "Oh, *ma'am!*" she breathed. "How did you escape?"

Skye shook her head. "That's just it, Moira. This dragon was, well … *nice*. Her name was Pathseeker. Ellis was nice, too. They didn't attack me, they *saved* me."

Moira stared at her.

DRAGON STORM

"It's true," said Skye. "Father had an Eye just like that one. And I, ah … borrowed it." She was embarrassed. She hadn't borrowed it — she'd stolen it from his chambers, and then it had been destroyed. She coughed. "The point is, Ellis and Pathseeker saved me. That's what I don't understand. He was there with some friends, and they must be in this Dragonseer Guild. Harald says they're trying to destroy us, but it makes no sense!"

Moira thought. "Where is this boy now?"

"I don't know." Skye sighed. "He could be anywhere."

She thought about the Dragon's Eye. Her father couldn't make it work. Harald had tried, too — she'd heard them talk about it.

But before it was destroyed, it *had* worked for Skye…

Of course. She stood up straight. "I know what to do."

That evening Prince Harald was meeting some of the city merchants. Skye waited until he entered the meeting hall and then slipped upstairs to his room. Two Silver Guards stood outside, guarding the door. They glared at Skye, and she went away, back downstairs…

She stopped one floor down, and crept into a storage room underneath Harald's room. No one knew the palace like a princess who had spent her whole life trying to follow her older brother! She climbed on to a stack of old crates and felt for the loose board in Harald's floor, the one that only she knew about. She removed it, heaved herself up...

And she was inside Harald's room.

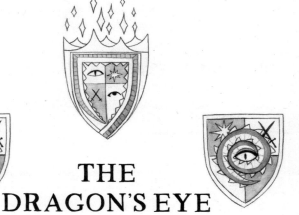

THE
DRAGON'S EYE

Skye replaced the loose floorboard and peered around Harald's room. It was as it had always been, with a large bed, wardrobe and desk, all carved from dark polished wood, and rich tapestries hanging against each wall. Skye opened the desk drawer, but it was empty.

She reached to the back of the drawer, found a catch and pulled it. A false back came away, revealing a hidden space. Skye smiled.

DRAGON STORM

She'd known *that* secret since she was eight. Sometimes Harald underestimated his little sister…

Inside the space was a small leather bag, and inside the bag was the Dragon's Eye.

Carefully Skye held it up. It was a diamond fixed into an eight-sided gold frame. Within the diamond, or perhaps painted underneath, was a beautifully drawn eye. It looked wild and a little cruel, like a cat's eye, or a wolf's.

Skye and Soulsinger

Skye had held a jewel like this before. She'd managed to make it come to life somehow. She tried to remember what she'd done before. She'd gazed into the diamond…

The eye moved!

Skye almost dropped it in shock. The eye flicked about, before glaring at her. The base felt suddenly warm, and Skye trembled. The last time she'd tried this, everything had gone wrong. The Dragon's Eye was a tool for finding things anywhere in the world, but Skye had asked it how to solve a maze and it had become confused. It had opened a gateway to *another* world – a maze world, where she, Ellis and Pathseeker had almost been stuck forever. But perhaps the question had been too strange? Perhaps something simpler...

Without quite meaning to, Skye whispered: "Where is Ellis the dragonseer?"

The Eye closed and the diamond became cloudy. Then the clouds parted to show the city of Rivven from above. For a moment Skye thought it was her dream. But then the view shifted and the city came closer. Now there was a narrow lane in a quiet area. And then a crumbling cottage...

Skye and Soulsinger

Skye frowned. Did Ellis live there? But the image moved again. Now it was inside the cottage and there was a wardrobe near the back —

"Hello, sis," said Prince Harald.

"Ah!" yelped Skye. She jumped backwards, and the Eye flew through the air.

Harald caught it with one hand and grinned. "Phew!" he said. "We wouldn't want to break *that*, would we?"

Skye gaped at him, and he chuckled. "Sorry for scaring you. But you *are* in my room. Going through my things…"

Skye swallowed. "I-I just wanted to see it," she stammered.

He frowned. "Why?"

"I … I don't know." She tried to make her voice sound normal, as if it didn't matter. "I wanted to see what the big fuss was…"

He gazed at her for several seconds. Then he shrugged. "It's magic, so people say. They *say* you can use it to find things. That would be useful, don't you think?" He smiled at her.

"Y-yes," she managed.

"Yes…" Harald sighed. "If it worked. But even with my … improvements, it seems not to. Look." He peeled off one glove and held the diamond in his red-stained hand. "Where is the Dragonseer Guild?" he demanded, glaring at it.

The diamond remained clear. After a few seconds, Harald relaxed and gave a rueful smile. "Nothing. But it has other powers, you know. In fact, there might be something else I can do now…"

He took a step closer. Suddenly his room felt rather small and Harald seemed taller. He squeezed the jewel, and the red of his hands shimmered through the diamond.

He closed his eyes and concentrated.

At first nothing happened. Then Skye noticed that the diamond wasn't just reflecting his red hands – it really *was* turning red. The painted eye inside moved around frantically.

"The Eye can find anything, they say," Harald muttered. "But it's much more than that. It can open doors *between worlds*…"

The room around them grew dark and shadows shifted in the corners. Skye had the strangest feeling that they weren't in the room any more, but somewhere completely different.

"Open them…" hissed Harald, his face fixed. "Or *close* them…"

DRAGON STORM

He relaxed and the room snapped back into place. Skye stared around her, but everything seemed normal again. Harald's hands throbbed with red. He wiped his forehead and chuckled. "Hard work!"

"I don't understand," said Skye.

Harald laughed. "Of course you don't, *little sister*," he said in a slightly sneering voice. "But this is real power. Something they won't expect..." He shook his head. "Enough for one day, I think."

He ushered her to the door and past the guards, who glared at her. "By the way," he said. "Best if you don't go sneaking into my room again, hmm? After all, the Dragon's Eye is a dangerous artefact, and not for children… We wouldn't want you to get hurt, would we?"

He smiled. It was a friendly, cheery smile, but Skye suddenly felt afraid.

She swallowed. "No," she said, keeping her voice steady.

Harald laughed and closed the door.

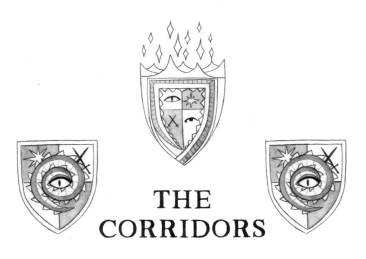

THE
CORRIDORS

The next morning, Prince Harald gave a speech to the people of Rivven.

It was in the King's Plaza, an open square in the centre of the city. Harald stood, with Skye and her father sitting behind him. Thousands of people lined the square holding banners. DRACONIS FOREVER! said one. DRAGON PRINCE said another.

Harald told them about dragons. He told them that Lord Smale had plotted to kill the king, and that the nations of Borolo and Venn were trying to destroy Draconis, but that Harald – under the command of his father, King Godfic, of course – would save them.

"This will be a new era for Draconis!" he declared. "For too long other nations have looked down at us!"

The crowd murmured.

"For too long foreigners have stolen our money!" shouted the prince.

"Yes," called one man near the front, a large merchant in a rich red cloak.

"We demand our rights!" continued the prince. "We demand our freedoms! We demand what is ours!"

"*Yes!*" shouted someone, and the crowd cheered.

Skye had to admit her brother was wonderful with people – charming, friendly, serious when he needed to be. He waved and smiled and looked confident, brave, trustworthy.

"Foreign dragonseers want to destroy us!" he bellowed. "We've stopped them once, but this threat will not go away … unless our proud nation rises up to defend ourselves! Who's with me? Who will help me save Draconis?"

The crowd cheered and clapped, and Harald grinned. "They thought they would crush us," he said, "but they have *unleashed* us! *We* will take our rightful place in the world and show them all! We will find these evil dragonseers of Borolo and bring them to justice! Draconis forever!"

"Draconis forever!" screamed the crowd.

Harald nodded and turned away from the noise. He rubbed his hands, like someone ticking off a list in his head. He saw Skye watching him and winked.

Skye gazed at him. When she was small, she had adored her big brother. Everyone did. He was kind, friendly, always helpful, never cross. Everyone said how nice he was – sometimes it drove Skye crazy hearing about her annoyingly perfect brother. But something had changed. It wasn't her imagination. She could see it – the small moments of cruelty, the way he twisted people. Harald was charming and clever. Everyone liked him. He was a natural leader.

And he was taking Draconis to war.

That afternoon, in her chambers, Skye summoned Moira.

Skye and Soulsinger

"I need your help," she said.

Moira let the palace staff know that poor delicate Princess Skye was tired out by the morning's business and had gone to bed. A maid left her room and headed down to the kitchens, with her bonnet pulled down low. Later, a boot boy, the lowest of all the servants, wandered out of the palace. He was covered in soot, and his hair was tucked into a filthy cap, and the guards hardly noticed him...

DRAGON STORM

And so Princess Skye slipped through the gates, down the hill and into the city.

She'd done this once or twice before, as an adventure, escaping the palace and wandering around Rivven, watching the people going about their lives. Today she could sense excitement in the air, like the faint smell of fire. More flags than usual fluttered in the breeze. She heard people gossiping about dragons and the evil Borolo. Children played dragon games in the streets, arguing about who got to be Prince Harald. And Silver Guards stood on street corners, watching and listening.

Skye slipped along the main street and down an old narrow lane to a small crumbling cottage. She glanced left and right before entering. Inside, it was just as she'd seen it in the Dragon's Eye. The room was dingy, and there was the battered wardrobe against the back wall. She opened it. Empty.

What now? The Dragon's Eye had shown her this – it must mean something. She examined the inside of the wardrobe. One corner at the top was worn away, as if someone had pushed there, again and again... Skye pressed the corner, heard a *click*, and the back of the wardrobe slid open to reveal a corridor.

Skye's heart thumped. She pulled a lantern from her bag and lit it, and hesitated for a moment. Then she stepped inside.

DRAGON STORM

The corridor looked old, but there was no dust. *Someone must use it a lot*, she thought. The floor was covered in strange wooden tiles that seemed to overlap. She walked a few steps, but then staggered as the walls suddenly shook. Was the tunnel collapsing? But then there was a clacking sound, and the tiles under her feet *moved*! Skye stared

down in shock, and when she looked up …
the corridor was different. Now it had an
opening off to the left. Had that been there
before? She turned and gasped – the way
behind was gone! It was a solid wall!

"What is this?" she muttered. It was like
a maze, but the walls were moving around
her – the maze was changing! There was

nothing she could do but keep going...

The floor beneath her *rippled*, and now she was facing a different direction! Skye spun and tried to catch her bearings, but the floors shuddered again. What was happening? Panic fluttered in her stomach. She walked faster, then she was running as fast as she could, but the corridors kept moving, clicking and shifting. She felt like a marble in a giant clockwork toy.

"Stop!" she cried out. "Stop this!" She spun and tried to push her way through a door, which became a wall, which slid and turned her round. "Help!" she screamed, and collapsed, down to the churning floor—

Skye and Soulsinger

Someone grabbed her hand.

"Hey," said a voice. "It's OK."

Skye looked up. In front of her was a girl about her age, with strong wiry arms. Her face was smeared with daubs of oil, and her black hair was tied up with a greasy rag. She was smiling and looked kind. Skye realised the corridors had stopped moving and were silent. They seemed to be waiting.

"I'm Mira," said the girl, and gave her a curious look. "Are you who I think you are?"

Skye tried to get her breath back. Her cap had fallen off, she realised. "Um…"

The girl smiled again. "It's OK. The corridors can be a bit scary. Come this way, Your Highness. Ellis has told us all about you."

THE GUILD

"They're called the Clockwork Corridors," said Mira, as she led Skye along them. "They're to stop anyone getting through, even if they find the entrance – and nobody's ever managed that." She gave Skye a curious look. "Except you…"

Skye followed her. The corridors seemed less hostile now. They moved smoothly, as if leading Skye and Mira somewhere. At last, they reached a huge ancient doorway and walked through it.

"Welcome to the Dragonseer Guild," said Mira.

Skye stared. They were in a hall, but a hall so huge that she could hardly see the far side. Above her, strange globes gave off a steady soft light, almost like the sun. There were buildings and offices, and what looked like training grounds. "Where *are* we?" she asked.

Mira shrugged. "No idea. It's a secret. I think Ellis knows – he's good at exploring – but he won't say."

A shout echoed from near the buildings, and now Skye could see birds flying towards them. No, not birds, she realised – these were too large, and didn't fly in the same way.

Skye and Soulsinger

They were a different shape. In fact…

They were *dragons*.

As they approached, she could make out their different shapes, sizes and colours. Some had powerful wings with steady beats, some were small fluttery things. Four, five, six, and each one was carrying a human…

DRAGON STORM

"Don't be alarmed," said Mira softly.

Skye turned and jumped. There was a dragon *right next to them*!

He was a peculiar creature, only as tall as Skye, with a stumpy body and a long neck. His skin was bronze and brown, like wood, and his shoulders and legs were stiff and straight. He looked almost like a machine. Skye gazed, half terrified, half fascinated.

He stretched his wings with a click-click sound. "Hello," he said.

Skye swallowed nervously. But she was a princess, so she drew herself up tall. "Um … hello," she managed.

"This is Flameteller," said Mira, smiling. "He's a dragon."

"I've ... seen one before," said Skye. "In the maze, with Ellis. Pathseeker..."

Mira nodded. "That's right. Here they come now, see?"

Skye looked up, and suddenly she was surrounded by dragons, as they landed in front of her, settling and stretching.

"Your Highness!" shouted a voice, and Ellis ran forward. He grinned. "What are you doing here? Did Mira bring you?"

"She found her way in by herself," said Mira. "The corridors alerted me."

Ellis looked surprised. "But how did you know where we were?"

"She's a dragonseer," said a red-haired boy next to Ellis. "That's what I've been saying!"

Skye and Soulsinger

The children stepped closer, and Skye leaned back a little.

Ellis laughed. "Give her some space!"

Beside Ellis was the dragon Skye had met at the Maze Festival months before. She wasn't very large but she was sturdy, with strong leathery wings. "Your Highness," she said, nodding her large head.

Skye bowed back. "Pathseeker."

Ellis smiled. "Let me introduce you to everyone else."

There was Cara, a thin girl with a cautious expression. Her dragon Silverthief had a strange mottled pattern on its skin and seemed to blend into the background. Then a tall girl named Erin, whose dragon was enormous, with a ridge of spikes along his back and ferocious features. He was Rockhammer. There was Connor, with a pale face and curly red hair. His dragon, Lightspirit, was long and thin, with very small wings and gleaming green eyes.

Tom, a strong wide-shouldered boy with a friendly face, stood next to a large dragon called Ironskin, who had dark red skin and a bony ridged forehead. And finally there was Kai, slim and smiling. His dragon Boneshadow was white, with a splash of red on her front, and a kind face.

Skye tried to remember all their names, but she could hardly believe what she was seeing. She should be terrified – these were *dragons*! – and yet part of her felt strangely comfortable around them.

"So how *did* you find us?" asked Ellis.

"I *told* you," said the red-haired boy, Connor. "She's a *dragonseer*!" He looked pleased with himself.

"Are you?" asked the tall girl, Erin.

"I don't think so," said Skye.

"Do you have a dragon?" asked Tom. "What's it like?"

"We *know* what it's like," said Connor. "That's what I've been telling you, her dragon is—"

"Good afternoon, Your Highness," said a voice, and a woman stepped forward.

She was tall, and wore deep blue robes.

She held a staff with
a bright blue jewel,
and her eyes glinted
with the same sharp
blue, though her face
was warm and smiling.

Skye realised she knew
her. "Lady Berin," she said in
surprise, "what are you doing here?" She
remembered Harald talking about her. He'd
wanted her to come to the Royal Address
to sign the Oath of Loyalty, hadn't he? The
clerk, Malik, had said she was unwell...

Berin smiled. "Welcome to the Dragonseer
Guild, Your Highness. It seems we have
things to discuss."

Skye and Soulsinger

Berin gently shooed away the other children and their dragons. "I need to talk to the princess alone for a moment," she said. The two of them walked slowly through the hall, away from the others.

"You used a Dragon's Eye to find us," said Berin at last. It wasn't a question, but Skye nodded.

Berin sighed. "We heard that Harald had found another one. Tell me – can he use it too? Could he use it to find us?"

"No," said Skye. "I mean, he can't use it to find things. But he can do something else. He said something about other worlds…"

"A Dragon's Eye is dangerous and potent,"

said Berin, frowning. "And Prince Harald has new powers."

"What is this place?" asked Skye.

Berin smiled. "This is the Dragonseer Guild," she said with pride. "It's been here for over a thousand years, since before the last Dragon Storm. Since dragons first visited our world."

"You mean, before we drove them out?"

Berin snorted. "Dragons were never our enemies. Look around!" She waved her staff. "Dragons *built* this, Princess. Humans and dragons created most of Rivven together – including the palace." Her face grew sad. "But there was a war between humans, and the dragons became drawn in. They were appalled at what they'd become and left our world. They are only now returning, to a very few humans. To dragonseers – humans who can reach out to the world of dragons and connect to one special dragon … and allow it back to *our* world."

Berin gazed at Skye. "Harald has a dragon at the palace."

Skye nodded. "Firedreamer," she whispered. Just saying the name reminded her of that horrible creature, with his huge claws, terrible growl and the smoke curling from his mouth. She shuddered.

"How do you think he came into this world?" Berin asked.

Skye frowned. "Harald said Lord Smale

sent him to attack Father, but that Harald was able to control him…" She looked at Berin. "Perhaps Harald is the dragonseer?"

"Prince Harald is *not* a dragonseer," said Berin with certainty. "And neither is poor Lord Smale, who could hardly summon a cup of tea. No, Skye."

"Well, then who?" asked Skye. Then she stopped. "Wait, you mean *me*? I don't think so. I'm not a dragonseer."

She thought of Firedreamer and was horrified. "And that *monster* is nothing to do with me!"

"It's the only thing that makes sense," said Berin. "Your Highness, you can use the Dragon's Eye. You *are* a dragonseer…" She nodded. "And Firedreamer is *your* dragon."

SUMMONING

Skye shook her head. "Firedreamer can't be my dragon! He's *horrible*!"

"It's strange," admitted Berin. "A dragon and their dragonseer have a bond, a way of seeing the world together. What I've heard of Firedreamer hardly seems like you! And yet..."

Berin led Skye towards a round stone hut, slightly away from the other buildings. "You were very ill last year," she said. "Is that right?"

Skye and Soulsinger

Skye nodded. "A fever. I don't remember much about it – I was delirious, they said. It all felt like a dream." She recalled lying in bed for weeks, shivering under hot sheets, hardly able to eat or even drink, surrounded by weird dreams and night terrors. "Harald had been away, on a tour of the southern states. I'd been looking forward to him coming home. But then when he returned, I got ill…"

Skye frowned. She'd been so pleased to see him, but he hadn't seemed pleased to see her. In fact, when she thought about it, that was about the time he'd changed. After that tour he'd become … cruel somehow. He wouldn't play games with her any more, and hardly even seemed to want to talk to her. Moira had said he was just growing, and that he'd soon be his nice self again. But then Skye had fallen ill...

"My vice chancellor, Mr Creedy, has learned of a form of magic control," said Berin. "A way to take power from someone. It's dangerous, and it would make the victim very ill. But if it worked ... you could summon *their* dragon."

Skye was shocked. "Are you saying Harald did that to me? Actually made me ill? He wouldn't do that!"

"The Harald you knew before would not," agreed Berin, "but the Harald who came back...? What do you really think, Your Highness?"

Skye and Soulsinger

Skye wanted to say no, but she bit her lip. She remembered her fever dreams. Some of them had been so vivid, and she *had* dreamed of dragons. She still did, sometimes. Could it be true – could Harald really have done that to her? And could Firedreamer, that horrible monster, really be *her* dragon?

They reached the hut. It had two large open doors, and a fire burned inside. Outside stood a man wearing a leather jerkin, his face hidden under a grey beard. He beamed at them as they approached.

"This is Drun," said Berin. "He helps the dragonseers with summoning. Drun, may I introduce Her Royal Highness Princess Skye."

"Hello, Yer Majesty," said Drun with a cheery nod. "You know about that Firedreamer then, eh? Poor little thing, kept prisoner like that. Such a shame."

Skye gaped at him in astonishment. "He's not a poor little thing! Have you seen him? He's a monster!"

"But he *is* a prisoner," said Berin. "Dragons cannot stay in this world by themselves. Without a dragonseer they return to their world. But Prince Harald has put an emerald chain round Firedreamer's neck to hold him here. He can't leave this world, and he can't break free of Harald's control."

"But with you here, we might fix that, eh?" Drun said.

"How?" asked Skye suspiciously.

"You can make a connection to him, girl!" said Drun. "That's what bein' a dragonseer is all about. If you *connect* with him, we can find out the truth."

"It's a lot to take in," said Berin, "but if you are Firedreamer's real dragonseer, you can help him. And if not ... there's no harm. Will you try?"

Skye chewed her lip. Firedreamer was terrifying. She couldn't believe she had anything to do with him. "All right," she said reluctantly, and Drun grinned.

DRAGON STORM

"Grand! Come inside, let's give it a go."

He led them into the hut. It was dark and a fire cast shadows and patterns on the walls as if the room were alive. Drun sat Skye down and sat on the other side of the firepit. "Now," he said, "you're going to try to connect with Firedreamer."

"How?" asked Skye.

Drun smiled. "Well, you've *seen* him, right?"

Skye shivered. "Yes."

"Then just think about him a bit. Imagine you can see him here. Tell me what you see…"

Skye gazed into the flames. "He breathes fire," she said. "That's what they say. He's huge and horrible, and he wants to destroy the world. I'm scared of him."

"Oh," said Drun, sounding surprised. "Um … anything else? Maybe something you like about him? What are his eyes like?"

"Yellow," whispered Skye. "He glares at everything like he hates it. He hates me. He hates *everything*."

DRAGON STORM

A circle of smoke drifted lazily up but didn't fade away. After a while, Skye thought it wasn't smoke but a shape – two round eyes peering out of the fire...

"There are flaps on his neck," she murmured. "To make flames. He wants to burn everything. He's red and green. His skin is covered in ridges. He looks..."

She blinked. A moment from a dream suddenly popped into her head. "No, he's blue," she said. "Pale blue, like the sky..."

Drun frowned. "Are you sure, miss?" But Skye was hardly listening. As if half asleep, she said, "And his eyes are brown, not yellow. He's blue." She hesitated. "No, red and green. No, blue..."

Skye and Soulsinger

The eyes stared at her from the fire. First brown, then yellow. First kind, then ferocious. She could see his head now, red with green stripes. Firedreamer's face was there in the fire. She was connecting with him, but this wasn't her dragon. *This wasn't her dragon.*

"No!" she shouted, turning away. "Stop! Get away! No!"

"It's all right, miss!" called Drun.

But somehow Skye knew that the creature in the flames was looking for her. And now she could hear it – a horrible screeching,

hissing voice. It roared—

"HELP ME!"

"Argh!" shouted Skye, and she pushed herself away and out of the hut, back into the soft light of the hall.

"You feelin' better, miss?" asked Drun, later. He gave her a cup of water and Skye drank it gratefully.

"He's not my dragon," she whispered. "I could feel him, but he ... he *hates*. He hates everything. He wants to burn the world."

Drun scratched his head. "But you connected with him," he said, frowning. "It's a mystery, it is."

"I'm sorry," said Berin. "I didn't mean to

upset you like this."

Skye nodded. "I know. I don't understand what's happening." She took a deep breath. "I need to return to the palace."

"Are you sure?" asked Berin.

"I have to or people will notice." Skye stood. "Harald is raising an army. I think he might really go to war. He's talking about invading Borolo…"

Berin nodded. "We've sent word to Queen Paulette. They're preparing, but how can they defend against a dragon? If we reveal ourselves, the Guild will be in terrible danger. But if we don't stand to help them, who will stand to help us?"

"I don't know what's happening," said

Skye. "Firedreamer is not my dragon. But I'll find out what I can."

"Thank you," said Berin. "Come, I'll take you back."

They walked to the entrance. The other dragonseers were waiting for them, but they saw Skye's face and said nothing.

"I'll show her out," said the tall girl, Erin.

"Thank you," said Berin. She bowed. "Your Highness."

Skye nodded. "Lady Berin." Then she followed Erin back through the Clockwork Corridors.

Erin was quiet at first. Then she said, "It's not as easy as they say."

Skye looked at her. "What isn't?"

"Summoning," said Erin. "I've been here longer than everyone, and I was the last one to manage it. Making a connection, drawing your dragon to this world... It's hard. So, you know, if that's the problem..."

"It's not," said Skye. She smiled. "Thank you, though."

Erin said, "I used to worry about my dragon, Rockhammer. Sometimes he'd come through ... *wild*. I get anxiety attacks, and he would, ah..." She grinned. "He destroyed a building once. Twice! But the thing is ... he's my dragon, and I'm his human. In the end, that's all that matters."

Skye tried to imagine Firedreamer as her dragon – his horrible glaring eyes, his smoking mouth, the dreadful claws, the *rage*...

They reached the little cottage, and Erin peered up and down the street. "There you are, Your Highness," she said. "I hope we'll see you again."

"Thank you," said Skye. She put her cap back on, slipped out on to the narrow lane, and made her way back to the palace, and to her brother and Firedreamer.

MARCHING

Prince Harald's army grew.

It all happened so quickly. People queued up to join. Banners fluttered all around, showing pictures of the prince and Firedreamer. There were home-made ones too – DEATH TO FOREIGN DRAGONS said one.

And Harald was everywhere. He gave speeches in the square, roaring about evil Borolans and foreign plots, and how

DRAGON STORM

Draconis would "rise up and take back what was ours". He never said what it was that Draconis needed to take back, or how Borolo was stopping them, but the crowd cheered anyway. To the merchants, he talked about lowering taxes. To the army, he promised better weapons. Important guests were invited to the Assembly Hall to meet Firedreamer for themselves. Sometimes Harald flew the dragon over the castle for the commoners to see.

And his army grew.

Between speeches, Harald worked with the Dragon's Eye, trying to learn its secrets, until one day he came to the hall with a gleam of triumph in his eyes. The red stain on his hands had spread further and now reached his elbows.

"We're ready," he said. He turned to the courtiers in the hall. "It is time!" he cried. "Time for Draconis to claim our rightful place!"

He gazed about him. "My subjects — prepare to march on Borolo!"

If it had seemed busy before, now it was chaos. Skye had never thought about how much was needed to supply an army — not just weapons and armour, but food, drink, cooks and equipment, boots to march in, tents to sleep in, spades to dig latrines... The water needed barrels, the barrels needed wagons, the wagons needed horses, and horses needed horseshoes, which needed blacksmiths, who needed forges, which needed coal and wood…

Clerks rushed through the palace, carrying stacks of papers and lists. Prince Harald stood in the centre of the chaos. He never seemed to sleep these days, and yet he always appeared alert. His eyes shone all the time.

Skye and Soulsinger

He would lead the army, he announced. King Godfic would stay in Rivven.

"You too, little sister," he said. "You can … keep morale up. Wave to the crowds. That kind of thing."

Skye started to protest. But then there was a rumble, which became a long growl. Firedreamer breathed in the shadows behind her. She clenched her jaw and nodded.

Back in her chambers, Skye stalked to and fro, fuming. *Wave to the crowds?* Harald treated her like she was nothing! But what could she do? How could she stop this madness?

Her chamber doors suddenly flew open, and Moira burst in. Skye turned in astonishment as her maid skidded to a stop in front of her, gave the quickest of bows and said, "They've arrested Alino!"

Skye gaped at her. "Alino the chef? Why?"

"They're rounding up everyone from Borolo. They're saying they might be enemy agents!" Moira looked like she was going to cry. "Ma'am, I don't understand. Are we at war?"

Skye chewed her lip. "No," she said. "Not yet. But we will be soon…"

She gazed out of the window at the city below. She thought of Harald's sneering joke. *Wave to the crowds*. That's what he thought princesses were for.

"There will be a war unless I stop it," she said. "Unless I stop Harald."

Moira trembled. "But *how*, ma'am? He has that horrible dragon…"

"Harald thinks I'm here to wave to crowds and wear pretty dresses," said Skye. "But I am a princess of Draconis. I will do what is *right*." She shook her head. "This war is not right. The dragon Firedreamer is not right. *Harald* is not right."

She looked up and tried to feel brave.

"So I will stop them."

The army of Draconis assembled beyond the city walls of Rivven. There were thousands of people – soldiers, cooks, servants, blacksmiths, carpenters, plus many others, and Silver Guards too. Huge machines of war – catapults, trebuchets and battering rams – trundled along on heavy wheels, pulled by oxen.

From the palace came the sound of brass horns, and Firedreamer appeared above the

towers. He flew towards the army, and soon everyone could see Prince Harald on his back. The crowd murmured in nervous excitement. Firedreamer circled once above them before settling on the grass and glaring about. His sides heaved as he panted.

Harald leapt off the dragon's back and gave the order to march. And the vast army,

and its followers, and Firedreamer, moved slowly forward.

Skye watched all this from behind a small supply wagon. She was wrapped in a dark wool cloak, her hair was tucked into a grey cap, and she'd smeared soot over her face. She worked her way slowly through the rows of soldiers, trying to get closer to Harald. She didn't know what she would do when she reached him. But, whatever happened, she would do what was right.

The army rumbled onwards, and Princess Skye crept closer.

They headed towards the southern hills, following the South Road beside the thundering River Seek. Silver Guards marched at the front and back to make sure no one strayed. The huge catapults groaned and creaked as they were dragged forward.

They passed the Rivven Wheel, a waterwheel that powered the grain mills. Two miles beyond was a ford, a shallow and calm part of the river. It was the only place to cross for thirty miles in any direction.

Standing before it was another army.

Harald's army halted. Harald rode forward on the back of Firedreamer and the crowd followed hesitantly. Skye crept along with them.

The other army wasn't as big as Harald's. Its soldiers weren't in uniforms. They looked like farmers and workers. Some of them carried hay forks for weapons. They had banners, and Skye thought they would be Borolan, but they weren't. Instead, they showed the Draconis coat of arms.

Skye and Soulsinger

Standing at the front was Lady Berin.

Harald grinned. "Lady Berin!" he called. "I see you're feeling better."

"Your Highness," said Berin, and gave a very small nod.

"Have you come to join us?" asked the prince.

"No." Berin spoke calmly, but her voice carried over the crowd. "It's not too late, you know. You can still end this madness."

Harald gestured towards his army. "It's the will of the people, my lady."

"Not *all* of them," said Berin. And Skye realised that Berin's army was *also* made up of people from Rivven and the surrounding lands. Ordinary people, not soldiers. Many of them looked scared, but they stood ready to stop Harald's army.

"We have no quarrel with you," the prince said. "We march on Borolo."

"You must not," said Berin. "Your Highness, this is *wrong*. You are *sick*. The heartbane is poisoning your mind—"

Harald dug his heels into Firedreamer's sides and the great dragon snarled. "Stand aside!" bellowed the prince. He was not smiling any more. "Stand aside, or we will *crush* you."

Skye watched in horror. This made no sense. Lady Berin wasn't the enemy! These people weren't the enemy – they were ordinary people of Rivven!

"We stand here," called Berin. "If we do not, who will stand for us?"

As she spoke, her eyes flicked away from Harald, and for a moment she seemed to stare straight at Skye. Then she lifted her staff.

"Dragonseers!" she cried.

And as Skye watched, the members of the Dragonseer Guild appeared.

WHO WILL STAND?

A dragon appeared next to Berin. It was huge and powerful, with black skin and green eyes. And Skye realised it was *Berin's* dragon. Of course Berin was a dragonseer!

Beside Berin, a pale man in a dark cloak scowled, and suddenly there was another large dragon, so black it was hard to see, with glaring red eyes. It lifted its head back and shrieked in fury.

A murmur of fear broke out in Harald's army.

And now more shapes appeared along the edge of the water. Skye saw the other dragonseers: Tom, with powerful Ironskin, Cara, with Silverthief, Ellis and Pathseeker, Mira and the strange Flameteller, Kai on his white and red dragon, Boneshadow, Erin on mighty Rockhammer, almost as huge as Firedreamer, Connor with Lightspirit, thin and wispy...

And there was Drun, standing with his arms folded and a determined expression. And beside him, a short woman in bright yellow leggings, holding a staff, and another woman with strong arms, her sleeves rolled up, and a woman who looked like Berin, holding another staff with a blue jewel…

And around them, people – ordinary people, not soldiers – readied their weapons.

"We stand here!" shouted Lady Berin. "Turn back, for we will not let you do this!"

Prince Harald grinned. "There!" he roared

to his army. "Do you see? Enemy dragons, just as I said!" Firedreamer's eyes flashed, and he seemed on the edge of bursting with fire. "Did you think I wasn't *expecting* this treachery?" Harald demanded.

He lifted something that glinted in the sunshine. It was the Dragon's Eye, glowing

golden red in his hands. The eye inside flicked frantically from side to side. Harald squeezed the jewel, and the air seemed to darken. It was as if a cloud had passed over the sun, though the sky was still clear and blue. Shadows crept towards them from all directions. Again Skye felt that strange feeling of *slipping*, as if there were two worlds overlaid. The Dragon's Eye could open doors to other worlds, Harald had said. What was he going to do?

"No!" she shouted. A ring of red light burst from the Eye and spread over both armies with a boom of thunder. Everyone leapt back, but it passed right through them...

Skye and Soulsinger

"Ironskin!" shouted a voice. Skye looked across the water and saw Tom staring up at where his dragon had been. She was gone. And Ellis's dragon, Pathseeker, was gone too. And Flameteller and Rockhammer... All the dragons were gone!

DRAGON STORM

The dragonseers stared at each other, and at Prince Harald, and then at Firedreamer. The dragon was still there, screeching in fury. His emerald necklace glinted in the sun.

"What have you done?" demanded Berin.

Harald laughed. "What's the point of owning a dragon if others have one?" he called. "*I'm* the Dragon Prince – and now Firedreamer is the only dragon in this world!"

And suddenly Skye understood. Open the doors to other worlds … or *close* them. Harald was closing the door to the dragon world, banishing all dragons! Only Firedreamer was left, and Skye realised the emerald chain was holding him in this world.

The Dragon's Eye pulsed and shimmered, red and horrible.

"Draconis will rise!" roared Harald. "The Dragonseer Guild is helpless, and nothing can stop us! *Draconis!*"

Lady Berin looked around her. Without their dragons the Guild could do nothing. The tiny force of ordinary citizens could not possibly face Harald's army.

"Marshall!" called Harald.

Marshall Flint rode forward. "Yes, my lord?"

"Send your men and arrest these traitors." Harald sneered at Berin. "They won't put up a fight. Lady Berin doesn't want to see anyone get *hurt.*"

DRAGON STORM

A line of Silver Guards moved forward, but Berin ignored them and stared into the crowd. She was looking straight at Skye, but Skye didn't know what to do. Firedreamer was bellowing and spitting, full of fury and fire. No matter what Berin thought, this could not be her dragon, surely?

The dragon swung his enormous head towards her and glared at her. His mouth opened in a snarl, but his eyes...

Skye looked up at Harald on Firedreamer's back, his hand clenched round the Dragon's Eye, his face lit with furious triumph. And suddenly she remembered what Erin had said to her about summoning. About how Rockhammer could appear wild, because

Erin summoned him when she was in a panic. Because the summoner *affected* the dragon...

Slowly Skye stepped forward.

"Harald!" she called.

Harald's guards drew their swords as she approached, but Harald recognised her and laughed.

"Sister! Goodness, what *are* you wearing?"

"Stop this!" she called up. "This is wrong, Harald! Stop it, or I will!"

Harald chuckled. "Will you? How, exactly?"

Skye set her jaw. "With *my* dragon, Harald," she said.

And she began to summon.

DRAGONSEER

Skye closed her eyes and summoned her dragon.

She had to see him in her mind, Drun had said. Skye understood now. She ignored Firedreamer. Instead, she thought about pale blue skin, dry and warm. She remembered a kind face, and the feeling of flying. She remembered the dream of him.

Above her, Prince Harald shook his head. "What are you doing, sister?" he asked in a mocking voice. "Trying to make your *own* little dragon?"

Skye ignored him. *Blue*, she thought. *And warm, and smooth, and his face is kind...*

"Even if you *could* summon a dragon, it can't enter this world. Not while I hold this!" He lifted the Dragon's Eye, still giving off its horrible golden red light.

Skye gritted her teeth. "He doesn't need to," she hissed. "He's already here. Isn't he, *brother*?"

Harald's face froze. He looked at her as if he'd only now realised she was a threat. "What are you doing?" he demanded. "Stop this!"

Blue, with warm skin, she thought. *Blue...*

DRAGON STORM

The Dragon's Eye was humming, and a wind rose around them until they were standing in the centre of a roaring, raging storm.

"Stop!" snarled Harald.

"Blue!" shouted Skye. "Smooth warm skin!"

Firedreamer howled at her, and drew a breath, ready to blast fire...

Then he shook his head. His body, red and green, shivered suddenly, and for a moment it seemed pale – almost ... blue...

"Berin was right!" shouted Skye. "*I'm* the dragonseer, not you! It was my power, and you stole it!"

"I'm the prince!" shouted Harald. "It's not fair, I *deserve* a dragon! You didn't even know I'd taken him!"

"I *knew*," hissed Skye. "He was in my dreams, Harald! I could feel him! He was my friend and look what you did to him!"

The wind howled. Firedreamer shuddered, and his colour returned. He glared at Skye with eyes full of hatred, but screeched, "HEEEEELPPP MEEEEEEE!"

"A dragon's form comes from their dragonseer!" said Skye. "But you *changed* him! You corrupted him! This is the form *you* wanted!"

Harald laughed. "Corrupted? He's more powerful than all the others! He's magnificent!"

"No," whispered Skye. *His face is kind*, she thought desperately. *He is kind, he is kind—*

DRAGON STORM

"Don't do that!" snarled Harald, and his red hands shone bright and horrible.

"You had everything!" shouted Skye. "You were the prince, and everyone loved you, and still you wanted more! You wanted everything of *mine*! You stole my power, Harald … but I'm taking it back!"

She faced the dragon. "Firedreamer, you are *free*!"

Firedreamer lifted his head back and *howled*. His ridged red skin turned pale, then blue, and smoothed out. His face became kind, his eyes brown. His sides heaved and he reared up, and Harald cursed, fell from his back and crashed to the ground.

Firedreamer was gone. In his place was something very different. Tall, blue, with the wide smiling face Skye remembered from her dreams, he gazed at her with gentle eyes.

"I know you," he whispered. His voice was soft and seemed to carry a note of music.

"Yes," murmured Skye. "My name is Skye."

"I am Soulsinger," he said. He nodded, as if hearing it for the first time. "Yes." He turned to Harald. "You kept me prisoner."

Harald glared at him. "You're not hers, you're *mine*!" he hissed.

Skye almost laughed. "How could you think you could *own* him? He's a dragon, Harald!"

Skye and Soulsinger

Harald gripped the Dragon's Eye so hard his fingers were almost white. Around them, the storm howled. "*Mine!*" he snarled. The red of his skin was reaching up to his face, almost glowing.

"Harald, *stop*," warned Skye. "You have to stop!"

Soulsinger flickered red for a moment, and his eyes glowed yellow.

"Yes!" roared Harald triumphantly. His hand clenched even tighter. "He's *MINE*!"

"No!"

And the Dragon's Eye shattered.

DRAGON STORM

The whirling wind shrieked and then collapsed. A shimmer like a mirror appeared above Harald's head and he stared up. "No!" he cried in fear. He seemed to *twist*—

And then he was gone.

Skye was thrown to the ground as the storm vanished, and felt something across her back. It was smooth, quite leathery but warm. She realised it was Soulsinger's wing, protecting her. She remembered the dry smell of him, like dust after the rain on a hot day, and smiled.

"I've missed you," she whispered.

"I've missed you too," he whispered back.

SOULSINGER

It was strangely quiet on the battlefield. Skye gazed into Soulsinger's eyes, and he gazed back, smiling. Then he staggered and almost fell.

"What's wrong?" asked Skye, alarmed. "Are you hurt?"

The dragon shook his head. "It is nothing. I am just tired."

On Lady Berin's side, the other dragons had returned, shimmering and flickering into the world. The Dragon's Eye was no longer stopping them. On the other side, Harald's army was starting to react.

"Where's Prince Harald?" demanded someone.

"There's another dragon!" shouted someone else, pointing at Soulsinger. "It's killed the prince!" Then everyone was shouting. Panic ripped through the crowd, turning to fury. The Silver Guards regrouped.

"For Prince Harald!" shouted a voice.

"For Draconis!" shouted another.

"Murdering dragons!"

"Get them!"

Skye groaned. They were going to attack.

Skye and Soulsinger

It was madness! The army lurched forward, and Skye and Soulsinger stumbled back. The Silver Guards drew their weapons, and Skye could see the strange oily pattern on their swords. She knew what they were; her father had talked about them before. They were *dragon* swords, made with ancient materials that could cut through a dragon's hide.

Skye gasped and turned to Soulsinger. "You have to go. They're out of control. You have to return to your own world!"

But Soulsinger drew himself up tall. "Not yet. Wait."

He stretched his wings and beat them steadily, climbing into the air. Then he faced the crowd. As Skye watched, he seemed to grow, as if he had somehow become more real than before. What was he going to do? She noticed that the undersides of his wings still had a trace of red, and for a moment he looked like Firedreamer, about to breathe fire. He opened his mouth…

Skye and Soulsinger

And sang.

His voice poured out over the crowd, into the air. It had no words, it was just a crooning, comforting noise, but it caught at Skye's heart as she heard it. It was the sound of the wind over a cornfield, or the gentle swish of waves on a beach. It was birdsong in the morning, and crickets late at night on a warm summer's evening. It was a sound of comfort and calm, and it washed over everyone and through them. And, as it did, the faces in the crowd lost their anger.

They became caught in the music, and paused, as if all they wanted was to hear one more note of that beautiful song…

There was a strange clattering sound, and Skye realised it was people dropping their swords. They hardly seemed to notice. All the hatred and fear drained out of them. All of Prince Harald's lies blew away.

The song drifted away, but the crowd stayed where they were, mesmerised. Soulsinger flew back down to earth. But his wings flapped strangely, and he landed off-balance, collapsing to the ground.

"Soulsinger?" asked Skye. She ran towards him. "Are you hurt?" He lay sprawled, hardly able to lift his head. "Soulsinger!"

Skye and Soulsinger

The dragon sighed. "I am … tired," he said. "It is all right."

Skye looked back and saw Berin on the back of her dragon, flying towards them. The dragon landed and she hurried across.

"I think he's injured!" sobbed Skye. "What's wrong with him?"

Berin looked into Soulsinger's eyes. She lifted her staff and held the blue gem at the end near his chest, and frowned. "He has been badly treated," she said. "Harald kept him in this world for too long. The poison corrupted him."

"Will he be all right?" asked Skye.

Berin thought. "He should recover in time. But…" She sighed. "But not here. Skye, you must let him go."

At first, Skye didn't know what she meant. But then she saw the emerald chain still wrapped round his neck.

Berin said, "The emerald is keeping him in this world, you see. He must return to his own world to recover."

Skye reached round to unclasp it, but hesitated. "If he goes," she whispered, "will he ... come back? To me?"

"Perhaps," said Berin. "I cannot say for sure."

Skye nodded. She rested her forehead against Soulsinger's, feeling his warm dry skin, smelling again the scent of summer rain.

Skye and Soulsinger

"I've only just found you," she said. "I don't want to lose you."

The dragon gazed at her but said nothing.

Eventually Skye sat up. "But I don't own you. Harald thought he could own dragons. Harald thought he could own *everything*. But I am a princess of Draconis, and I will do what is right."

She wiped her tears away. Then she reached behind Soulsinger's neck and unfastened the clasp, and the emerald fell away.

Soulsinger sighed. "Thank you," he whispered. "Skye…"

Already he was fading, and Skye had to lean in close to hear him.

"You are my human," he murmured. "I will always be your dragon."

And then he was gone.

A MISSION...

The army that returned to Rivven was very different from the one that had set out.

Instead of marching in time, they wandered back in small groups of ones and twos. They looked faintly lost, as if trying to remember something. Occasionally they hummed or whistled part of a tune.

The city guards didn't know what to make of it, and neither did the people left behind. Was the war won already? Had the horrible dragons of Borolo been defeated?

But the returning soldiers didn't seem to understand their questions. They just shrugged and hugged their wives or husbands, and kissed their children. They were quiet but not unhappy. They chatted about small things – the thatch that needed mending above the door, or the loose wheel on the wagon, or what to make for dinner. Quietly, without anyone noticing, someone took down Prince Harald's banners.

"But what *happened*?" demanded the others.

The soldiers thought, deeply, before answering. "There was music," they said. "It went like … like…" And they became quiet again and smiled.

And, somehow, the city breathed in and out and returned to normal.

"Marshall Flint has gone," said Berin.

She and Skye stood on top of the wall of the Royal Palace, gazing at Rivven. It was a bright day but not warm, and Skye realised that summer was ending. Many of the younger folk were out in the fields surrounding the city, harvesting and preparing for winter.

Berin said, "She and the Silver Guards disappeared. Harald was paying them, and when he ... left, they did too."

Skye nodded. "Father believes Harald

was being controlled by evil dragons," she said. "He thinks Firedreamer was the one controlling Harald, can you believe?" She knew she sounded bitter, but she couldn't help herself. "Because Harald was *perfect*."

Berin smiled sadly. "Some people can make themselves believe anything."

There was a pause. Then Skye said, "Where is he? My brother?"

Skye and Soulsinger

"I don't know." Berin frowned. "The Dragon's Eye can open paths between all worlds. You and Ellis saw one before, the maze world. He may be there, or anywhere." She sighed. "We're searching some of the ancient books for clues. We may find him."

Skye nodded. She wasn't sure how to think about Harald yet. He had been her hero for years. Despite everything he had done to her and to Soulsinger, she found that she missed him. The palace seemed empty, and her father was distant.

She had not seen Soulsinger, or dreamed of him, since the battle.

"Princess Skye, what will you do now?" asked Berin.

Skye looked up. "Oh, the usual, I suppose," she said, trying to smile. "Princess duties. Waving, wearing dresses, that sort of thing."

"King Godfic is planning a diplomatic mission to Borolo and Venn," said Berin. "For some reason they're not very happy with Draconis right now."

Skye snorted.

"He needs someone to represent Draconis," continued Berin. "Normally it would be the prince. But perhaps someone else could step in…"

It took Skye a moment to realise what Berin meant. "Oh! Hmm." She thought. "I don't have much experience. Harald was the one who did all that. I might not be what they need."

Berin smiled. "Perhaps all they need is someone who will do what is right. I think you'd do a fine job." She looked across at the houses and streets. "You know, young Harald was a good person. I remember him well. All of this… He went south, and when he came back, he was changed. He had heartbane. And somehow he knew you were a dragonseer even before you knew it yourself, and he knew how to steal that power."

Skye frowned. "You think something happened to him?"

"I don't know," said Berin. "But someone gave him the heartbane and told him how to use its power. Perhaps the answers are out there. And, you know, Borolo and Venn had dragons of their own once, just like we did. They may be returning there as well..."

Skye looked at her. "Are you sending me on a secret mission?" she said in a teasing voice, and Berin laughed.

"Perhaps! If you want. There are dragons out there, Princess. And new young dragonseers like yourself. They'll need our help..."

They watched the sun set over the city.

"Hmm," said Skye at last.

A month later, Skye stood at Rivven docks with Moira, ready for her diplomatic mission. She was surrounded by servants

Skye and Soulsinger

and porters, courtiers and guards, and dozens of clerks. The king himself was there. A crowd had gathered and there was music. Their ship lay moored and ready.

DRAGON STORM

"Captain Hork will be in charge of your bodyguards," said her father.

Skye nodded. Hork was watching the ship bob gently up and down, and he already looked green.

"And Malik will lead the negotiations," continued the king.

"Yes, Father."

"Hmm," he muttered. "And you're quite sure about this, are you?" For a moment his voice quivered, and he looked away as if embarrassed.

"Yes, Father," said Skye. "I am a princess of Draconis."

"Yes. Well," he murmured. "I'll … miss you, daughter."

Skye smiled gently. "I'll miss you too. And I'll be back soon, I promise."

"My lord," said Malik, "the tide is turning. We must away."

King Godfic nodded and stood straight. "I know you'll represent Draconis well," he said. "Be safe."

They hugged, and then Skye boarded the ship. The crowd cheered as they cast off. Looking down, Skye realised she could see the dragonseers, Ellis and the others, waving and grinning, and she waved back. Berin bowed to her, smiling.

Skye looked out towards the ocean. She could smell salt and feel a fresh breeze. Above her, the sails billowed white as they

caught the wind. And as she watched the
sails flutter, she imagined them against the
blue sky, as if they were flying… And, just
for a moment, she saw the beat of pale blue
wings, and remembered the feel of smooth
dry skin, and the smell of dust after the rain,
and heard a whisper in her mind…

Skye and Soulsinger

Skye…

Skye smiled, turned to face the wind, and heard the call of dragons.